MANAGING
PERFORMANCE
STRESS

RACE AND ETHNICITY

Culture, identity and representation

Stephen Spencer

Taylor & Francis Group

LONDON AND NEW YORK

First published 2006
by Routledge
2 Park Square, Milton Park, Abingdon, Oxon, OX14 4RN

Simultaneously published in the USA and Canada
by Routledge
270 Madison Avenue, New York, NY 10016

Routledge is an imprint of the Taylor & Francis Group, an informa business

© 2006 Stephen Spencer

British Library Cataloguing in Publication Data
A catalogue record for this book is available from the British Library

Library of Congress Cataloging in Publication Data
A catalog record for this book has been requested

ISBN10: 0–415–35124–3 (hbk)
ISBN13: 978–0–415–35124–9 (hbk)

ISBN10: 0–415–35125–1 (pbk)
ISBN13: 978–0–415–35125–6 (pbk)

◼ CONTENTS

ILLUSTRATIONS

FIGURES

TABLES

ACKNOWLEDGEMENTS

Many thanks to all of those who contributed their voices to this book. Special thanks to Chas Critcher, for allowing me to use extracts from a filmed interview; to Mark Quah for the interviews with British Chinese people and to Stuart who added an articulate personal perspective on the British-Born Chinese identity. Thanks to Dr Yvonne Howard-Bunt for providing some thoughts on mixed-race identity and also to Diego Uribe for his insightful comments on the eve of his return to Mexico. I am indebted to David Timber and the Kumbutjil Community at One Mile Dam in Darwin for allowing me to use interview material and some stills from a film made there, and to Mick Lambe, a stalwart campaigner and now Kumbutjil Project Officer (in residence), for his assistance in understanding a complex situation and for permission in using imagery from the Pariah website which he developed and hosts. Thank you also to the Malaysian students whose candid comments provided insight into the situation there.

Certain sections of this book draws on case-study material from Guyana which is due to be part of a text called *A Dream Deferred: Ethnic Identity in Guyana* (to be published by Dido Press). The case study in Chapter 6 (concerning Aboriginal community in Darwin) is a modification of an article to be published in the *Pacific Journalism Review*, Auckland University, April 2005.

Thanks also to:

The Commission for Racial Equality for permission to use the *Scared?* poster from their 1998 campaign.

Northern Territory News for the use of the front page, 15 April 2003.

Ross Woodrow, Newcastle University, NSW, Australia for his permission to include three illustrations: *Amongst the Queensland Blacks, Queensland Figaro, 10 December 1888; Nature – Civilization, Queensland Figaro, 6 August 1887*, and *England – Blackfellows at home: They are kindly received in fashionable circles – ladies play the piano to them etc. Sydney Punch, 15 August 1868.*

New Scotland Yard for permission to use the *Life Savers* police anti-terrorist poster.

Every effort has been made to contact copyright holders for their permission to reprint material in this book. The publisher would be grateful to hear from any copyright holder who is not here acknowledged and will undertake to rectify any errors or omissions in future editions of the book.

■ INTRODUCTION

Images of others, images of ourselves

Consider the following image. Paul Sharrad comments on a press photo from the 1991 Gulf War:

> In a camp of refugee workers from Kuwait containing amongst others, Indians, Pakistanis, Nepalis and Arabs of inconvenient nationality without the means of getting home, there huddled a group of Filipinos, triangulated like paintings of Custer's Last Stand or the Iwo Jima statue under a flag which pleaded 'Don't leave us among Asians'.
>
> (Sharrad 1993: 1)

This strange image is an excellent example of the complex negotiated identities that exist amongst global diasporas. It provides a graphic example of the urgency of striking a distinct identity and finding means to 'flag' this to others as well as the complex and ambiguous cosmopolitan relations in which identity and otherness are defined. The Filipinos in this story came to recognise themselves as a distinct group, united by common characteristics which to them made their difference self-evident; their identity then was quite removed from the category 'Asian' within which any western observer would almost certainly pigeonhole them. Under conditions of extreme anxiety their common history as a people at once united them and separated them from 'others' – now those attributes of their unique and complex colonial ancestry had to be urgently signalled.

How does this 'alienation of body and soul' come about? Diaspora is of increasing significance in a post-Fordist decentralised world, more than ever dependent upon flows of migrant labour, where outbreaks of conciliatory multi-culturalism are punctuated with policies of regressive racism and moral panics about refugees, asylum seekers and economic migrants in western democracies. The shared histories and transitory cultures are the breaking news of our global-ising world. Without some recognition of the multilayered history of Filipinos, their struggle and colonial history of connection to the USA, such scenes may appear surreal.

What can such examples tell us about the way we make sense of our identity and the way in which these meanings are constructed and communicated? It is examples like these that make us recognise the reflexive and constantly negotiated nature of ethnicity. As Sharrad and others suggest, the growing emphasis on post-colonial identities reflected in courses of study and literature pose an important challenge to one-dimensional approaches to ethnic identity.

Historical divisions from a long colonial era are a legacy embedded in many national cultures. Nations have been shaped by the exploitation and racism of a handful of European colonial empires. Today, contemporary literature bears witness to the same exploitation and racism 'the doctrine of divide and conquer persists, the pattern of varying psychic upheavals continues to be registered in "diaspora literature"' (Sharrad 1993: 1).

The purpose of this book is to examine the portrayal and meanings we attach to groups differentiated by 'ethnicity' or 'race' through analyses of examples from around the world as well as those we are confronted with every day.

Chapter 1 focuses specifically on the way in which issues and images of race and ethnicity are represented, examining the process by which we make sense of the 'other'. The social world in which we live is saturated with signs, images and stories projected through every form of media, permeating our consumer culture and all levels of social relationships. It is argued that the media is a powerful source of – in McQuail's term – 'referent power' (1978) presenting persuasive and author-itative messages from celebrities and experts, and that the media plays the role of a bard in our culture functioning as 'a *mediator of language*' (Hartley 1998: 85–6).

In other words, some of the complex negotiated views that form our self-identity are shaped by the media. This chapter serves to introduce and discuss the way in which social reality is constructed and yet appears to be 'natural'. One way that this is achieved is through a process by which identities are formed contingently based not only on who 'we' are or who 'we' like and relate to but also 'who "we" are not', 'who' "we" fear or hate'. This process of drawing mutually exclusive boundaries is clearly socially constructed, yet appears preordained – a 'natural' order. In this regard the concept of 'myth' as used by Roland Barthes and Claude Lévi-Strauss, has gained some value in discussions of new cultural ideologies, showing the process by which inequality is made to appear natural and everyday, and how we are inoculated to gross generalisations about others – and of course about ourselves. Will this help to understand the strange alienated case of our stranded Filipinos? Perhaps not entirely but certainly it helps to explain how such identity conflicts might arise. This chapter discusses one of Barthes's most famous essays in which racism and colonial paternalism take on the banal commonplace status of myth. Other recent examples are presented that will allow the reader to recognise the signifying practices employed in deconstructing images.

Chapter 2 examines the problem of naming, going further into the analysis of race, ethnicity and racism. The 'problem of definition' is, in many ways, a recognition that the reality of ethnicity as a lived experience is never static, and making assumptions based on well-worn definitions – attempting to fix identities – misses the point that how 'they' can be defined at any one time and place is entirely dependent on the unique coordinates in operation; it depends on the 'us' as well as the 'them' axes. The meaning of otherness changes with social context over time, drawing upon political issues and ideologies and shifting regimes of social and scientific thought. A notable shift is the change from more essentialist views of race and biological determinants to a politics of identity based upon cultural differences.

Who are you? What are the givens of identity? Concepts of 'race' and ethnicity, gender, sexuality, citizenship and nation are discussed along with the attendant problems of categorisation that beset cosmopolitan society. Are these rational, essential differences or 'socially imagined'? Social sciences have not been neutral in this process of categorisation, and their role will be highlighted here. A brief history of the development of terms and conceptions of the other will be included drawing on the work of Brackette Williams, Stuart Hall, Theo Goldberg and others.

Certainly ethnicity does generally describe groups with a shared identity, shared origins, interests and codes, but just as with class, where there is a tension between the concepts of a 'class in itself' and a 'class for itself' (where the latter represents class consciousness) ethnicity has both internal and external definitions. Individuals belonging to the dominant culture may find it unnecessary and peculiar to consider *themselves* an ethnic group, yet officialdom readily monitors and catalogues ethnic distinctiveness within 'ethnic minorities'. This is an example of the process of delineating ethnicity as an external phenomenon. (The example of the exnominated nature of 'whiteness' is used as a case in point here.) Conversely, the internal definition of a group as united by common culture, language, beliefs and aspirations may draw boundaries in quite a different fashion. The book explores the way internal and external ethnic boundaries are drawn and reviews key areas of theory used to explain the dynamics of ethnic divisions.

The examination of boundaries and their constant drawing and redrawing is of fundamental importance to issues of 'race' and 'ethnicity'. These should be considered as terms indicative of change and fluidity rather than a fixed or static identity. Racial or ethnic boundaries are subject to periodic softening or hardening, blurring or sharpening of emphasis. These boundaries are not only structures of state power and legislation, geographical or political lines drawn on a map to delineate territorial rights, they are part of the internal landscape of people living on either side of ethnic boundaries. 'Boundaries define the borders of nations and territories as well as the imaginations of minds and communities' (Cottle 2000: 2).

In Chapter 3, 'Colonialism: Invisible Histories', the intention is to give some illustrative examples from the history of colonialism, the legacy of which has so moulded contemporary ethnic relations. Through the re-examination of histories of colonialism, comparisons are drawn between several nations and their construction of the colonial subject. Several examples from early twentieth-century texts are included to critically appraise the romantic and racist discourses prevalent in representing the Other. This section also considers the infra-human treatment of the colonial subject and the need to come to terms with histories that have been disguised, revised or simply ignored. There is also discussion of Fanon's ground-breaking analysis of the damaging internalisation of colonial values. Finally, the chapter considers forms of neo-colonialism which operate today through structures of global economic domination.

Does this explain the Filipinos' rejection of Asian identity? Has the construction of a view of the East as disorganised, heathen and imbued with mysticism created a negative and belittling image of their views of how powerful Western countries perceive Asia? Images from *Goldsmith's Animated Nature* and Baron Cuvier's *The Animal Kingdom* – popular nineteenth-century natural histories, and twentieth-century works such as Hammerton's *People of All Nations* (1933), are used in the discussion of the construction of the Other. By examining the discourses that have constituted such images, it is possible to open a window onto the jingoism, racism and fascination with diversity typical of these popular ethnographies.

Chapter 4 reviews a number of social theories that have sought to give explanations for ethnic divisions, including various Marxist-inspired viewpoints, neo-Weberian and feminist strands of theory, and a glance at post-structuralist ideas. It becomes increasingly clear that 'race' and racism are the result of social and political discourses that change between times and places. Theories, when they compete for a universal explanation of 'race' and the dynamics of racism, show their weaknesses all too quickly. Is it more realistic as John Rex stated to consider that:

> The study of race relations, in common with a number of other politically charged areas in social sciences, seems beset by feuds and conflicts of a quite theological intensity. Thus such approaches as plural society theory, sociobiology, Marxism, Weberianism, the anthropological theory of ethnicity and psychological theories of identity all seem to be making imperialist demands to command the whole field to the exclusion of all other theories. . . . Closer investigation of these theories, however, reveals that they are in large measure complementary.
>
> (Rex 1986: 64)

While a synthetic approach that merely cuts together disparate explanations may not necessarily give greater insight, Rex's willingness to remain open to the value of different theories may be valuable in assessing their relative adequacy as explanations to unique expressions of ethnic identity and racism.

Racism, its forms, causes and consequences, is discussed here as a phenomenon occurring at all levels of society, from the undermining experience of many visibly different minorities characterised by occasional but steady verbal assaults, using derogatory terms, stereotypes, often defended as jokes or off-hand remarks, to violent and organised abuse and institutional racism that have been identified to operate in education, health care, the legal system, media reporting, employment and policing. However, as well as these institutional agents of discrimination it can be argued that racism is implicit in our conceptions and structures of differ-ence. Miles argues that 'race' and 'race relations' are invalid terms that merely perpetuate the hegemony of racist culture (Miles 1989). One of the concerns here is how far race or ethnicity could constitute a primary site of social division and a genuine category for critical social analyses. Is race a strictly instrumental category derived from the economic base and relations of production? Or is it instead a category with semi- or complete autonomy from other determinants of inequality such as class?

The chapter considers the social-constructionist viewpoint that discourses or discursive practices play a significant role in constructing race and ethnicity. This is achieved through a variety of disciplinary and institutional structures that define the borders of social consensus and difference. The term 'discourse' has come to mean 'a whole field or domain within which language is used in particular ways, such as economics, anthropology, psychiatry and the way these regimes of thought influence social reality, through their schemes of classification in different periods of time. This approach has been heavily influenced by the so-called 'linguistic turn' in philosophy and social theory. Especially influential in this discussion is the work of Foucault, Pecheux and others. However, the chapter focuses on the work of theorists who have effectively applied the approach to studies of racial and ethnic others. Stephen Muecke, for example, has shown how entire ethnic groups of Aboriginal Australians have been positioned by restricted categories of discourse.

The chapter also looks at the dual burden of oppressions experienced by women within ethnic groups. Black feminism has drawn attention to the intersection of gender and race and to quite different forms of oppression and resistance experienced by black women to those emphasised by white middle-class feminists.

While Chapter 4 introduces the increasing fragmentation and syntheticism of theories of race and ethnicity, Chapter 5 specifically addresses postmodern and post-colonial readings of ethnicity that highlight how avoiding essentialist and universalising views of the Other in favour of specific localised subjects can have the uneasy consequence of developing an uncritical acceptance of relativism at any price. However, the complexity and fragmentation of these postmodern anaylses more closely mirrors the complex and hybrid forms of ethnic identities.

Following on from the previous chapter, post-colonial feminist critiques are discussed. Portrayals of Asian women are, as Yegenoglu (1998) suggests, instrumental, if not pivotal in the maintenance of Western cultural hegemony. The portrayal of Asian women as passive, exploited, in a culture presented as backward when compared with the growing independence of women in the West, she argues, merely helps to reinforce the myth of Orientalism. The chapter also examines traditional leftist criticisms of identity politics which are seen as an obstacle to socialist ideals.

Chapter 6 focuses on the situation of indigenous ethnicity and one multi-faceted case study. Based on research in Darwin in northern Australia, the chapter highlights the realities of life in an urban Aboriginal community on the fringes of white Australia's monocultural affluence, and considers the consequences of historical exclusionary treatment of Aborigines and discourses used today that show the persistence and function of white Australian attitudes. At the end of the chapter the case is further analysed through the prism of several different theoretical approaches. This is hoped to provide the student with a case to consider from a variety of different theoretical positions.

Building on the theoretical discussions of the previous chapters, Chapter 7 explores conflict in ethnically divided societies. One intention is to show that imagery, stereotypes and other popular representations embody ingrained political differences and are employed situationally. Some examples are given of tensions within multicultural societies, changes and threats to the orthodoxy of social meanings and the struggle for symbolic dominance between groupings in ethnically divided post-colonial nations. The chapter will draw upon research into cases of bipolar ethnic relations in Guyana as well as similar rivalry in Malaysia.

Chapter 8, 'Living the Contradiction', is concerned with issues of diaspora, hybridity and multiculturalist responses to ethnic diversity. In some societies, adaptation is apparent through a process of creolisation; in others circumstances there is less 'middle ground', and 'ethnic enclaves' develop, or assimilation policies are implemented with the purpose of extinguishing cultural difference. Multiculturalism has always been a highly contentious term. Here it is examined from both sides of the political divide. Despite the optimism with which it was asserted to provide inter-ethnic harmony and respect, the term has become fraught with tensions. The problems encountered in multi-ethnic society are highlighted by interviews. There are examples of boundary crossing between ethnic divides (examples are reported from Mexico and Guyana). This chapter indicates the permeability of ethnic boundaries and again emphasises the essential contingency of ethnic identity.

Chapter 9 draws together several strands and considers the impact of emerging cultural forms. What trends are observable in our globalising world? Three forms of emergent cultural forms and the social meanings through which they are represented are briefly discussed. These are 'mixed race' relations, cyberspace and terrorism.

'Britain currently has one of the highest rates of inter-racial relationships in the western world, with 50% of all black children born having one white parent. Whether we view such unions as positive multiculturalism or not, the truth is that mixed race relationships are a fact of life' (BBC World Service, 1 September). What future can the children from interracial relationships expect in twenty-first-century Britain. Are they a sign of a post-racial future? The fragile global situation, fears, real and imagined, of global terror, neo-imperialism and homogenising global forces have led to new struggles for cultural hegemony and widespread resistance that has divided society. The future significance of terms like 'race' and 'ethnicity' cannot be divorced from wider societal (or global) dynamics.

USING THIS TEXT

It is important that we recognise the central importance of understanding race and ethnicity not as an academic exercise in which exotic cultures are studied in far-flung outposts or under benighted colonial regimes in another era, but instead as one of the defining aspects of social identity today. Along with class, gender and sexuality, ethnicity (within which the uneasy concept of 'race' is often implicit) is one of the central problematics of social existence, yet one that is both elusive and a source of anxiety and confusion.

This book asks students of race and ethnicity to look into the mirror and reflect on aspects of identity rendered invisible by convention. Identity, culture and representation are intimately interlinked in socialisation and in our constant monitoring of the social world and ideas about ourselves. The world around us is an inescapable mirror held up for us in which we see an image of what we are supposed to be. The social meanings gleaned are produced from the selective words and images of the mass media, whether its news or what passes for entertainment, documentary or fiction, and also from the political system – its rhetoric, policies and debates – and, of course, peers and family, attitudes, values and beliefs. Even everyday objects such as stamps, coins, flags and consumer products are imbued with values and understandings of nationalism, citizenship and what makes 'us' different from 'them'.

This book provides a series of contemporary contexts from which key questions are drawn. It sets out to illustrate the complex processes through which race and ethnicity are socially constructed and disseminated. The realities of life in post-colonial contexts are illustrated through images, anecdotes and popular representations as well as through interview material.

Each chapter has a summary and poses a number of questions for further consideration. For those wishing to gain an understanding of contemporary issues, this book provides some critical markers in the contested theoretical landscape of race and ethnicity.

CHAPTER 1

Representation

This book began life as a series of images, with the notion that images convey immediacy about the complex issues of race and ethnicity that written texts cannot always deliver. The problem, especially for many students, is how to make sense of theories of race and ethnicity, which are often confusing and hedged about with sensitivities. Two key aspects of race and ethnicity should be highlighted here: first, neither 'race' nor 'ethnicity' have simple referents 'out there', they are not stable definitions of some static social reality, rather they are central concepts of identity that constantly change and adapt to social contexts. Second, the way we understand race and ethnicity is through the circulation of social meanings. Apart from recognising and deconstructing our own socialised values, we have available to us a vast array of popular representations, advertising, films, television and newspapers, organisational culture, everyday conversations and opinions. These representations are not fixed and eternal, some positivist's 'social fact', but the products of history.

How can images, words and media representations of others assist in the task of unravelling the construction of race? This inevitably depends on the cultural forms used and the ideas about representation employed. There are a number of books that attempt to trace the significance of whiteness, empire and race through a review of dominant representations. Stuart Hall (1997) has been influential here, especially in using illustrations that show how race and ethnicity are associated with ideas about sexuality and gender identity. In addition to illustrating the process of 'racialising the other' through popular imagery of colonial domination, Hall has suggested counter-strategies through which representation could contest, parody, reverse or confront the 'dominant gendered and sexual definitions of racial difference by *working on black sexuality*' (1997: 274).

Dyer, in his seminal text *White*, recognised the naturalised and invisible nature of 'whiteness': 'Whites must be seen to be white, yet whiteness as race resides in invisible properties and whiteness as power is maintained by being unseen' (Dyer 1997: 45). To counter this invisibility, Dyer proceeds to expose the white iconography from classical painting to films like *Alien* and *Falling Down*, imagery that serves to legitimise and maintain white dominance.

More recently Knowles (2004) has criticised Dyer's claims to have exposed the 'mechanisms of race making' (188) through a lexicon of images as flawed and unsustained. Further, she refutes the claim made by Dyer and others that racist discourses and imagery of the past are still active and influential. Instead she suggests that 'If the past lives on in the present – it most certainly does so in *new* social forms' (2004: 189). However, while Knowles quite correctly points out the dangers of conflating the complexities of 'race making' with images of white domination and the domestication of empire, through such imagery, the cultural-studies approach (of which these two are exponents) has opened up a front that penetrates popular opinion and offers some strategies to counter the tacit acceptance of whiteness. Also it seems clear that stereotypes of race can endure over long periods of time and that while their articulation in each era may be nuanced rather differently, the core values may remain starkly preserved. Having said this (and examples of persistent ethnic stereotypes in Chapter 8 bear this out), one should be mindful of the possibility of **aberrant decoding** (see Glossary for terms in bold) by which textual material, especially imagery, is misrecognised due to shifts in the cultural reference points; meanings can shift markedly from one period to the next and the meanings of race and ethnicity are clearly pre-eminent examples.

Undoubtedly, it is not enough focusing on representation simply to enumerate images of colonialism and whiteness (or blackness) and hope to have uncovered the construction of race. Hall's schema, the 'circuit of culture', offers a more fluid and holistic view of the practices involved in the production of culture (see Hall 1997, Woodward 1997). In this model 'representation' is one position in a matrix alongside processes of Identity, production, consumption and regulation. This focus on the circulation of shared meanings shows that meanings and ideas have material consequences. For example, the racial thinking that led to ideas about eugenics, racial purity and paternalistic views of whites towards indigenous peoples had consequences for millions of people under colonial rule in Australia, and, up to the 1970s, 'half-caste' children were removed from their Aboriginal families and adopted out to white families, in a clear attempt to 'breed out' mixed individuals. Similarly, images and notions of whiteness or blackness are also converted into items for consumption, television programmes, hair products, toys, and so on. Products are often purchased because we feel some affinity to their style or the brand image and identity being communicated much more than for their utility or material value. What this is beginning to make explicit is that the underlying values and beliefs in a society are forms of representation themselves that mediate our experience of the social world and constitute elements with which the individual identifies and understands him- or herself.

This internal process could be considered to be affected by ideologies. An ideology, according to Louis Althusser, is a 'system of representations' (1971). This system underpins our social and cultural life and mediates between people and their relationship to society as well as their social identities. These representations operate at the level of unconscious desires as well as through an individual's rationality. To explain the process of **interpellation**, by which people are hailed as a particular subject, Althusser uses the example of a policeman, teacher or priest calling to a person on the street 'Hey you!' As the person turns around, they have become the subject. This hailing takes place in reality at many levels (conscious as well as unconscious callings) and aligns them with specific identities or cultural roles. Ideology in this way constitutes the person's 'lived' relation to the real. One major and authoritative source for ideologies is the national news. Take one particular day—

AND NOW THE NEWS . . .13 JANUARY 2005

As I write this, the daily news features several stories all of which are directly or indirectly connected to issues of race, ethnicity, global politics and neo-colonialism. Here (with my brief commentaries) are some of the days' stories from the *Guardian* Unlimited web site, <http://www.guardian.co.uk>

> **Thatcher avoids jail for coup role**
> **9.15 a.m.:** Mark Thatcher pleads guilty to involvement in a failed coup attempt in Equatorial Guinea under a plea bargain that saves him from prison.
> **The chronicle of a coup foretold**
> **Special report: Equatorial Guinea**

Son of the former British Prime Minister is bailed out from a possible jail sentence for admitting his part in investing in an attempted (and badly bundled) coup in Equatorial Guinea, involving plot leader ex-SAS officer Simon Mann, a friend of Sir Mark, now serving four years in Zimbabwe for trying to illegally buy weapons. The small oil-rich country was probably considered a safe and potentially enormously lucrative risk. An example of the fact that carpet-bagging forms of capitalism are still alive and well?

Royal family in Nazi row
Prince Harry pictured in Nazi uniform
Special report: the monarchy

On the sixtieth anniversary of the closing of Auschwitz – the twenty-year-old Prince (third in line to the throne) makes a bad choice of costume at a fancy-dress party: Africa corps uniform with swastika armband. Another instalment in the ongoing soap opera that is the 'Royals' (see Ros Coward's 1984 essay), the story became one of the most debated across the whole spectrum of daily newspapers from the *Sun* to the *Independent*. However, as with all such controversies about the royals, the key question is not 'Well should he be allowed to attend Sandhurst [Britain's premier officer training establishment]?' but 'Why do we retain this anachronistic and totally redundant institution?'

Bones of contention – the discovery of a new species of human astounded the world. But is it what it seems, asks John Vidal.

A story about the discovery of the remains of a new type of human, the small humanoid dubbed 'hobbit man' was discovered on the Indonesian island of Flores and who, if genuine, would mark a turning point in our understanding of human evolution. However, the story here reveals the possibility that it may not be anything more than a pygmy version of *Homo sapiens* actually related directly to people of small stature who are living in a nearby village to the cave where the remains were discovered.

US gives up search for Saddam's WMD
World: Iraq Survey Group concludes dictator destroyed weapons years before invasion.
Comment: Seamus Milne
Special report: Iraq

At the time of writing this, the ongoing disaster of the invasion of Iraq and the bloodshed that ensued since 'victory' was achieved by the US and UK's military in 2003 had begun to fade into the background in western media, although US failure to contain 'insurgency' and the ferocity of 'insurgent' action, despite the destruction of centres like Fallujah, was undiminished. The story is very old news for millions of people who opposed the war and realised the WMD claims were a fiction from the start. One could argue that the protracted search and gradual admission presented here was a clear tactical move by the US administration, because by now the story is barely newsworthy and will only rate a short mention towards the back of the paper.

In terms of gravity, two events that were also ongoing at the time had briefly eclipsed all others. First, a natural disaster of unprecedented ferocity: the Indian Ocean region tsunami had devastated the Indian-Pacific region with over 60,000 likely to be lost to Indonesia, Sri Lanka, India, Bangladesh, Thailand and numerous small archipelagos that never usually make the news, and millions more of the world's poorest threatened with disease and privation. This event on Boxing Day 2004 brought the world rushing into western consciousness in a way it rarely does. Second, another horrifying chapter in genocidal ethnic cleansing (arguably the most systematic genocide since Kosovo and Rwanda, in which 800,000 Tutsi people were murdered by their Hutu neighbours) had been unfolding from earlier in 2004:

> Armed by the Sudanese Government, the Arab 'Janjaweed' militias murder, rape, and pillage African villages with impunity. Their leaders from the 'Arab Gathering' credit the 'Arab race' with 'civilization,' and consider black Africans to be 'abd' (male slaves) and 'kahdim' (female slaves.) In Tweila, North Darfur, on 27 February 2004, according to the U.N. Darfur Task Force, the Janjaweed and Sudanese army murdered at least 200 people and gang-raped over 200 girls and women, many in front of their fathers and husbands, whom they then killed. The Janjaweed branded those they raped on their hands to mark them permanently so they would be shunned.
>
> (Stanton 2004)

Headlines such as these give a sense of local and global relations of power, signs of the manner in which the western nations divide the world and their own consciousness of those people in it. An immense chasm exists between these worlds, our knowledge of the suffering that occurs in Africa and elsewhere is partial and fragmentary and, like our acquiescence to US foreign policy, most certainly reflects dominant interests. So little coverage seemed to emerge from other ongoing conflicts. The war in the Congo, for example, is reported to have claimed between 2.5 and 3 million victims. Why then did the western media not focus on this war? Bob Franklin (Professor of Journalism at Cardiff University) made a very salient point in a recent interview (Franklin 2004): 'Philip Knightley's famous book about the media coverage of war suggested that the truth is the first victim. Well, the first victim isn't truth, it's complexity.'

This is quite likely to be one of the main reasons why this war has not been under scrutiny: reporting during warfare is notoriously confusing but the situation in the Congo seemed more tangled than most with at least five African countries taking part and complex divisions and factions within those nations.

COMPLEX WAR

It's unknown who's responsible for last week's attack. The situation in Congo is totally confused. Backed by forces from Namibia, Angola and Zimbabwe, the Congolese government army is fighting rebels supported by Uganda and Rwanda. Conflicts are being fought out within these coalitions, too. Last year, for instance, troops from Uganda and Rwanda clashed with each other. Besides, the region has a long history of ethnic strife. Ethnic Hema and Lendu are currently at war in eastern Congo.

(Gruppen 2001)

However, another reason for the comparative media silence could be that there is less interest in the relatively remote areas of southern Africa and western interests are notably not involved (nor is there any question of the war involving oil which is an apparent issue in the Sudanese ethnic cleansing). There is journalistic convention known as McLurg's Law which I have seen posted up on the wall near a journalist's desk: '1 dead Briton is worth 5 dead Frenchmen, 20 dead Egyptians, 500 dead Indians and 1,000 dead Chinese'.

Stories with more potential for dramatic conflict are also more likely to appear; many 'news stories' are interpreted in terms of conflict anyway since this is more dramatically interesting. There is thus a bias in favour of 'bad news', a featuring of negativity. (The Glasgow University Media Group made this point long ago with their famous series 'Bad News' (1976) and 'More Bad News' (1980).)

Like drama, the news does tell a story. On landing in the (Belgian) Congo during its evacuation, an American journalist rushed over to a group of white women asking, 'Has anyone here been raped, and speaks English?' As Fiske comments, 'His story had been "written" before landing, all he needed was a few local details' (Fiske 1987: 283).

An extension of this journalistic convention that narrows the focus to appeal to the home market has been put forward by Herman and Chomsky.

So you tend to have a serious double standard, you have what Herman and Chomsky called 'worthy' and 'unworthy' victims. So, for example, in the bombing of Istanbul – clearly a terrible attack which claimed a number of civilian lives You had wall-to-wall coverage of that, but you don't have wall-to-wall coverage of things happening at the same time with greater consequences for human lives – such as the dropping by the US of one-ton bombs on Northern Iraq, which had virtually no coverage in the mainstream media – partly because it's not being put out by their authorised sources – sources of the government and the political elite.

(David Miller, interview 2003)

That there is clearly a double standard relating to casualties in times of war is obvious. The journalistic convention in which the relative cultural and geographic distances give a cynical rule of thumb in determining news values is well known. British foreign policy is no different. Mark Curtis in *Web of Deceit* gives a long list of 'unpeople' who are, as Salleh writes,

> the victims of this global order, Curtis [2001] places the million or so Indonesians who were slaughtered during General Suharto's bloody seizure of power in 1965. Declassified documents show British complicity in the killings – the then Labour government supplied Suharto with warships, logistics and intelligence, as well as secret messages of support.
>
> (Salleh 2003)

This brief foray into the media mechanisms, the realpolitik behind the news, illustrates the value of an approach that looks critically at cultural production, casting a critical eye on the western value system that presents us with such anomalies: 3 million people (or unpeople) on the one hand receive barely a flicker of interest, whereas the hue and cry following the tsunami (or the Asian tsunami as it is being called) sent shock waves around the world and encouraged politicians to talk about a moratorium on national debts that the affected countries owe to the World Bank. Is this because, again, there is more sympathy for the regions hit by natural disasters? Or that Africa is routinely presented as an area of unremitting disaster (AIDS, drought, war and famine)? Certainly equatorial Africa is a long way from the western tourist itinerary, whereas south-east Asia is a prime tourist destination and some 7,000 British and 3,000 Swedes, amongst others, were reportedly in the affected region at the time of the earthquake. On the other hand, Prince Harry's appearance in Nazi regalia totally dominates the media for several days and all the more complex and serious international stories are sidelined as controversy rages on all channels about the ill-advised costume – boyish impetuosity or callous disregard by a highly educated member of the elite?

This volume attempts to give the student an understanding of race/ethnicity grounded in the materiality of representation, popular imagery and dialogues with people who have first-hand accounts of the effects of the western legacy of colonialism and who talk about aspects of their ethnic identity. These voices highlight the increasing need to recognise common themes, problems and potential solutions amongst the Babel of world cultures. In her Nobel Peace Prize speech Aung San Suu Kyi noted succinctly the increasing importance of universal human rights as a means of bringing harmony: 'It is precisely because of the cultural diversity of the world that it is necessary for different nations and peoples to agree on those basic human values which will act as a unifying factor' (Aung San Suu Kyi 1994).

READING IMAGES OF OTHERS

In everyday life, we are often separated from other ethnic groups by boundaries that are not only physical and geographical but also social, economic and cultural. How 'otherness' is recognised can turn on visible differences or clusters of these: skin colour, clothing, location and cultural practices are at times used as an 'Identikit' to exclude, single out, scapegoat, even to murder and ethnically 'cleanse' or, conversely, to find allegiance with and to celebrate (perhaps superficially) as a paean of multiculturalism. We can revel in diverse cuisines and ancient traditions and religious practices that add spice to the normal fare of our own cultural traditions. Boundaries are socially drawn and may be redrawn, heightened or lowered and, in some instances, crossed. In the following examples, some of the contradictions, stereotypes and political determinants of otherness are highlighted.

WHAT IS THE OTHER?

The simple answer is 'not self'; in other words, an alien subjectivity, a being who exhibits characteristics notably different from our own, whether gender, race, class, custom or behaviour. To a certain extent we are each born into a social system – constantly evolving certainly – but nevertheless a pre-existing moulding influence on our behaviour and outlook and on our understanding of difference. The 'Other' exists as a metaphysical concept rather than as a genuine entity. The Other represents an area of consensus, a way of delineating self, and the shared values of our culture or subculture. We create ideals and typifications and the Other presents us with tests and measures for these ideals. The process of forging an identity at the individual as well as the group level is dependent on interaction with others. So the existence of a group of people – a 'them' rather than an 'us' – can be seen to be important in human society as it affirms qualities and characteristics that a group sees as normal as the rules by which they live. In the most obvious cases these affirmations gain official and legal status and those breaking the rules are portrayed as 'criminals', 'insane', 'deviants' or 'anti-social'. They may live and work on the fringes of 'respectable' society, and make up a marginalised group or underclass, but they are also frequently associated with racial or ethnic groups. Such boundaries are, by their very nature, implicitly political and strike to the heart of personal and social identity.

The role of the media as a 'mediator' in this process of identity formation is a continuous and pre-eminent one. Media representations of race mediate meaning between complex networks of people and political ideologies. But 'Is it the reflector or the director?' as the song goes.[1] The social world in which we live is awash

---

1 Disposable Heroes of Hiphoprisy – *Television – the drug of a nation.*

with signs, images, stories and complex symbols projected through every form of media, permeating our consumer culture, and all levels of social relationships. It is argued that the media is a powerful source of – in McQuail's term – 'referent power' (1987: 294), the influence of attractive and powerful celebrities or authority figures in the media is frequently acknowledged. Fiske and Hartley used the term 'bardic function' to explain the process by which the media broadcasts 'a series of consciously structured messages which serve to communicate to the members of that culture a confirming, reinforcing version of themselves' (1978: 85–6). In other words, some of the complex negotiated views that form our self-identity derive from the media's images of 'others' as well as images of ourselves as we would aspire to be. Our language itself mirrors and reproduces social divisions, at times it may serve to fix definitions or bound the debate, at others to challenge them.

The media can be seen as 'the most generalised of generalised others' (King 2004: 185). Inevitably we build views of our own identity from these disparate communications. One way in which we do this is by interpreting signs presented to us that contain embedded views and values of national, cultural or common subcultural identities and, conversely, the identities of others with whom the communicative opportunities are few. As Hartley suggests (1992: 207), 'The only real contact with others is, paradoxically, symbolic, and rendered in the form of stories, both factual and fictional'. On the outer boundaries of this unknowable 'imagined community' is what Hartley calls 'Theydom' (as opposed to our own or Wedom). The rules of representation for these two kingdoms are quite different.

> People from Theydom, such as Aboriginals in news stories . . . are exempted from the established systems of balance which apply to Wedom's own adversarial politics; there are not 'two sides' to an Aboriginal story – not two *Aboriginal* sides, that is, only an Aboriginal side and a 'balance' supplied by, for instance police, welfare, legal or governmental authorities.
>
> (Hartley 1992: 207)

Whilst we are not aware on a daily basis of the manner in which our subjectivity is constructed, we are constantly monitoring our environment and establishing reference points, alignments with shared values and beliefs and contradistinction with others with whom we have less in common – or who are portrayed as enemies of our society. These relations of inclusion and exclusion are far from simple and tend to be organised around different identities at different times in our history. For example, at the time of writing there is a heightened fear of terrorist activity and in some quarters this is also equated with asylum seekers, refugees or, as these displaced people may not always be so visibly apparent, anyone who has a different ethnic appearance.

As Frederick Barth in his seminal study *Ethnic Groups and Social Boundaries* (1969) persuasively argues, the existence of ethnic groups depends less on the

9

intrinsically shared common culture of an ethnic group than on the maintenance of social boundaries. 'For social boundaries to be actively maintained, they need to be continually validated, and this requires regular interaction with members of out-groups' (Barth 1969: 32–3). While the media may play a key role in this validation, it should not be conceived of as a mere conduit for racist propaganda. While studies of British media in the 1970s and 1980s set out to show that black youth had become demonised by the media, particularly in the moral panic over 'mugging' (Hall et al. 1978), this emphasis reflected the New Conservative agenda that has been dubbed a reactionary common-sense view, which helped to affirm and popularise increasingly authoritarian policies. In fact the media cannot be seen as operating in a vacuum. Media interests and advertising revenues often imply an agenda constrained by political and economic forces (see Herman and Chomsky 1995).

A number of recent studies indicate that the portrayal of race in the media reflects ideologies of multiculturalism and has moved away from crude stereotypes in favour of a representation of more subtle cultural differences. Cottle (2000) warns that 'the dynamic nature and subtleties of media discourse and representation, . . . cannot always be captured through simplistic and static applications of the concept of "stereotype"' (2000: 124). It appears that despite the wayward tabloid examples of invective against asylum seekers and others, media discourses of race are inevitably parasitic on social and political formations in the wider society.

At certain times, the media draws on crude popular stereotypes (see the example below of Englishness and Frenchness). While we know these are probably stereotypes we still recognise them and they may have the appearance of 'home truths' cemented into place by habitual usage and familiarity. Such stereotypes abound; they could be gender based or relate to generalised national characteristics; for example, of the French, Chinese, Australian, English, or African-Caribbean culture. While such common-sense viewpoints are subject to historical shifts, the basic oppositions that outline an 'us' and a 'them', a dominant and a subordinate and, in terms of the media, an 'ideal reader' (Kress 1988) are relatively unchanging, these are interpreted differently. Particularly in times of crisis – as in the 'apple war' (see Box 1.1) or, more recently, in the war with Iraq in which the French were vilified by Murdoch's *New York Post* as 'weasels'. Because of the French refusal to join the alliance with Bush, old grievances and stereotypes were reactivated:

The 'petulant prima donna of realpolitik' is leading the 'axis of weasels', in 'a chorus of cowards'. It is an unholy alliance of 'wimps' and ingrates which includes one country that is little more than a 'mini-me minion', another that is in league with Cuba and Libya, with a bunch of 'cheese-eating surrender monkeys' at the helm.

(Younge and Henley 2003)

BOX 1.1 THEY EAT HORSES, DON'T THEY?

A world survey by a French magazine says that the best friends of France are the English, which will surprise a great many Englishmen who think we hate each other. Noel Coward summarised the Anglo attitude to the French when he said; 'There's always something fishy about them.' *The fact is that what we don't know them very well and what we don't know we don't trust.*

It is true we have often fought in the same wars. But the only time we came to losing was when they were on our side. Maybe they do have the best wine, the most glamorous women, the cleverest cuisine and the most elegant style. But do they deserve any of them? It is said that they cook while the British only open tins. But what do they cook? Snails (disgusting). Frogs legs (distasteful). And horses (barbaric).

They grow an apple called Golden Delicious which is green, not gold, and about as delicious as a ball of wool marinated in castor oil. What's more, it's putting our growers out of business.

And now we are told we are their best friends. It's ridiculous. The only thing we've got in common is the Channel. The English Channel.

(*Daily Mirror*, 10 September 1980, p. 2)

Groups that constitute 'Other' are not a constant – the manner in which the aspects of difference that are constructed as problematic or, popularly, as a 'moral panic' change over time and between nations (see Table 1.1 below). The construction of a group as 'other' depends on the social and historical character of a nation and is parasitic on developments in science, social theory and belief systems that function to create an identity a sense of nation. Table 1.1 shows the shift from the primacy of religious belief (social solidarity based upon collective worship, a belief in a battle between supernatural forces) through the beginnings of race science and the ranking of colonial and imperial subjects within an order based variously upon civilisation and evolutionary (Darwinist) notions of development to more pragmatic criteria, geographical and economic notions of development and modernisation.

Pieterese (2002) identifies the changing face of otherness within Europe. These shifts in discursive structures generated by economic and cultural globalisation seem to encourage more porous national boundaries and yet also – perhaps as a result of these lowered frontiers and cultural homogeneity – there are heightened anxieties. For example, disputes around the expansion of the EU and the concern that the future inclusion of Turkey – a predominantly Muslim nation – may

Table 1.1 Shifting faces of the Other

TIME	BOUNDARIES	EXTERNAL DIFFERENCES	INTERNAL DIFFERENCES
CE–present	Religion	Pagans, non-believers Christianity v. Islam	Heathens, heretics witchcraft, Roman v. Orthodox
1790–1950	Race	Race, language	Class, status, Nation Ranking among European countries
1800–1970	Imperialism, colonialism, neo-colonialism Internal colonialism	Civilisation & savagery Darwinism Orientalism	'Backward areas' within Europe (e.g. Celtic fringe, 'urban jungle')
1950–present	Developing North/South Divide	Developed/Advanced Industrial/PostIndustrial Information Age Core/periphery	Uneven patterns of development
1900–present	Europe	European civilisation, identity, boundaries	Europe of multiple speeds Tension between deepening and widening of EU
1960–present	Cultural difference	Cultural difference Identity politics Foucauldian discourses	Multiculturalism, sub-cultural differences in lifestyle, sexual preference, age
1980–present	Citizenship, legal status	'Fortress Europe'. Illegal immigrants, asylum seekers, 'financial migrants, guest workers, terrorists, etc.	Citizens, denizens, terrorism

(Adapted from J.N. Pieterese ('Europe and Its Others Over Time') in Goldberg and Solomos 2002: 18)

threaten the core values of European identity. The displacement of millions of people throughout the world (often as a result of wars and global poverty) has resulted in fears of mass migration of asylum seekers and the development of a 'fortress Europe' mentality, although it is ironic that Britain, for example, is often reliant on migrant workers from Eastern Europe and elsewhere for basic services – just as parts of America are dependent on Hispanic workers.

Finally, there is the current trend to define groups by an emphasis upon cultural differences, an ethos at the heart of western forms of multiculturalism, often manifest in a superficial celebration of difference. However, as discussed in Chapter 7, some critics see multiculturalism as racism behind a mask of political correctness. Pieterese has shown that the need for creating 'others' plays a role in cementing social relations and defining the identity of the nation state, whether the outsiders are heretics, pagans or 'illegal aliens'. These boundaries are keenly felt and create a moral consensus uniting people under the core values of society. Therefore 'race' and ethnicity are markers of difference that reflect the social construction at a particular time. As Hall (1997) suggests, race is a 'floating signifier', where and how it is used to draw boundaries and determine rules of inclusion and exclusion will depend upon historically specific conditions.

Similarly, the recent rhetoric exhibited in the media against the French not only was a result of France's refusal to be drawn into the Iraq war, but also indicative of Britain's ambivalent role in Europe and its unwillingness to relinquish ties with the USA or to abandon its relative separatism within Europe. In each case, the (often derogatory) imagery and tabloid characterisation of the ritually reviled group(s) has a ready-made stock of stereotypical traits and insults derived from a shifting historical lexicon of economic, political and military rivalry. The so called 'Dunkirk spirit' has been invoked many times over the years at times of economic crisis (for example, in the 'apple war' referred to in the *Mirror* story, or French ferry strikes and blockades). Interestingly, a military retreat is lauded as a historic victory and heroic indication of British steadfastness representing the powerful image of unity against oppression and willing sacrifice.

These trends of defining the Other are certainly tied to global and national shifts and boundary drawing. The other may be physically (i.e. geographically) distant, or othered due to cultural labelling, seen as deviant, beyond the Pale.[2] More recently, groups that had been striving for equality are in some cases effectively othered by the pluralist thinking that sets out to recognise and even celebrate difference.

---

2 'Beyond the Pale' (see Curtis 1984) derives from the Norman attempts to conquer Ireland in the thirteenth century. The Pale (meaning boundary) was an area that fluctuated widely over the centuries and represented the territory around Dublin held by the English monarchy. 'Beyond the Pale' became established in English as meaning 'uncivilised' and 'socially unacceptable' (Curtis 1984: 12).

BARTHES AND THE READER'S ROLE IN CONSTRUCTING MEANINGS

Meaning in some schools of thought is very much dependent on the intentions of the sender, but in semiotics, however, 'the message is a construction of signs which, through interacting with the receivers, produce meanings. The sender defined as transmitter of the message, declines in importance. The emphasis shifts to the text and how it is "read"' (Fiske 1990: 3). Meanings from our social world are not so much 'out there' but reside within the reader and are actively decoded by knowledge of conventional codes. Hence the intended nuances in a word, a photograph, a dance or a piece of film are only recognised if our cultural understanding of these meanings allows us to decode the intended meaning. For example, cultural knowledge is required to recognise that the red rose is a symbol for New Labour or a traditional sign for romance and chivalry. The famous line 'A rose by any other name would smell as sweet' (Shakespeare, *Romeo and Juliet*) is true in the sense that the word 'rose' is an agreed convention, the word itself has nothing intrinsic to do with the scented flower: language is an arbitrary conventional code. This is an important point as it indicates that we are actively making meanings and that, while people might show general agreement on some signs, there are a range of interpretations possible depending on our own subjective identity, ethnicity, class, gender, generation, education, experience and state of mind.

Roland Barthes, using the structuralist linguistic principles of Saussure and others, mapped out the **process of signification** as shown in Figure 1.1.

The reader interprets the surface meanings (signifier) and from the word or image recognises the implied social, cultural meanings (signified). First we perceive the signifier; this could be written, spoken or a graphic element, and we interpret this conventional code based on our cultural knowledge. In this example, 'the rose' refers to a flower (amongst other things). These aspects make up the first level of signification, that of denotation. However, the denotative sign is also a signifier at the deeper level of connotation. This connotative sign in turn can be seen as

SIGNIFIER 1	SIGNIFIED 2
'the rose' (words or image)	Object in the world i.e. a flower
3. SIGN	
a single red rose	Chivalry, romance, New Labour etc
I SIGNIFIER	II SIGNIFIED
III SIGN	

Figure 1.1 The process of signification

another layer of meaning, which again becomes the signifier at a third level – the level of myth. For example, the word or image of a rose carries the connotations of romance, part of the lexicon of courtly love; it can also more narrowly be a political emblem developed to reinvent the Labour Party in the UK under Tony Blair to mark a new centrist appeal to the electorate, while keeping the socialist iconography of the red rose. The way in which we interpret these signs and the process by which we make meaning is largely dependent on the context in which we are 'reading' the signs.

Images of race can be analysed in this way, recognising the layering of socio-cultural meanings and paying attention to the manner in which the image is chosen and framed to contextualise and foreground a 'preferred reading',[3] while maintaining the myth of the image as 'natural'. These deeply embedded conventional values are illustrated in Barthes ground-breaking 1957 article 'Myth Today'. Consider Barthes' **deconstruction** of a specific image of 'otherness' (from *Mythologies*, 1972).

> And here is now another example: I am at the barber's, and a copy of *Paris-Match* is offered to me. On the cover, a young Negro in a French uniform is saluting, with his eyes uplifted, probably fixed on a fold of the tricolour. All this is the meaning of the picture. But, whether naively or not, I see very well what it signifies to me: that France is a great Empire, that all her sons, without any colour discrimination, faithfully serve under her flag, and that there is no better answer to the detractors of an alleged colonialism than the zeal shown by this Negro in serving his so-called oppressors. I am therefore again faced with a greater semiological system: there is a signifier, itself already formed with a previous system (a black soldier is giving the French salute); there is a signified (it is here a purposeful mixture of Frenchness and militariness); finally, there is a presence of the signified through the signifier.
>
> (Barthes 1972: 116)

Barthes is suggesting that images like this one are elements in a myth – superficially benign and obvious (at the denotative level) but underlying this surface are connotations of colonialism and deference to French paternalism by her subjects. It was also obviously important to maintain a sense of order and control during struggles against French colonial rule in North Africa and very harsh and repressive actions of the French in defence of their colonies, especially in Algeria.

Such imagery could be viewed as elements within a reified language of common sense, statement of fact, the bourgeois efforts (as Barthes saw it) to continuously

---

3 Texts are potentially open to multiple readings, but in practice one is 'preferred'. The analysis of the text often exposes this preference.

disguise the complex process of historical change. In this process the struggle of the colonial subject or the proletariat disappear into reified objects that can be measured and hoarded up. We talk of *the* stock exchange and *the* balance of payments. These alienated objects obscure conflict and manipulation by the elite. Such nominalised terms disguise the reality of human toil.

This is how myth in Barthes' sense operates: the second level of signification becomes the signifier for a third level that is disguised and naturalised by association with the simply denotative (and 'innocent') objects in the world:

> Just as the cuttlefish squirts ink in order to protect itself, it cannot rest until it has obscured the ceaseless making of the world, fixated this world into an object which can be forever possessed, catalogued its riches, embalmed it, and injected into reality some purifying essence which will stop its transformation, its flight towards other forms of existence.
>
> (Barthes 1972: 155)

Every day we are inundated with images, words, non-verbal signs, advertising, television and posters that communicate to us, in a similar way to Barthes' encounter with *Paris-Match*, information about the society we are in and affirm, reinforce or question and oppose this mythical common-sense view of the world. Yet such meanings are dependent on the codes and practices we bring to their interpretation. We are intimately bound to the codes that are presented to us and our cultural knowledge allows us to make sense of these messages. However, some social meanings are taken as a self-evident part of an unquestionable social order. For example, the ownership of the wealth of the nation is in the hands of a privileged elite, or the status 'white' is not nominated as an ethnic status but rather as 'natural' in our common-sense reality. There is a sense of closure, a myth of naturalness, about the operations of capitalism.

These are the invisible yet dominant codes that underpin our experience of social reality, so familiar and habitual that they are effectively unspoken conventions. Many of our everyday assumptions are based on these myths – they are unnamed conventions – subject to a process of **ex-nomination** as Barthes remarks: 'the bourgeoisie is defined as *the social class which does not want to be named.* "Bourgeoisie", "petit-bourgeoisie", "capitalism", "proletariat" are the locus of an unceasing haemorrhage: meaning flows out of them until their very name becomes unnecessary' (Barthes 1972: 138, italics in original). In a very similar way, whiteness is constructed as natural, innocent and omnipresent, the attributes of 'depoliticised speech' – of myth.

RHETORICAL IMAGES

The implication of this realisation that language is a conventional and arbitrary code became central to the culturalist analyses of society. Raymond Williams, Stuart Hall, John Fiske and John Hartley among many others have applied these structuralist understandings to their interpretations of popular culture.

Barthes' essay 'The Rhetoric of the Image' (1984a) was an important contribution to the study of the process of signification in photographic images, especially those images in popular cultural forms such as advertising. The idea that 'every picture tells a story' is very old, but Barthes focused upon the internal process of signification played out in our 'reading' of images, the dialogue between the denotative level and the symbolic connotative level. The manner in which this denotative, literal level is coded 'prepares and facilitates' (Barthes 1984a: 43) our reading of the connotative level. Hence, slight changes in the mode of portrayal (for instance, transformation of a still life into a painting or recording an event photographically) will inevitably change the relationship to consciousness and the manner of interpretation the viewer employs. Barthes highlights the contrast between the interpretation of photographic images as opposed to film: 'the photograph must be related to a pure spectatorial consciousness and not to the more projective, more "magical" fictional consciousness on which film by and large exists' (1984a: 45). He talks about a process of 'eviction' that takes place when we perceive an image, a conscious suspension of the faculty through which the connotative potential becomes associated with the denotative sign. This is necessary when coping with the barrage of mundane subjects (e.g. advertising images). Deeper meanings are necessarily 'mentally deleted'. Yet the naturalistic codes through which photographs are encoded are not experienced as manipulations of reality, as illusions, rather they indicate the actuality of 'having been there'. Photographs appear to be objective evidence of existence. This complex cognitive process that occurs as we perceive an image means that, in Barthes words, 'the denoted image naturalizes the symbolic message, it innocents the semantic artifice of connotation' (1984a: 45). This implies that photographs underwrite the objectivity of an event. Stuart Hall argues (in his 1973 analysis, see Hall 1980) that news photographs neutralise the ideological function of the newspaper (Hall 1980: 188). The authority and supposed objectivity of news photographs seems to counter the political bias that we know the paper to have.

Ethnographic images, the type employed in many early twentieth-century volumes gave the reader a neat summation of 'peoples of the world': banal, ethnocentric and trivialising, they present a collation of the traits and livelihoods. Egypt is the Nile, camel trains, the pyramids, veiled women; the Arctic is Eskimos fishing through ice holes, building igloos, dogs pulling sleds and Argentina is gauchos on the Pampas, drinking maté from a gourd; Australia is Aborigines holding spears

Figure 1.2 Stone Age people of the desert

Figure 1.3 Negro women tending young sugar canes

or boomerangs, roustabouts in the shearing sheds; Malaysia is sarong-wearing Malays tapping rubber trees, and so on. These lantern-show slides reduce the world to maps showing characteristic ethnic types, symbols of produce and industry. The world effectively reduced seems manageable, apolitical. Figures 1.2 and 1.3 below are two of this ilk; published before the Second World War, they present the world pictorially as a pageant that parades before our eyes, to be consumed. For your pleasure the diverse typifications of the world's peoples are assembled, the images are sought out that seem to embody the essence of each nation.

> If it were possible for a pageant of the world's peoples to be shown on the silver screen of your nearest cinema, and each individual took no more than a second to play his part, the performance would go on night and day without cessation for over sixty years. Of the 2,000,000,000 men, women and children in the grand march past, the majority would be of the white race, followed by members of the yellow, brown, black and red races in decreasing but amazing numbers.
>
> (Wheeler 1935: 7)

Looking at Figure 1.2, the manner in which a whole people is reduced to an icon becomes apparent. The racism is deeply embedded in the project of these trivialising taxonomies. Such images show elements of anthropological and romantic discourses that Muecke (1982) argues are amongst the narrow lexicon available when talking about Indigenous Australians. The anthropological discourse, with its focus on kinship, ceremony, totemism and mythology creates the other as totally removed from the viewer, remote, fixed in time. Significantly, they are portrayed as an evolutionary 'cul-de-sac' and doubts are expressed about their survival. Such images are instructive not only for what they reveal about the people in question but also for what is revealed about how white European culture sees itself through the objectification of others.

How 'they' are catalogued, the iconic postures and cultural artefacts, the use of the landscape, positioning of the family groups as well as the continuity with imagery used today suggests that this view of indigenous Australians as a timeless 'primitive' culture serves a marked social function that helps to define and legitimate white Australian culture.

Figure 1.3 is surprising. Compared to the stereotypical images that I have just described it seems to have an authenticity, a lack of posing that is unusual. The text describes this as 'a pleasant rural scene'. The women's clothing – at once puritanical and ragged – encumbers their exhausted bodies giving an oppressive sense of stifling, back-breaking physical labour in oppressive heat. This makes the scene anything but 'pleasant'. It is a reminder of colonialism and slavery and the description makes attempts to draw a clear distinction between slavery and this 'pleasant' scene – informing us that 'For many years Jamaica was one of the world's greatest slave marts; the emancipation of the slaves took place in 1834.

The negro peasant population is chiefly employed on the sugar plantation, and here we have a typical group of women busily working among the young canes' (Hammerton 1933: 203).

Yet in pictures like this that objectify the colonial subject there are no attempts to consider them as people oppressed. They are burdened by transgressionary signs that undermine the superficial voyeurism employed in the text. The face of the woman in the centre of the picture, half turned and regarding the photographer narrowly with suspicion and resentment, forms in Barthes terminology the **punctum** of this image and transforms it from the artifice of the popular trivial ethnography by opening up other readings to this intended apolitical diorama, in which separate subjects are entirely removed from the perception of Hammerton's **ideal reader**. In this way, a small sign, a look, a gesture, the set of a body (a feature unintended by the photographer who composed the image) transforms and denies the dominant reading's implied closure.

WHITENESS AS MYTH

'Whiteness' is an example of a dominant yet naturalised and mythologised cultural form. Michael Pickering exposes the underlying truth about the discourse of race as a marker of difference from a position of invisible white domination:

> In contemporary discourse, 'race' refers to people who are non-white, and denotes cultural 'difference'. 'Race' is used as a way of designating certain categories within our culture, and it does this from an invisible, undesignated position. This is the position of whiteness. As a normative position, whiteness is taken to be a natural fact, existing beyond the bounds of consideration. It is not racially marked *as* white in the way that black is so marked.
>
> (Pickering 2004: 91)

This is easy to illustrate in everyday language: to specify something is 'white' may seem nonsensical or transgressive, while black or Asian may seem quite justifiable. The song by the Clash (1977), 'White Riot', breaks our assumptions of what a riot can or should be. The prevalence of 'White' Studies is an interesting phenomenon recognising and scrutinising 'whiteness' in an attempt to reveal what is typically rendered invisible and normative. The unearned privilege accorded to 'white' people in our societies operates in a similar way to other markers of power in society. For example, young, male, able-bodied, heterosexual, middle-class people may reap the benefits of special privileges simply by accident of birth.

Writer Kimberly Hohman (2000) comments on several aspect of white privilege that can be taken for granted by the white mainstream culture but which, she suggests, are a constant source of unease for others:

- being able to turn on the television and see people of their race widely represented;
- never being asked to speak on behalf of their entire race;
- being able to succeed without being called a credit to their race;
- being able to have a bad day without wondering what their race had to do with specific negative incidents.

Frantz Fanon was one of the first to articulate the seamless dominance of white ideology – an ideological field that distorted the psyche of the post-colonial subject – recognition that whiteness was normalised and permeated every aspect of the metropolitan culture in which black people found themselves. Such insights about the damage and distortion suffered as a result of this have been of profound importance to the civil rights movement of the 1960s and to the politics of resistance around the world. Fanon's insight into the experience of metropolitan and colonial racism has created a critical consciousness of the linkages between racialism and white western culture that present whiteness as a platform of unspoken, invisible superiority. The effects of white colonialism are not just on the outer material shell of the colonised but also on their insides through the psychological damage caused by this inescapable whiteness. Fanon reflects this sense of fragmentation of the psyche and the feeling that the entire world of discourse is permeated and possessed by whiteness:

> To speak a language is to take on a world, a culture. The Antilles Negro who wants to be white will be the whiter as he gains greater mastery of the cultural tool that language is. Rather more than a year ago in Lyon, I remember, in a lecture I had drawn a parallel between the Negro and European poetry, and a French acquaintance told me enthusiastically, 'At the bottom you are a white man.' The fact that I had been able to investigate so interesting a problem through the white man's language gave me honorary citizenship.'
>
> (Fanon 1967a: 38)

It is clear that Fanon had deep insight into the battle for symbolic dominance and the way in which signs (linguistic or otherwise) were the tokens by which post-colonial power operated. Newly arrived in Paris from Martinique he describes the shattering experience of racism. Brought up in a colonial society, the son of a white French father and a black mother, he had never thought of himself as 'black' or experienced the hostile forms of metropolitan racism. He describes the experience as shattering, his self-image shattered into pieces as a small French boy called out to his mother in alarm, 'Look a negro!'

> 'Dirty nigger!' Or simply, 'Look, a Negro!' I came into the world imbued with the will to find a meaning in things, my spirit filled with the desire to attain

to the source of the world, and then I found that I was an object in the midst of other objects. Sealed into that crushing objecthood.

(Fanon 1967a: 109)

This reduction of people to mere clusters of physical features and invented signs of difference; a Jewish nose, Asian eyes, African pigmentation, renders their individuality null and void.

More recently, Richard Dyer's *White* (1997) draws up an important analysis of whiteness, a state that on the surface seems mundane and unexceptional. However, when whiteness comes under scrutiny the profound depths of racialist ideologies and their link to culture are exposed. By contrast, non-whiteness is always marked as different, out of the ordinary. A focus on the naturalised form is an important moment of recognition that race and racism are not just adjuncts, afterthoughts to the cultural practices of a group, rather they are discourses that are intrinsic to white cultural superiority. Dyer illustrates the all-pervasive whiteness of western culture through paintings of classical antiquity and the modern filmic portrayal of white heroes including Tarzan, Hercules and Rambo. These latter popular icons could be considered a manifestation of a form of excessive whiteness that functions as a sign of an idealised whiteness aspired to by the commonplace whiteness, and also feared. This is similar to ideas about gender. Connell (1987) posits several kinds of masculinity, including a hegemonic masculinity that portrays the extreme position of maleness, other forms are either complicit or subordinated. Whiteness (and patriarchy) attains invisibility and bodies of the Other, black or female can be rendered unproblematically as objects.

SCARED?

Travelling through the urban wasteland of a city in northern England, surrounded by the decaying remnants of a once-thriving industrial hinterland, I was confronted by this disconcerting and incomprehensible image: a huge black face brooding, threateningly lit and the word 'SCARED' in blood red. In what way does this text anchor the image – is it addressed to us or to the face itself? We are, I suppose, far from innocent observers of advertising – a cultural form that has learnt to derive maximum benefit from manipulating our expectations and the intertextual nature of our visual knowledge. Behind a poster such as this there lies a lexicon of well-worn cultural expressions: the style of under-lighting, passive trance-like facial expression, the size and form of the lettering. A face emerging from the gloom like Brando's in *Apocalypse Now*.

To construct meaning, we refer back through images associated with film, TV, poster art and archive imagery. Our understanding of this is certainly dependent on a matrix of cultural knowledge. Is this a 'teaser ad' for a forthcoming movie or a public-safety ad? We might look at it with a certain cynicism, with humour or

Figure 1.4 Scared? Poster from Commission for Racial Equality's controversial campaign – Sheffield 1999

irony as we are frequently confronted by advertising campaigns that make abstract metaphoric allusions to branded products. Is this simply the signifier for a product or brand that we have missed the television ad for? Or a sinisterly lit face of another TV celebrity we have not paid attention to?

Depending on the currency of popular concerns at the time we view such an image, we might well consider it to be about the threat of terrorism or even about the popular anxieties exacerbated by tabloids over asylum seekers. Yet the starkness of the poster does suggest another somehow subversive and less likely meaning: that the poster is addressing our fear of 'blackness', a primordial myth bolstered and reaffirmed by hundreds of images of drug-related black street crime, tabloid panics of mugging and violence, lurid Hollywood images of gangsters in films such as *Boyz from the Hood* and *New Jack City*. Indeed, a whole genre of film from the 'blaxploitation' era of the 1970s onwards portrays black culture in the USA in gross physical terms of sexual and aggressive action. These are the very attributes that were perpetuated as stereotypes throughout the colonial period. Constructing the black body as physically powerful and menacing and with enormous sexual energy can be seen to persist in these genres of popular culture.

But, driving past the billboard, one can make out another line of print in white 'YOU SHOULD BE. HE'S A DENTIST'. This denouement serves to both explode and expose the unspoken cultural meaning, blackness, without a biography, is a signifier, and the connotations it refers to are all too often negative.

Our culture has marked out blackness as Other as deviant and whiteness as ex-nominated and inherently privileged. So, by juxtaposing a deviant assumption, a white professional category 'it' becomes 'he'; it is this shocking transformation that so exposes the racist expectations popularly harboured. This is the message – the rhetoric of the image. The campaign had intended to address complicit racism by allowing the viewer to expose, through the readers' practices of signification, their implicit cultural bias. We recognise the gross stereotypes, disturbing and distasteful as they may be, and at some level they may influence judgement, may become naturalised despite their banality.

Another poster, ostensibly an advert for a recruitment agency with a slogan 'Dominate the Race', pictured a besuited white executive climbing a ladder and treading on the hands of a similar dressed black candidate who was grasping the lower rungs. These posters may have left people gasping in amazement at the extraordinary breaches in political correctness, but by all accounts there were not many complaints registered. The 'Scared?' poster (a Commission for Racial Equality administrator informed me) had more complaints from dentists who felt this was scornful of their profession than from individuals concerned about racism. The Director of the Commission for Racial Equality (CRE) at the time, Sir Herman Ouseley, had decided to use shock tactics. A series of posters were put up around the country. Overtly racist billboards were planted in hope of a reaction. One, claiming to promote the 'TDX-5 rape alarm,' showed a white woman sitting on a bus anxiously eyeing a young black man. The ad line read, 'Because it's a jungle out there'. This ad clearly alluded to the pernicious myth of threatening black sexuality. They were alarming, distasteful and arguably in danger of reaffirming popular stereotypes rather than shaming people for recognising them. However, the entrenched nature and invisibility of white prejudices is clearly the obstacle that the CRE was trying to hold up a mirror to.

THE MATRIX OF CULTURAL IDENTITY

Figure 1.5 shoes a Matrix of Cultural Identity (adapted from Hall and du Gay (1997)). The matrix shows five interrelated processes in the way social meanings are circulated within culture: production, consumption, regulation, representation and identity. Looking at each of these in turn sheds light on the importance of how meaning is produced, affirmed or challenged, and the central place of culture in defining personal identity. The diagram shows the dynamic relationship between five interacting loci of cultural practices. Figure 1.4 will be considered as an example of the way in which the five interlinked processes may operate. Although the emphasis here is on the construction of identity as the centre point of these processes, identity itself is simply another domain in the construction of social meaning. Any point in the matrix could be considered first.

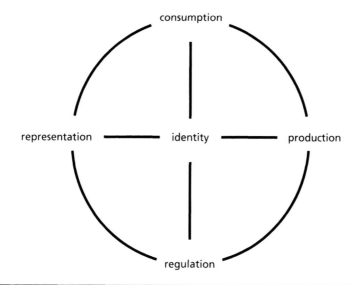

Figure 1.5 Matrix of Cultural Identity adapted from the Circuit of Culture (Hall and du Gay, 1996)

Production

The poster is a result of cultural meanings and cultural economies. It is the product of a poster campaign by the CRE – an institution whose role is circumscribed by commercial and social policies for the dissemination of effective and positive portrayals of diversity. It is, like many mass media forms, an attempt to produce an artefact that reflects beliefs about consumers of images. The image itself is a product of the genealogy of ideas of representation about blackness and its popular meanings. Yet in terms of encoded rhetoric we are aware of a possible attempt to choose the imagery that epitomises the lowest common denominator of racism. Hence a hyperreal grossness, an obviousness in these posters that may be akin to the recognition of artifice that Barthes (1977) suggested in his writing about the 'obtuse meaning' that 'declares its artifice but without in so doing abandoning the "good faith" of its referent' (Barthes 1977: 58). Here the referent is determined by each reader's recognition of the larger domain of cultural assumptions about generic blackness, a face without a biography.

Consumption

Consumption is an intrinsic link to our relationship to the forces of production and occurs, therefore, in very different forms depending on our social position. Consumption preserves and enhances the economic system. In the consumption of meanings – such as those implicit in this poster – culture divides us into different types of consumer. Hence, it is a fair assumption that there will be a range of possible meanings and interpretations to open images such as this one. Consumption, and the choices we make within it, is central to the ways in which our identity is constructed. **Cultural capital**, as Bourdieu suggests (1989a), is linked to class-related differences in consumption. So the codes and aesthetic sensibilities we have, or believe we have, shape our sense of identity and difference. Hence, an image such as this is a cultural product that can be consumed in various ways depending on our social and cultural location. Status and social class can be reproduced through patterns of consumption. Ideas of High Culture, aesthetics and popular cultural forms divide readers sharply, as they embody class distinctions of taste made about cultural products: identity is certainly linked to consumption in many ways. Consumption is not just about commercial and economic activity it is an intrinsically cultural process and one which is increasingly central to definitions of identity (Bourdieu 1989).

Identity

The way in which individual and shared identity is constructed will determine how an individual relates to this image. Ethnicity, gender, nationality, social class, sexuality and community are aspects of the self that may lead to complex and conflicted interpretations of this image and its meaning as a public-message part of an organised campaign. Indeed, the interplay of all such images and ideas of self create a constant dialectic within the individual's identity.

> Identity is a work in progress, a negotiated space between ourselves and others; constantly being re-appraised and very much linked to the circulation of cultural meanings in a society. Furthermore identity is intensely political. There are constant efforts to escape, fix or perpetuate images and meanings of others. These transformations are apparent in every domain, and the relationships between these constructions reflect and reinforce power relations.
>
> (Taylor and Spencer 2004: 4)

Hence, the ways different groups identify with the image are not fixed either. A black man's face is enormously meaningful in our culture but for very different reasons. The accumulation of imagery of metaphors of blackness and whiteness raises questions for the construction of identity. It is only because of identities'

potential for exclusion that they can serve as points of commonality and identification, 'every identity naming as its necessary, even if silenced and unspoken
other, that which it "lacks"' (Hall and du Gay 1996: 5). This has psycho-social
consequences for those identities that are marginalised. Cornel West asks, 'How
does one come to accept and affirm a body despised by one's fellow citizens?'
West considers that 'demythologizing' of black sexuality is crucial for black America
because much of black self-hatred and self-contempt has to do with the refusal of
many black Americans to love their own black bodies (West 1995).

Regulation

Like other economies, the cultural economy is subject to regulation and sanctions.
The poster campaign led to police covering up some of the posters for fear that
they might incite racial hatred. Yet while regulation and production depend on
formal policies and decision-making, the CRE had a mandate to address the issues
of societal racism and to attempt to intervene. They hence employed 'creatives'
who tried to design a campaign that would reflect the meanings coherently to
the public. Individuals as they observe the poster may assess whether it affirms or
contradicts their values. Indeed, it later became apparent that the CRE was
anticipating mass complaints against the posters that they felt would show robust
public outrage against assumptions being made implicitly in the campaign.
A follow-up campaign was planned with posters that would carry smaller versions
of the original 'Shocked' posters framed with the words, 'What was worse? This
advert or your failure to complain?' However, this never eventuated as official
regulation was imposed:

> The CRE has not had a chance to put up the second set of ads. The police of
> Avon and Somerset have threatened to prosecute the CRE under the Race
> Relations Act – the very law that established the CRE, and forbids 'racism.' In
> some areas, the original ads were ordered covered with white paper. The CRE
> stands by its campaign. It says there were only 82 complaints about the posters,
> adding that thousands of Britons saw them and did nothing – proof that the
> campaign is badly needed.
>
> (Tweedie 1998)

Representation

Every culture uses signs and symbols to represent concepts, ideas, values and
feelings. The face shown in the poster could act as a cultural icon, i.e., a multilayered image that reflects dominant values and beliefs, as well as conflicts and

contradictions of the time. It begs the question 'What is the meaning of blackness?'. In semiotics of the image, it is recognised that words anchor images and their significance. Here, the word 'SCARED' contains a rhetoric that suggests certain features of blackness are being highlighted. We might see within the image other icons of our time and make those associations. In a similar way, these images that perhaps form part of a western lexicon of images of black males are anchored by their slogans.

Interestingly, the image in the SCARED? poster is reminiscent of a demonised popular icon, O.J. Simpson, whose public trial gave media channels opportunities to dwell on his impassive features and re-invoke notions of primordial racial evil. Apparently some media channels went further and actually darkened his features to emphasise primordial blackness.

> During the trial of O. J. Simpson, *Time* magazine published a picture on the cover in which Simpson's skin tone had been darkened by digital manipulation in order to make him seem more 'black' – at the same time *Newsweek* ran an OJ cover which shows his un-enhanced complexion. The effect of *Time's* manipulation is obvious when seen alongside *Newsweek*.
>
> (Duggan 2000: 2)

These are only some of the possible interpretations of the complex synthesis of social meanings. The limits to possible interpretation are dependent on individual subject location; the image is potentially open to meanings that entirely contradict and resist any of the supposedly popular meanings I have suggested.

CHAPTER SUMMARY

The chapter attempts to present the reader with some of the concepts and tools used in cultural studies, and sociology. It is important to recognise that the manner in which the understanding of 'others' has been constructed is contingent on the implicit values of whiteness which are ex-nominated and therefore so often not recognised. Race is not about whiteness or blackness per se but rather about difference from a platform of unnamed dominance. The inclusion of Barthes' ideas about myth are important for two reasons: First Saussure's notion that all elements in a linguistic system are meaningless without their relation to other elements is the foundation of the understanding taken up by Barthes that our most central cultural precepts are nothing other than artefacts, totems of our belief, and secondly that this recognition allows us to expose them for what they are. It has been illustrated that images can be understood as cultural products, and meanings which social agents produce and consume, and that such meanings and values are an inevitable part of our identity regulating our behaviours and drawing boundaries around our perceptions.

EXERCISE 1.1 MYTHOLOGIES

1   Consider what Barthes means by 'myth'. Can you think of contemporary examples?
2   Advertising typically uses these given, conventional meanings (myths) to persuade us that a product's attributes are important. Choose one or two examples from advertising and explain how the myths operate.
3   Give examples of myths of masculinity and whiteness in our society. (These can be seen to operate in literature, television, film or from popular anecdotes, urban myths or jokes.)
4   Apart from the list from Kimberly Hohman, what other aspects of white privilege can you think of that are taken for granted in western societies?

   • being able to turn on the television and see people of their race widely represented;
   • never being asked to speak on behalf of their entire race;
   • being able to succeed without being called a credit to their race;
   • being able to have a bad day without wondering what their race had to do with specific negative incidents.

5   Choose a photograph from a book or an advertisement from a magazine and show how the interplay of signs works:

   (a) within the 'Matrix of Cultural Identity';
   (b) to disguise or mythologise ideas as natural that are in fact socially constructed.

EXERCISE 1.2 SCARED?

1   At first glance at this image, what is your initial response? Write down your impressions. What is the context of this image? Who is it aimed at?
2   How did you arrive at this interpretation of the poster? What cultural sources informed your view?
3   Consider the cultural aesthetics that come into play when we interpret such images. Which of the following oppositions (or points in between) are useful in considering?

(a) your response or ability to interpret this poster;

(b) another image you have seen.

easy ↔ difficult
realism ↔ abstraction
proximity ↔ distance
polemical ↔ neutral
function ↔ form
necessity ↔ luxury

4 How do you locate this image in a cultural genealogy? Can you site other similar images that are known to you from other media such as film, television, news stories, etc.?

5 What is the effect of the word 'SCARED'? How does it function in relation to the image? Compare other pictures, ads or posters, and the effect of any wording (or absence of wording).

6 Compare your interpretation with that of two or three others. List their responses.

(a) Was there a consensus or was the diversity of views a sign of the openness of the poster?

(b) What did the different or similar readings say about your backgrounds?

7 Imagine the face on the poster was white instead of black. What codes might we use to make sense of it?

CHAPTER 2

The Politics of Naming

In this section, the importance of language and other cultural codes are explored in more depth. We have shown that the connotations of cultural codes are actively interpreted by the 'reader' and that, while they are open to different readings in practice, these tend to be constrained by dominant social values and popular conventions of interpretation that can be dissected along the lines of key social divisions from which they are viewed. Language can be a source of intense ethnic rivalry; in some instances it can be used to belittle, abuse or, as in the example quoted below, almost to deny the separate existence of unique and complex cultures.

> A single English word can effectively, in an instant, disembowel the vast 100,000 year histories and culture of about five hundred different peoples in Australia by naming us 'Aborigines'. That language was used by the colonisers as a weapon can be seen in the experience of numerous colonised peoples (here and in other countries) who were forced to use the coloniser's language.
>
> (Foley 1997)

It is exactly because language is so intrinsically linked to culture, identity and meaning that colonisers were at pains to control its use, and also why it may become a flashpoint in ethnic struggles of resistance as in. For example, the unique Basque language and the desire for Basque autonomy within Spain. There are many such struggles (Welsh, Catalan) that are examples of what Hechter (1975) has termed 'internal colonialism', suggesting ethnic enclaves' struggle for autonomy within the boundaries of the nation-state. The means by which regional languages were discouraged has been a source of long-standing enmity to those who felt the power of the state at school and elsewhere.[1]

One of the indications that race and ethnicity do not have fixed referents but rather belong to the domain of shifting social and cultural meanings in which boundaries are constantly negotiated is the fact that conventions of naming are a constantly changing and sensitive area. How a group is denoted is not experienced as an arbitrary label but as a deeply meaningful and often challenging semantic field. Naming and categorising of individuals is highly political. The way in which these boundaries are established at times admits individual choice and self-determination. At other times it is enforced by the dominant culture, colonial power or government. At the level of popular understandings, there are frequently issues about what is the correct (and politically correct) term to describe ethnic groups. It is significant that students are often concerned to ensure they have the right terminology. At times our **misrecognition** of others reflects the lack of communication between mainstream culture and minority groups by our using terms from another era such as 'coloured people' ('people of colour' is still used in the USA). While these terms are considered deeply patronising to those to whom they are directed in the UK, it is not surprising that white middle-class students feel unable to keep up with trends that have little impact on mainstream white culture. Indeed as Kohn (1996) notes, 'we' harbour anxieties about 'race'. 'We feel that the subject is covered by a taboo, but we don't know exactly what the rules of the taboo are. It seems important if not obligatory, to discuss cultural differences, but dangerous even to mention physical differences' (Kohn 1996: 1). Ironically, elements of black culture – especially music and fashion – are frequently appropriated, filtered and commodified for a mainstream white consumer market.

DEFINING RACE AND ETHNICITY

It is important to recognise that the shifting meanings of these terms are a consequence of the fact that they refer to socially constructed concepts. At times they have been used interchangeably (in Europe); at others they are strongly differentiated. 'The modernist connotation of "race" and "ethnicity" sees "race" either subsumed in "ethnicity", or referred to euphemistically through "ethnicity"' (Popeau 1998: 177). Popeau indicates that the term 'ethnicity' is typically used as a 'polite and less controversial term for "race"' (1998: 166).

---

1 Consider the example of the treacherous 'Welsh Not', A piece of wood that had to be carried by a child at school if caught using the Welsh language. They could, though, pass it on to other children who were heard to speak Welsh, so it encouraged betrayal as the last child carrying the hated object at the end of the day was the one to be punished.

'Race'

'Race' is an extraordinarily problematic term, debated and reviled and contested so fiercely yet still employed as it is clearly so intrinsically woven into the fabric of western cultural history (inverted commas are often employed to indicate that the term is, at best, part of a dubious fossil record of an inglorious history. It is certainly a candidate for being placed 'under erasure' (Derrida's convention '**sous rature**') a process by which such terms are used with a line through them to indicate their problematic or spurious nature. However, despite this, many nations continue to use the term. For example, Malaysia and the USA both employ the term in contexts where Europeans would prefer the term 'ethnicity'. This use of the term 'race' as a marker of difference derives from differing social histories, stark divisions and, in the case of Malaysia, a long period of colonial rule. Furthermore, the term is woven into understandings about definitions of citizenship and lineage. Ideas of blood quantum are still used to determine identities and rights of membership to cultural and national groups. For example, membership of an ethnic grouping can be determined by lineage or blood quantum or by fact of birth within a country or by self-determination. The official status of people with different 'blood quantums' could equate to material reward being different for full blood, half-caste, quadroon, octoroon. Amongst indigenous peoples of Australia and America, it has been a means of determining rights to belong or to be excluded. It was the basis on which decisions were made about taking certain mixed children from their Aboriginal parents (a practice that was carried on into the 1970s). 'Quadroons and octoroons, under 10 or 12 years of age, should, where such can be done without inflicting cruelty on the half-caste mother, be placed in an European institution, where they can be given a reasonable chance of absorption into the white community to which they rightly belong' (Bleakley 1929: 17).

Not only were many thousands of Aboriginal families devastated by these forced removals, based on ideas of actively 'breeding out' aboriginality, but Aboriginal people of mixed ancestry encountered the dilemma of being caught in the middle of a harshly divisive system as the next example shows:

In 1935 a fair-skinned Australian of part-indigenous descent was ejected from a hotel for being an Aboriginal. He returned to his home on the mission station to find himself refused entry because he was not an Aboriginal. He tried to remove his children but was told he could not because they were Aboriginal. He walked to the next town where he was arrested for being an Aboriginal vagrant and placed on the local reserve. During the Second World War he tried to enlist but was told he could not because he was Aboriginal. He went interstate and joined up as a non-Aboriginal. After the war he could not acquire a passport without permission because he was Aboriginal. He received exemption from the Aborigines Protection Act – and was told that he could no longer visit his relations on the reserve because he was not an Aboriginal. He was denied permission to enter the Returned Servicemen's Club because he was.

(Read 1996)

Race is central to ideas of culture that emerged during the Enlightenment. The concept emerged in European languages in the late fourteenth early fifteenth centuries. 'Race' was first used in English in the sixteenth century. In *Keywords*, Raymond Williams (1983) cites its earliest uses as 'offspring in the sense of line of descent'. Young (1995) and Malik (1996) show that the divergent views about race and racial categories stem from the Enlightenment when divisive categorising and pseudo-scientific views of racial difference emerged albeit with resistance from some philosophers who held fast to ideas of universal humanity united by given capacity for reasoning and civil life and that differences were in fact due to climatic or agricultural variations. As a discourse, the concept has a long and complex history of shifting meanings 'parasitic on theoretical and social discourses for the meaning it assumes at given historical moments' (Goldberg 1992: 553).

This suggests that different uses of the term can be traced within historically specific discourses. The interpretation of race as a 'floating signifier' (see Hall 1996b) is anchored to the prevailing social realities of the time.

Table 2.1 is based on the discourse of race as expressed by Theo Goldberg (1992) and charts some of the strands that have composed the socially interwoven ideas about the construction of race. These will be given some consideration in turn.

SHIFTING MEANINGS OF RACE

Monogenism

With regard to questions of origin, religious orthodoxy maintained a strong and constant influence on thought. The Great Chain of Being from the Middle Ages to the Enlightenment provided a fixed and immutable order for creation. God's creations were set out in layers from the infernal regions below the Earth, to the lowliest terrestrial life, to animals, birds, humanity, and above them to celestial beings, to God the Father. All linked by a chain. However, there were anomalous gaps between the realms that were not easily accounted for. The Bible was treated as an accurate text explaining the process of creation (the world was calculated to be only 5,500 years old). Humankind sprang from Adam and Eve. As non-Europeans were more frequently encountered and as the slave trade progressed, other biblical explanations were needed to safeguard Christian morality. There was the notion that black-skinned people were the descendents of Ham, the son

Table 2.1 Evolving discourses of race

DISCOURSE	DESCRIPTION	CONSEQUENCES
Monogenism (fourteenth–eighteenth century)	focus on origin, breed, stock; descent from Adam and Eve	commitment to race as lineage, pedigree
Polygenism (eighteenth–nineteenth century)	biological inheritance and hierarchy	species; population; rigid categories
Evolutionism (late nineteenth century)	more fluid taxonomies; race as sub-species genetically interpreted	breeding populations are species; races are sub-species.
Race as class (nineteenth-century on)	socio-economic status or relation to mode of production, or status	race as determined by class; reductionist – ignores cultural dimension
Race as culture (nineteenth-century on)	identification with language, religion, customs, mores encultured characteristics	group-bound dictum 'manners (or language) maketh man'
Race as ethnicity (twentieth-century on)	use of term 'race' inherently; ethnocentric 'ethnicity' used interchangeably with race; social choice to identify by natural rather than social criteria	reflects reification of concepts over time; ethnicity shifts back to objectified category 'them' rather than 'us'
Race as nation (late nineteenth-century on)	race as nation; similar to early concept of lineage, rallying force behind nationalist movements	for example, White Australia Policy; also current concerns about immigration and asylum seekers, etc.

that Noah cursed and banished to the land of Nod – East of Eden. And there were also notions that there were pre-Adamic beings that were outside of the regular Christian remit. These views, which are not supported in the Bible, were nevertheless influential.

The voyages of discovery that began in earnest in the fifteenth and sixteenth centuries and the consequent acts of colonialism and empire-building began to broaden ideas about the world and its inhabitants. Initially shrouded in mystery and prone to mythological invention, 'other' peoples became the object of increased interest and study and even collection and exhibition. McCaskell (1994) gives the example of how a chimpanzee was brought back to Britain in 1699 and efforts made to over-represent certain features to make it appear much more human, as it was considered a potential candidate for a missing link between monkeys and humankind. There was a desire to eradicate the anomalous areas and gaps on the Great Chain.

Polygenism

Monogenism, which was maintained by many Enlightenment thinkers, gradually gave way to notions of hierarchical ordering and separate generation of races as species. As early as 1677, William Petty proposed that 'savages were a permanently distinct and inferior species of humanity located between (white) men and animals on the Great Chain' (Frederickson 1981). Fifty years later, the consequences of Petty's classifications and their far-ranging consequences were realised by Swedish biologist Linnaeus whose *General System of Nature* (1806) established four basic colour types in descending order:

- White Europeans
- Red Americans
- Yellow Asians
- Black Africans.

By the tenth edition, the colour categories had also been linked to attributes of character that showed the gradual influence of the idea that the stamp of character was innate and implicitly linked to physical differences. This had the consequence of forming much more fixed and inviolable traits and further emphasised the hierarchical and mutually exclusive natures of the 'races'. A century later, these categories and the ready stereotypical traits were apparently accepted and commonplace.

Works such as Oliver Goldsmith's *Animated Nature* (1876) portray the races as separate. Well into the twentieth century, the influence of such stereotypes and an acceptance of a **Manichean divide** were being reproduced in popular 'everyman' sort of sentiments. Take, for example, the morally superior tone of *Savage Survivals* (1933) which states that:

Savages cry easily and are afraid of the dark; they are fond of pets and toys; they have weak wills and feeble reasoning powers; they are notoriously fickle

and unreliable and exceedingly given to exaggeration of their own importance
– in all of these particulars being much like the children of the higher races.
(Moore 1933: 73)

The frequently apocryphal and stereotyped traits seem to have remained fixed
and resilient (obviously due to remoteness and lack of contact in many cases). Take
the entry in Goldsmith's on Laplanders:

These nations not only resemble each other in their deformity, their
dwarfishness, the colour of their hair and eyes, but they have in a great measure,
the same inclinations, and the same manners, being all equally rude, super-
stitious, and stupid. The Danish Laplanders have a large black cat, to which
they communicate their secrets, and consult in all their affairs. Among
the Swedish Laplanders there is in every family a drum for consulting the
devil; and although these nations are robust and nimble, yet they are so cowardly
that they never can be brought into the field.
(Goldsmith 1876: 209)

It is quite clear that no attempt is made to understand indigenous practices and
belief systems other than through a veil of ethnocentric Victorian values.

What impact did such classifications of human beings have? The consequences
of these classifications were far ranging. A major error was to assume that the
human species was clearly divided into subgroups, such as sub-species.

1   Human differences once classified seemed more fixed. Once terms are
    habitually used they become naturalised and embedded in the culture and
    the language.
2   The linking of physical and behavioural characteristics fitted with long-
    standing, common-sense values; that differences in physical appearance
    betoken differences in habit and temperament.
3   These typologies tended to ignore the geographically gradual nature of
    biological differences and examples which didn't fit. Gross differences are
    recognisable subtle variations are not recognised as easily.
4   All of these above aspects helped to reinforce a value-laden hierarchical view
    of different peoples. It could be argued that powerful Christian images like
    the Great Chain of Being had already predisposed European culture to such
    notions.
5   Legitimized as God-given and 'natural' supposed inferiority of non- Europeans.
    The views of scientists such as Blumenbach and Linnaeus who were widely
    renowned lent authority to such views.
6   History suggests that the hardening racialisation which had already occurred
    in the USA began to become more prevalent in Europe. A consequence is

that black thinkers, writers, scientists, philosophers were removed from the records and histories, their considerable achievements were negated.

Evolutionism

Ideas about evolution did not begin with Darwin. Hierarchical schemes of varying sophistication were developed from the seventeenth and eighteenth centuries onwards. Count Arthur Gobineau's pessimism about the outcome of the French Revolution of 1789 stemmed from a belief that inequality was a natural state and that the democratic views that stripped the aristocracy of their elevated positions were the outcome of racial miscegenation leading to a degraded racial stock, which would inevitably level a naturally uneven playing field. Again this early conception linked race with social strata as well as racial types. This view, as we will see, took hold and was maintained into the nineteenth and twentieth centuries. The interpretation of Darwin's radical view of biology had already been framed by earlier conceptualisations of evolution. Lamarck had suggested that acquired traits of the parents could be inherited by their offspring. His ideas were appealing at the time as the suggestion that acquired social traits could be inherited biologically was looked at favourably by social reformers. At the same time, Lamarck maintained that there was a grand design towards greater perfection and elaboration: 'Nature, in producing in succession every species of animal, and beginning with the least perfect or simplest to end her work with the most perfect, has gradually complicated their structure' (Lamarck 1801: 16). This did not send out the same shock waves to devout believers as Darwin's suggestion that the process of natural selection was apparently random.

Darwin's *On the Origin of Species* had a major impact on nineteenth-century thought and ran contrary to racial theory, which 'required the fixity of characteristics – race only had meaning if characters which defined a racial group remained constant over time' (Malik 1996: 90). However, in natural selection, biological types or species do not have a fixed, static existence but exist in permanent states of change and flux. This startling theory, which was supported by Darwin's empirical work (owing much to the younger Darwin's passage as a naturalist on board the *Beagle*), presented all living organisms in a struggle for survival, a struggle to produce offspring, of which only the best adapted to conditions will survive. One of the catalysts for Darwin's ground-breaking vision of change was the work of Charles Lyell's *Principles of Geology* (1830) which showed the Earth to be in a continuous process of change from ongoing geological forces and also indicated, by reference to fossil records, that mankind was much older than biblical accounts. The immense periods of time that Darwin suggested implied that change was more random and accidental than pre-ordained.

The effect of all these points was to move human beings away from the centre of creation and imply that they could hardly be its crowning glory. Some writers and cataloguers of humanity seemed to take note of this greater fluidity and, while they used racial categories, illustrated the extraordinary diversity within these groups.

The plates from Baron Cuvier's *Animal Kingdom* (1890), which portray the human race are divided into four categories: American Indian, Caucasian, Mongol and Negro (the same as Linnaeus's red, white, yellow and black), show the varieties within these colour-coded groups (see Figures 2.1 and 2.2). Each plate purports to show details of human types. The inclusion of the skull indicates the preoccupation with materialist anthropology and physiognomy at the time. The studies, from drawings by Thomas Landseer, are sensitive and sympathetic to the dignity and character of their subjects, and a long way removed from the crude stereotypes that can be seen in other works of the period. The accompanying text explains that these categories of humankind are not considered separate species, as this precludes interbreeding between species, whereas it is clearly possible between human groups. However, the physical boundaries of race are affirmed by the presence of 'hereditary peculiarities of conformance':

> Although the human species would appear to be single, since the union of any of its members produces individuals capable of propagation, there are nevertheless, certain hereditary peculiarities of conformation observable, which constitute what are termed *races, Three of these* in particular appear eminently distinct: the *Caucasian*, or white, the *Mongolian*, or yellow, and the *Ethiopian*, or negro.
>
> (Cuvier 1890: 37, italics in original)

Yet the hierarchical connotations noted in the text are seemingly at odds with the sensitive *individual* portraits of Landseer. Each Mongolian or Negro type is based on a specific portrait. The Negro race (Figure 2.1), for example, are far from animalistic, but show people from diverse, sentient and complex cultures. These portraits illustrate the wide physical differences *within* a category and further contradict rigid ascription of race. However, Cuvier's text falls back on crude racist stereotypes, drawing them as debased and irrevocably primitive:

> The Negro race is confined to the southward of the Atlas chain of mountains: its colour is black. Its hair crisped, the cranium compressed, the nose flattened. The projecting muzzle and thick lips evidently approximate it to the Apes: the hordes of which it is composed have always continued barbarous.
>
> (Cuvier 1890: 38)

Social critics of the time were scornful of these attempts to caricature attributes of the world's human varieties. It is not difficult to imagine how weaknesses

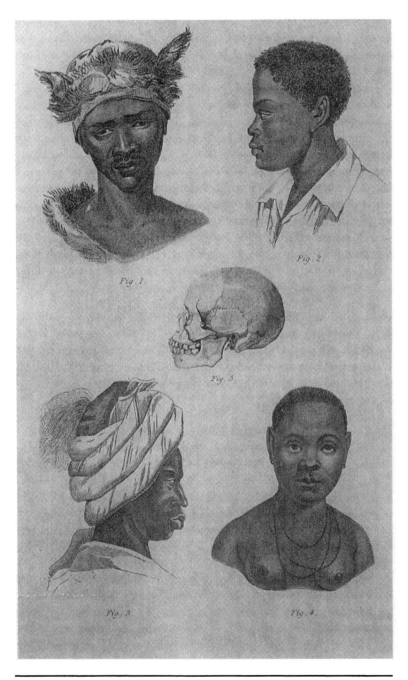

Figure 2.1 Negroes. Negro race – portraits by Landseer in Baron Cuvier's *Animal Kingdom*

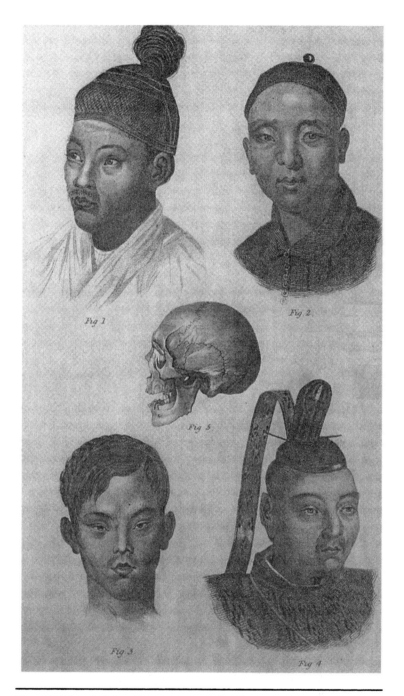

Figure 2.2 Mongols. Mongolian race – portraits by Thomas Landseer in Baron Cuvier's *Animal Kingdom*

and negative values observed in one's own society were projected onto the individuals of groups that the race scientists had never encountered. In the 1890 volume an additional note is made by W. B. Carpenter and J. O. Westwood: 'With all deference, I would suggest that naturalists are much too prone to confound resemblance with identity' (Cuvier 1890: 39).

The Origin of Species (1859), while it led to recognition of the non-uniqueness of the human race, also

> gave the rationale for a racially stratified view of evolution based on an ethnocentric colonial view of the subjugated nations who, with reference to their relative lack of western technology, were deemed more lowly. Europeans represented the highest point of evolution, diverse Asians and Indians fell in somewhere behind, and Africans brought up the rear, with Aboriginal and Papuan peoples allocated the very bottom.
>
> (Young 1976: 50)

> Imperialists, calling upon Darwin in defense of the subjugation of weaker races, could point to the 'Origin of Species', which had referred in its subtitle to 'The Preservation of Favoured Races in the Struggle for Life'. Darwin had been talking about pigeons, but the imperialists saw no reason why his theories should not apply to men.
>
> (Hofstader 1955: 171)

Use of the discourse of social Darwinist thought accords with a popular view of the inherent morality and civilised virtue of the 'white race'. There was a proliferation of popular pseudo-scientific treatises on the evolution of human types that had foundations in the physical analogies made to identity, character, intelligence, criminality, etc, popularised by phrenology, physiognomy and craniology. Shape and size of skull or other features for example, the Jewish nose (which was 'discovered' in 1711 (Mosse 1978)) and came to be seen as measurable means of assessing an individual's position on an imagined genetic ladder.

Social Darwinism was the theory that societies and classes evolve under the principle of 'survival of the fittest'. Natural selection eliminated weak persons and groups. Most Social Darwinists were, therefore, against improving the conditions of the poor. To let nature run its course was considered best, as natural equilibrium would eventually result. The theory in effect justified poverty and social stratification by combining Darwinism with individualistic and liberal values.

Laissez-faire economics and the Industrial Revolution produced a large, underpaid and exploited wage-earning class. Capitalists grew rich and the poor stayed poor. Industrial nations grew into large empires and exploited colonies to further fund the industrial expansion and the growing desire for consumer products through the plunder of booty capitalism. In such a context, the concepts of 'struggle' and 'survival of the fittest' were a useful justifications for exploitation.

Ideas of 'progress', which underpinned the drive towards greater industrialisation and scientific rationalisation, seemed analogous to 'progress' in evolution. However, the meanings embraced by the term were quite different. Industrialists and social reformers saw progress as the expansion of capitalism and the nation's productive capacity; Social Darwinists saw the improvement of the race; and biologists the selective adaptation of living things to their ecological environment.

Herbert Spencer (1820–1903) was an English philosopher who developed a theory of evolution even before Darwin's *On the Origin of Species*. Spencer developed the principle of 'survival of the fittest' to society, arguing that societies grow from an initial militant phase into large organized social units, from 'an indefinite incoherent homogeneity, to a definite coherent heterogeneity' (Spencer 1860). The pre-scientific basis of early hierarchies such as the belief in a Great Chain of Being in Christianity made ranked tiers of evolution already seem plausible. Darwin developed the theory of natural selection to explain differences between species, but many of his contemporaries, including Spencer and Darwin's own cousin Francis Galton, used his ideas to promote Social Darwinism and eugenics. Social Darwinism maintains that certain groups of people are poorer than others and more likely to be used as slave labour because they're 'less evolved' and therefore inferior.

However, the initial principle of eugenics, defined by Galton (1996), was directly in connection with the teaching and work of Darwin, himself very influenced by Malthus. According to Darwin, the mechanisms of natural selection are thwarted by human civilisation. One of the objectives of civilisation is somehow to help the underprivileged ones, therefore to be opposed to the natural selection responsible for extinction of the weakest. According to eugenicists, this intervention could affect the natural balance, leading to an increase in individuals who were weaker genetically and who would have normally been eliminated through natural-selection processes.

RACE AND CLASS

In the nineteenth century, racial differences, which effectively drew species divides between people, were applied on grounds of class position also. 'What we would now consider to be class or social distinctions were seen as racial ones' (Malik 1996: 81). Race can be associated with measures of social status, where one lives, occupation, language, style of dress, and so on. There is, as Goldberg points out, the sense that if one behaves 'white', one is seen as white. So, race is composed of conventional discourses and if performers 'play white' then they are likely to be considered white. A more Marxist interpretation suggests that race is a relationship to the means of production (see Chapter 3). In this view, race is seen to be a mask for other forms of social inequality and is reducible to socio-economics. Accepting racialisation by creating inviolable genetic boundaries legitimised inequality and allowed unequal treatment to become institutionalised.

It could be argued that the use of racial divisions emerged as a way of resolving the conflict between, on the one hand, the ideology of equality for all and universal reason and, on the other, facts of social inequality. We might think of Orwell's *Animal Farm* and the pig Napoleon's dictum: 'All animals are equal but some animals are more equal than others' (Orwell 1945). The development of a contradictory concept of 'race' stems from just this style of reasoning. Indeed, without such a concept, inequality might have been a much more bitter pill to swallow: 'Racial ideology was the inevitable product of the persistence of differences of rank, class and peoples in a society that had accepted the concept of equality' (Malik 2002: 5).

RACE AS CULTURE

Whether 'culture' is taken to mean a whole way of life or as signifying discursive practices through which hegemony is produced, it is nevertheless integral both to the lived realities of race as well as the construction of boundaries that make it an intensely political concept.

Race, from a culturalist viewpoint (such as that espoused by Stuart Hall), is a series of shifting and unfinished points of identification. While these may have some biological referents, they are quite removed from inheritable biological concepts of race. As Goldberg explains, 'In its non-biological interpretation, then, race stands for historically specific forms of cultural connectedness and solidarity' (Goldberg 1993: 59). It is here that the concept of ethnicity seems to overlap with this discourse of race. Culture has taken a central place in many areas of social science. There has been a marked 'cultural turn' away from structuralist paradigms, with their focus on macro-level forces of social change that obscure the more individual experiences of social actors. The cultural stuff that is contained within the lived experience of ethnic boundaries becomes the focus for a differentialist approach. However, culture is also prone to reification and correlates, at times, closely to more physical attributes. As Frederickson states, it's 'difficult in specific historical cases to say whether appearance or 'culture' is the source of the salient differences because culture can be reified and essentialised to the point where it has the same deterministic effect as skin colour' (2002: 169).

ETHNICITY

Ethnicity derives from *ethnikos*, the Greek word for 'heathen'. 'It was widely used in the senses of heathen, pagan or Gentile, until C19, when this sense was generally superseded by the sense of a racial characteristic' (Williams 1983: 119). However, in the modern era, ethnicity has come to be generally used as a term for collective cultural identity (while race categorises 'them' from outside, ethnicity is used for shared values and beliefs, the self definition of a group, 'us'). Van den Berghe drew the influential distinction between ethnicity as 'socially defined but on the basis of cultural criteria' whereas race is 'socially defined but on the basis of physical criteria' (Van den Berghe 1967: 9).

In the context of western multicultural societies, ethnicity has become the preferred used term to avoid 'race' and its implications of a discredited 'scientific' racism. Ethnicity is generally taken to be a more inclusive and less objectifying concept; indicating the constantly negotiated nature of boundaries between ethnic groups rather than the essentialism implicit in divisions of 'race'. The crossing of ethnic borders and encounters with those of different ethnic background is one of the most significant experiences in the formation of our identities. In the same vein Stuart Hall writes that:

> To be English is to be your self in relation to the French and the hot-blooded Mediterranean, and the passionate, traumatized Russian soul. You go round the entire globe: when you know what everybody else is, then you are what they are not. Identity is always, in that sense, a structured representation which only achieves its positive through the narrow eye of the negative.
>
> (1991: 21)

The way in which ethnic boundaries reflect often heartfelt values and ideas of maintaining national integrity is frequently portrayed through the use of every-day discourses about others that often involve hackneyed images. These might include jokes, urban legends and stereotypes. However, there is also evidence that ethnicity can be an instrumental category that is activated during times of external threat. It is a functional aspect of groups that allows them to compete, often using a predetermined values and beliefs (self-affirming stereotypes and negative stereotypes of the other), to strengthen their case.

Guyanese academic and author Brackette Williams points out that it is impor-tant to consider the way groups produce meaning and which signs and symbols they attach meaning to. Perhaps there is no final, definitive 'ethnicity', only specific readings of ethnic identity at specific times and places.

> What is the use of these categories in studying the production of meaning and its relationship to power? For me, these terms and concepts are simply working

tools. I'm not especially concerned with the ultimate meaning of 'ethnicity,' but rather with the reasons it keeps intervening as a category through which people shift kaleidoscopic kinds of meanings in relation to economic regimes and shifts in those regimes.

(Williams 1995)

Charles Taylor points out the dangers of classification becoming a practice that has distorting and belittling consequences: 'our identity is partly shaped by recognition or its absence. Often by the misrecognition of others. Non recognition or misrecognition can inflict harm can be a form of oppression imprisoning someone in a false distorted and reduced mode of being (Taylor 1992: 25).

The way in which ethnic identity is ascribed is important to consider. Is the shared characteristic the feature of a 'group' (which implies shared goals and coherency) or is it merely a pattern? The implication of being a member of an ethnic group is that at some level one has an awareness of shared values and interests and would be motivated to take collective action using this sense of common ethnic identity as an organising principle. Conversely, individuals who share common origins and cultural traits could be counted as belonging objectively to that ethnic group, yet when membership is not operational and genuinely shared motives do not exist, then this could be described as an ethnic category. What makes an ethnic category an ethnic group is the sense of 'we-feeling' and common interests in advancing the group's position in society through collective actions.

In Guyana for instance the creolese term 'ahwe people' is a uniting term that designates a Guyanese identity across ethnic boundaries, as in the following exhortation on the Guyanese Land of Six Peoples web site – a plea to bring back the old practices before the ethnic unrest of the late 1960s:

Is wha it gon tek fu bring back some a dem ting wha we talk bout – leh we tink, what about forming groups to plant up de land either in we backyard or in de back dam, forming a steel band, youth group(s), drama group(s), and so on.

My people yu interested? Alright, afta dis village day leh we organse ahwe self and show dem big people dat ahwe can du ting like dem and even betta – Right!

Leh we try.

(Hazel Robinson, *Guyana Chronicle*, 23 May 2004)

The strong sense of communal identity in Robinson's statement shows the intentionality of ethnic identity. Here, a strong memory forms a potent exhortation for collective action across ethnic boundaries united by shared creolised language and culture. It shows how an 'imagined community' can perhaps mobilise sense of identity and possibly action. In a similar vein, Jenkins (1996: 23) relates the Marxist concept of 'class in itself' and 'class for itself' to this character of group identity. In other words a class can be a passive term, which simply describes apparently common features, but when the class recognises its true nature in relation to the means of production, then the identity is activated and class consciousness occurs. In a similar way, ethnicity, like race, can be an imposed category or, conversely, it can become central to a revolutionary sense of identity in a struggle for independence or political power, or simply a recognition of shared experiences or attributes. This tension between externally proscribed and internally held identities is extremely political and may lead to conflicts, civil war, persecution or, conversely, it may be the catalyst to restore a sense of positive community.

Ethnicity can then be considered as a transient concept. It is not necessarily useful to try and pin down a final meaning. Rather, the different possible dimensions reflect the shifting terrain of social theories about difference. As we shall see, attempts to pin down or reify terms like 'ethnicity' are part of the problem as they reduce a complex ever-changing phenomenon. Loomba addresses this issue:

> The term 'ethnicity' has dominantly been used to indicate biologically and culturally stable identities, but Hall asks us to decouple it from its imperial, racist or nationalist deployment and to appropriate it to designate identity as a constructed process rather than a given essence. For Hall, the new black ethnicities visible in contemporary Britain are results of the 'cut-and-mix' processes of 'cultural *diaspora-ization*.'
>
> (Loomba 1998: 176)

RACE AS ETHNICITY

In the concept of 'ethnorace', as Goldberg suggests (1992), the phenomena that are ostensibly separated by the terms 'ethnicity' and 'race' are liable at times to overlap. For example, 'Jews, Blacks, Hispanics, and Japanese in the United States may now be referred to as either race or ethnic group' (Goldberg 1992: 554). These categories may have different connotations, and ethnicity tends to be seen as less tendentious. Furthermore, more recent US data (2000 Census) define ethnicity as the broader term cutting across possible divisions of race:

> In general, the Census Bureau defines ethnicity or origin as the heritage, nationality group, lineage, or country of birth of the person or the person's parents or ancestors before their arrival in the United States. People who identify their origin as Spanish, Hispanic, or Latino may be of any race. According to the revised Office of Management and Budget standards noted above, race

is considered a separate concept from Hispanic origin (ethnicity) and, wherever possible, separate questions should be asked on each concept.

(US Census Bureau 1999)

The association of 'race' with scientific racism and Nazism and the lack of any evidence for basic biological differences in the genetic composition of 'races' have led to the cautionary use of inverted commas and the preference for the term 'ethnicity' which has become the acceptable term used for otherness in multi-cultural societies like Britain, Canada and Australia, and yet the term has different and sometimes contradictory meanings. As a means of categorisation, the term 'ethnicity' can be another manifestation of the dominant culture marginalising minority groups in its midst. In Australia, for example, over recent years, the term 'ethnic' has become a generic noun for anyone of other than Anglo-Celtic origin (and is especially associated with Greeks and Italians, as the term 'wog'[2] becomes recognised as racist and unacceptable) as in 'He (or she) is ethnic'. This reification of terms is exactly why Hall (1996a) is concerned to reclaim the process of construction in the term 'ethnicity' and to avoid ready-made labels, indicating that ethnic identity is a process of becoming, a question of intersubjective negotiation, not a final state. However, in popular culture as well as in 'official' documents, ethnicity is conflated with race. A prime example of this semantic confusion is demonstrated by the census categories used in the UK and the USA.

In our society we are frequently confused about the correct term to use to describe people. The term 'background' (as suggested by Soysal 2000) could be argued to indicate the subject's loss of continuity, perhaps as a member of one of many diasporic communities (see Chapter 8). A 'background' might be an expression of an imagined community, a constant reminder that one has been separated from one's past – or that the past is constantly being reshaped by the present. Appropriate titles and forms of address change rapidly and, as can be seen, in Figure 2.3, the process of eliciting ethnic identity can be fraught with problems. There is a noticeable lag between official forms used for the census and the social reality of people's self-identifications.

In the 1991 UK Census, the form in Figure 2.3 had become a familiar sight and one that served as a constant reminder of the difficulties inherent in cate-gorising people. Forms like this telegraph certain imagined identities, but they do not appear to actually be considering 'ethnicity', or at least, if they are, they do so in a most contradictory fashion. As Ratcliffe (2004: 37–8) points out, '"White" is clearly a pseudo-"racial" term based on phenotype, "Black-Caribbean"

---

2 A term used to denote Greek/Italian Australians. An interesting phenomenon is the re-claiming of this derogatory term by the Greek/Italian communities, this has been seen in several popular TV and stage comedies *Wogs Life* and *Wogs Out of Work*.

White	☐	
Black Caribbean	☐	
Black African	☐	
Black other	☐	(please specify)
Bangladeshi	☐	
Chinese	☐	
Indian	☐	
Pakistani	☐	
Asian other	☐	(please specify)
Other	☐	(please specify)

Figure 2.3 Ethnic categories used in the 1991 Census

also prioritizes phenotype and conflates a variety of island origins and language groups . . . "Indian", for example, brings together under one label those of many different religious, linguistic and regional backgrounds'. In short, there is little suggestion of the collective cultural identifiers that we might consider to be included in ethnicity.

The disparity between Figure 2.3 and 2.4 illustrates this constant process of reinventing and reshaping past identities and forming new, hybrid identities more realistically aligned with one's social experiences. However, the categories used are, again, problematic. Origins, allegiances to cultural heritage, questions of citizenship and belonging as well as the marked interethnic relationships in the United Kingdom are all issues that underpin the decisions in constructing census categories and that have informed the changes that can be noted between the two censuses.

In the 2001 Census, a range of more detailed categories were included. Although there seems to be some attempt to recognise the changing perceptions and dynamism within communities, there are still fundamental problems. The white category has been extended, which breaks down the hegemonic and monolithic nature of whiteness into several categories. However, the ascriptive choices offered give little recognition of ethnic identity. These labels are by themselves unable to address questions of the multifaceted forms of cultural identification that cut across the borders of such broad categories. However, a question on religious identity that was used in the 2001 Census does begin to collate a more refined picture.

The category of black again takes on a different meaning here as a master category, arguably asserted as more inviolable. Asian too is now recognised as a unifying category in parallel to black (but Chinese has separate status/identity).

White – British

White – Irish

White – Other

Mixed – White/Black Caribbean

Mixed – White/Black African

Mixed – White/Asian

Mixed – Other

Black/Black British – Caribbean

Black/Black British – African

Black/Black British – Other

Asian/Asian British – Indian

Asian/Asian British – Pakistani

Asian/Asian British – Bangladeshi

Asian/Asian British – Other Asian

Chinese

Other Ethnic Group

Figure 2.4 Ethnic categories used in the 2001 Census

These decisions are of course intensely political. The self-identity of Asians within this frame is extraordinarily complex and, within the national categories recognised here, is also defined by regional ethnic and religious cleavages. One of the most significant shifts over the ten years is the inclusion of 'mixed' as a category. This begs the question, how a significant percentage of people chose to designate themselves in 1991. The term 'mixed' could also be considered problematic as it implies there are pure ethnicities. The preferred term today is 'dual heritage' (or 'multiple heritage').

The presumption of Britishness as a distinct and unified ethnic category is increasingly problematic. This does not only apply to the devolving of Scotland, Northern Ireland and Wales away from immediate Westminster control or the complex hybrid identities that comprise the mix of Asian, Caribbean and African groups that make up nearly 9 per cent of the UK's population, but also movement towards defined regionalism. It is argued that: 'more people can define themselves as Londoners, Brummies, Mancunians or Geordies first, and English second. Scots often divide on east-west lines in terms of instinctive local identities' (from a speech by MP Barbara Roche, 2002). In 2004, the idea of the North East warranting a separate regional assembly was mooted and overwhelmingly rejected by the people themselves in a referendum. But many would argue that 'Geordies are distinctive in their character, dialect and in their identity forged through strong associations with the working-class occupations of mining, ship-building and the steel industry'.

In the USA, similar semantic struggles are being conducted as Brackette Williams (1995) comments on referring to the significance of the detailed semiotic process of naming. For members of the majority white culture who have, perhaps, had less cause to feel marginal, such concerns might seem surprising, but in the USA, as in many multi-ethnic nations, citizenship and identity are often struggles for equality and recognition in the face of political and economic marginalisation.

> In the United States, when you look at categories like Asian American, African American, Hispanic American and then look at the category *black*, you notice that it remains one of the few uncapitalized categories. Part of the reason for people wanting to change this label is precisely to acquire that capitalization. That may seem trivial, but to have that capital, as opposed to being lowercased, is a way of speaking semiotically about status positioning. It does not create the position. It does not really alter status. But what one attempts to do is to reorient one's position in this struggle to attain that status one doesn't yet have. By capitalizing everybody, perhaps one puts everyone on the same terrain of struggle.
>
> So you look at things like that and you think, how have categories changed? We now talk about Native Americans instead of Indians, but we don't hyphenate Native and American. What does acquiring a hyphen, acquiring a capitalization, altering it from a color category to a socalled cultural or transcontinental category, mean for the political positioning of that group? Does it alter that positioning? Is it archaeological? That is, is it a trace of what has already been accomplished? Or is it a signal for what will happen, for what one expects to happen in the future? If you want to be hyphenated in an environment where everyone else is not hyphenated, what is the motivation?
>
> (Williams 1995)

This semiotic struggle indicates a shifting identification, pride and assertion in identity. It could reflect shifts between ideas of race (colour based) and the ascendancy of ethnicity. However, the US Census has fewer racial categories, and the typical breakdown of results makes certain interesting distinctions to the British model as shown in Figure 2.5.

The striking fact about these categories is that they are based on race and, in fact, are not far removed from some of the oldest forms of racial categorising (based on colour and other phenotypical attributes). Therefore, because Hispanics (who are a significant population in the USA) are not seen as a race, they are not measured in this census as it is assumed that ethnic is the wider category and race is subsumed under this broader term. So it is possible for black people or

Population Counts for City X	
Total Population	500,000
One Race – Total	450,000
White	400,000
Black or African American	10,000
American Indian and Alaska Native	5,000
Asian	500
Native Hawaiian and Other Pacific Islander	100
Some Other Race	34,400
Two or more races – Total	50,000

Figure 2.5 Typical breakdown of ethnic categories in the US Census

(Source: US Census Bureau, Public Information Office, 2001)

Asians to also be Hispanic. This could be interpreted as a positive practice in the sense that it actively resists the conflation of race with ethnicity. However, the selecting on the basis of race gives power and credence to one of the most dubious and divisive terms. Interestingly, here there is no recognition of 'mixed' categories, although in reality the USA has very significant mixed (or dual heritage) populations.

> Between 1970 and 1990, the number of multiracial children under age 18 has quadrupled to 2 million according to the U.S. Census Bureau. That number will grow as interracial marriages continue to soar. There were 1.4 million interracial couples in 1995, a 114% increase since 1980, the Census Bureau said.
>
> (*USA Today*, 8 May 1997)

The unwillingness to utilise a category that would affirm people's mixed or dual identities is puzzling. (In 2000, the US Census Bureau gave some ground on this issue permitting individuals to mark several boxes to indicate their mix of ethnicities.) Although by all accounts the decision may be motivated by political resistance of African Americans who may see a significant 'mixed' category as undermining the resource base received.

■ CHAPTER SUMMARY

Race and ethnicity, like other cultural terms that are central to social identity, are especially complex and difficult to define. Some scholars and census takers might insist on separating the terms and seeing race as a very different category based on physical and objective differences, hinting at a nature–culture divide between the terms race and ethnicity. Yet, from the Spanish origins of the term (*raza*), as Sollors (2002: 102) points out, 'race' was used to designate not only Moors and Jews, but also heretics and their descendants. Pieterse has shown the manner in which boundaries have been drawn over history to include and exclude different groups in Europe, and Goldberg's work has traced discursive changes that reflect social and political realities in different historical periods. While race-makers categorised human types and suggested sharply demarked physical differences, there was always dispute about where and how to draw boundaries.

EXERCISE 2.1

1 When you look at the census forms (Figures 2.3 and 2.4), do you feel confident that your identity is adequately captured? Why?/Why not?

2 Which one allowed you the most approximate identification? Why?

3 What are the implications of the category 'white' or 'black other'?

4 How would you decide on a category if you were of 'mixed race'?

5 What does the form suggest about the manner in which such categories have come into being?

6 What is your regional identity? How defined is it? Are you aware of distinct cultural history, or regional dialect or accent? Do you choose to identify or dis-identify with this? Why?

7 What role does class play in regional identities?

8 Discuss images of regional identities (e.g. of Geordies) in magazines (like *Viz*'s Basher Bacon, etc. and in cartoons like 'Andy Capp'). Do such caricatures capture anything enduring?

9 Consider the speculative comments made by Brackette Williams. What differences do you think would occur between USA and the United Kingdom in terms of the drawing of ethnic boundaries and the sense of identity experienced in each country?

10 Compare the British Census to the more limited categories in the US Census.

11 What might be the reasoning behind not using a 'mixed' category on a national basis? (Several states have instituted this, but it has been resisted nationally.)

12 Consider other semiotic forms of expression of citizenship and nation. How do the following reflect identity?

(a) flags

(b) coins/notes.

13 Consider words that we commonly use to designate other peoples, such as Asians, Arabs, Caribbean, Europeans. These terms generalise and obscure differences. When does it become necessary to use more specific terms and why? What is the possible impact on your identity to be subsumed under an umbrella term?

14 What signs are there today that there is still some belief and support for eugenics or eugenic-type policies? Are such policies always wrong?

15 The strand of evolutionist biology that was applied to Social Darwinism has survived today in certain theoretical ideas and principles. What are they, and do they have any credence?

16 There is, as Goldberg points out the sense that if one behaves 'white' one is seen as white. So race is composed of conventional discourses and if the performer 'plays white' then he/she is likely to be considered white. Discuss this observation and relate it to situations of adaptation to the dominant culture. Are visible differences partly or wholly negated by impression management? (You might relate this to Indians who take on the 'dreadfully English' stereotypes or to other ethnic minority groups. Such presentation is frequently parodied on TV – consider *Goodness Gracious Me*.)

Colonialism
Invisible Histories

'You were the first to teach us something absolutely fundamental: the indignity of speaking for others.'

(Gilles Deleuze in conversation with Foucault, from Foucault 1977b)

Guyana: 'Look what they done to the mother',

Indian-Guyanese bus driver commenting on the defaced statue of Queen Victoria in Georgetown (conversation on a minibus, Georgetown, recorded 15 April 1991).

Figure 3.1 Defaced statue of Queen Victoria, Georgetown, Guyana

BUS DRIVER (EAST INDIAN): See see, thas how this country run like [.] Queen Victoria they pushed he to the back of the Promenade Gardens [.]

SS: They chucked her out?

DRIVER: Queen Victoria [. . .] the mother [.]

SS: Yeah I heard [.]

DRIVER: Queen Victoria who gave us this country [. . .] its independence [. . .] put her at the back [.]

SS: Desmond Hoyte[1] pulled her out again?

DRIVER: *Not Desmond Hoyte!* No [.] Not Desmond Hoyte [. . .] the people [.] is the people [.] When they elect a new mayor for this town[,] the people call on the Mayor[,] 'Why have you got the Queen, the statue at the back of [. . .] Burnham[2] used to go shit on her [.] This government just trying to squeeze this nation[,] they trying to see this nation wasting [. . .] they just going over the world and just asking for aid and help and all them ting [.] What are they doing with our own resource?

SS: They've got their export market haven't they?

DRIVER: We main crop is sugar and rice [. . .] and it more expensive than the stuff they bring in [.] They exporting sugar [. . .] tha fair?

SS: No it's crazy [.]

DRIVER: The rice [. . .] long brown rice[,] the polished rice [. . .] they exporting it and they giving we to eat the white rice [. . .] and the low grade of rice [. . .] low grade [.]

SS: Yeah [.]

DRIVER: You know like rice umm we use to feed umm pigs [.] Yes pig[,] this the food we eating[,] majority food we eat is fertilizer[,] fertilizer!

---

1 Desmond Hoyte was the African-Guyanese President at the time of the recording (1991).

2 Forbes Burnham was the African-Guyanese President (1965–85)

This brief excerpt from an interview invokes some of the dynamics of a country facing an economic crisis and divided along ethnic lines. The Indian-Guyanese had economic power largely through holdings in agriculture whereas African-Guyanese (at the time of recording) held political power and dominated the public sector. The reference to the damaged statue is a story, almost a social and political allegory, that I heard from several Indians, that when the African-Guyanese leader Burnham finally got into office one of his first acts was the almost ritual desecration of this colonial icon. He had it tossed into the ditch at the back of the parliament buildings and, or so a number of Indian respondents claimed, defecated on the statue.

The powerful imagery and bitterness expressed were typical. Interestingly the stage-managed calm that could be witnessed in public places when both groups were together quickly dispersed when the spatial boundaries were redrawn (as in this case in which an Indian conductor and driver were alone with me in a minibus).

CONSTRUCTION OF THE COLONIAL SUBJECT

The division of the world between a handful of European empires, which only began to unravel after the Second World War, has had the most profound impact on human groups the world over. The advantage this pillage provided the western nations was a springboard for their relatively superior economic and commercial power right up to today. Yet the records of what really took place and the way each generation has been taught about colonialism has rendered it part of an invisible history, an exercise in collective amnesia on a monumental scale.

I remember visiting Liverpool in 1984, when it was a rebel Labour stronghold. Derek Hatton was making a stand against the rate capping imposed by Margaret Thatcher's government. The streets were covered in litter because basic services were breaking down, the dockers, the miners and other heavy industries were against the wall or had already sunk. In a charity shop I found a book, a late-nineteenth-century encyclopaedia, and under 'Liverpool' it mentioned that by the early 1800s the western seaboard port was one of the wealthiest cities in the world. I looked at it in wonder not quite believing what I had read.

SLAVERY

Slavery existed centuries before the concept of race was invented, back more than 4,000 years into antiquity. Drescher agrees that people of all physical variations have been enslaved at different times, and yet there is no evidence that 'before the last four centuries that any society invented race ideology as a reason for enslaving others' (Drescher and Engerman 1998: 322). More than thirteen centuries before Aristotle, the Hammurabi Code in Babylonia[1] defined a concept of chattel slavery that served as a way of classifying the lowliest and most dependent workers in society: 'slaves could be sold or inherited; the same features would reappear through the ages in scores of cultures' (Drescher and Engerman 1998: ix).

---

1 Laws compiled during the reign of Hammurabi (1792–50 BC), King of Babylon, include regulations governing slavery. These are amongst the oldest known civic regulations.

On the eve of the millennium, the Mayor of Liverpool made a public and unreserved apology for the city's role in the Atlantic slave trade.

> 'This was the proudest moment of my political life,' says Lord Mayor Joseph A Devaney. The resolution stated that while the city had been bequeathed a rich diversity of people and cultures, learning, architecture and financial wealth, the human suffering had been obscured. 'The untold misery which was caused has left a legacy which affects Black people in Liverpool today.' The Council expressed its shame and remorse for the city's role in 'this trade in human misery'.
>
> (Henderson 2000)

Indeed, at the height of the slave trade with Bristol and London, Liverpool was the main British port involved with the slave trade. Around 500 ships sailed from Liverpool in just the years 1785 to 1787, collecting African slaves to trade in the Americas and bringing back produce from the plantations. At the time, the city was amongst the wealthiest in the world. The so-called triangular trade was the reason for this growth. Walking through the city, it is hard to believe this city was responsible for such shocking atrocities leading to the deaths of countless hundreds in the thousands of crossings made, with people packed into specially layered ship's holds by their hundreds, in conditions that beggar belief. There are not many accounts of the conditions from the point of view of the slaves themselves. However, there is one famous account that has survived, that of Olaudah Equiano who wrote of the conditions in the slave ship:

> The white people looked and acted, as I thought, in so savage a manner; for I had never seen among my people such instances of brutal cruelty. The closeness of the place, and the heat of the climate, added to the number in the ship, which was so crowded that each had scarcely room to turn himself, almost suffocated us. [. . .] The air soon became unfit for respiration, from a variety of loathsome smells, and brought on a sickness among the slaves, of which many died. The wretched situation was again aggravated by the chains, now unsupportable, and the filth of the necessary tubs, into which the children often fell, and were almost suffocated. The shrieks of the women, and the groans of the dying, rendered the whole a scene of horror almost inconceivable.
>
> (Equiano 1789: 58)

Slavery has always been problematic: the attempts to bestialise human beings (i.e. to reduce them to the state of beasts of burden) have never been easily achieved. Aristotle believed it possible to distinguish 'the natural slave' as being similar to other domestic animals for the service of their human masters. The very fact of their subservience – he believed – was evidence of their natural role. The trade was barbaric and treated people as mere objects that could be used and disposed of without any danger of moral outrage. The African trade vied for by European powers (the Portuguese, Dutch and French and then the dominance by Britain) led to the systematic pillage of the whole of Africa and, as argued by many scholars (see e.g. Walter Rodney 1972), underdeveloped the continent.

By the seventeenth century in New World colonies, the foundations were being laid for a racial ideology, 'as the English were institutionalising a form of slavery for which they had no precedents, they were also constructing the ideological components of race' (Drescher and Engerman 1998: 322). This historical linkage gave rise to a new form of servitude known as racial slavery. However, both slavery and race were incompatible with the Christian principles and social values espoused by the English colonists. The result was that slavery and the idea of race functioned to reinforce each other in complex ways. These colonists were driven by an insatiable desire for land and the labour to work it – both primary sources of wealth. Enormous profits could be turned and fortunes were made across the Caribbean.

Use of indigenous peoples as slaves was largely unsuccessful. They had no immunity to Old World diseases, often escaped as they had intimate knowledge of the land, or died from overwork.

> The decision to restrict chattel slavery to those of African ancestry was a pragmatic one. Africans were visibly different; they were on alien soil with no familiar places to go even if they escaped; and they had no powerful political supporters or allies in the international Christian community to object to their enslavement.
>
> (Drescher and Engerman 1998: 323)

This practical set of differences was widened and overwritten as the realities of colonial life evolved. 'Laws forbidding intermarriage between "racial" groups, laws increasingly restricted the freedom of slaves, and practices prohibiting the education and training of slaves exacerbated the cultural differences between slaves and free whites' (ibid.: 323). There were laws against interracial marriage (see McCaskell 1994: 11). Any white person who married a 'negro, mulatto or Indian' was liable to permanent banishment from the colony. The Carolina Law of 1741 sought to prevent an 'abominable Mixture and spurious issue' by levying a prohibitive fine against any white person who married 'an Indian, Negro Mustee or Mulatto Man or woman, or any Person of Mix Blood, to the Third Generation' (Vaughan 1982: 995).

Black slaves had no human rights. Casual killings of black people became legal by the mid-seventeenth century, interracial marriage became punishable by law in 1705 and, six years earlier, 'white' became a recognised racial category in law. Colonialism and slavery permitted such ruthless treatment of people who could not be permitted to retain human dignity. The colonial regime dealt with slaves and other subjugated people with unrelenting barbarity, their conditions in the slave houses were infrahuman. Casual murder and rape and executions were commonplace. Further into Equiano's account (Equiano 1789: 107) he relates the conditions on the Southern States plantations in which cruel dispiriting conditions prevailed:

> I have often asked many of the men slaves (who used to go several miles to their wives, and late in the night, after having been wearied with a hard day's labour) why they went so far for wives, and why they did not take them of their own master's negro women, and particularly those who lived together as household slaves? Their answers have ever been – "Because when the master or mistress choose to punish the women, they made the husbands flog their own wives, and that they could not bear to do." Is it surprising that usage like this should drive the poor creatures to despair, and make them seek a refuge in death from those evils which render their lives intolerable – while
>
> With shuddering horror pale, and eyes aghast
> They view their lamentable lot, and find –
> No rest.

As Drescher and Engerman point out (1998: xiv) 'the basic "problem of slavery" [. . .] arises from the irreducible humanness of the slave'. Drescher gives examples of slaves that are contrary to the typical notions of them as broken and subservient to the end: 'throughout history slaves have run away, outwitted their masters, rebelled, murdered, raped, stolen, divulged plots for insurrection, and helped protect the state from external danger'.

Perhaps the most famous rebellion was that of the black Jacobins and the formation of the first free black state in Haiti. Toussaint l'Ouverture whose troops defeated first the Spanish and the British, then internal insurrection and finally the Napoleonic French army of 20,000 by brilliant military strategy before being captured (see Beard 1970, James 1963).

ENLIGHTENMENT VIEWS

As discussed in the previous chapter, the Enlightenment was an era in which profound consideration was given to understanding human difference. Released in part from the dogmas of Christianity and the rigid world order, speculation grew about origins, ideas of reason, ethics and morality. Some of the themes that emerged had certainly been visited before. Was society natural? Greeks in fourth century BC had considered this question. In the Enlightenment, questions arose about the nature of human societies, their various forms and cultural practices and about whether universals of human nature existed that dictated human relations and the structure of society. Did societies evolve naturally and organically or were they due to human agency?

Several historical encounters had already been influential in these debates. Columbus reported that natives from some islands that he visited, as who were receptive to Christianity were 'simple children of nature' and other natives who had met them with hostility and resistance as 'cannibals' who should be subdued or exterminated. This early nature/culture dichotomy is perhaps the beginning of that Manichean divide that was further elaborated during the Enlightenment. Rousseau's idealised conception of the 'noble savage' was an intermediate position between the dehumanising effects of culture and the rawness of nature. On the other hand, the growth of interest in cataloguing human types along with other species of plants and animals eventually led to suggestions that certain human types were more evolved than others and had more claims to full human status than others.

Two hundred years earlier, in 1550, another landmark debate took place in the city of Valladolid between the Spanish jurist Sepulveda and a Dominican Friar Bartolome de Las Casas, who had witnessed the killing and enslaving of native people in South America under Pizarro earlier that century and who had been arguing for the freeing of indigenous people since 1519. Sepulveda argued, using Aristotle's conception of 'natural slavery', that all Indians were 'non-rational beings' and hence should be forcibly enslaved. They were, he said, 'barbarous and inhuman peoples abhorring all civil life, customs and virtue' (Frederickson 1981: 36–7). On the contrary, argued Las Casas, they 'possessed reason and a capacity for civil life' (Frederickson 2002: 36–7). Although Las Casas won the debate, the support of the Pope Paul III and the eventual agreement from Emperor Charles to abolish Indian slavery in 1542, the pragmatism of colonialism that brought hundreds of tons of gold and silver to Europe had enabled the development of a new source of labour in Africa.

Most European societies were involved in African slavery in one way or another. And, in general, the image that most Europeans had of Africans was that of slaves, of subordinate and powerless peoples. Similarly, their knowledge and under-standing of Native Americans was distorted by the facts of their conquest and apparent demise. By then it was widely accepted that the indigenous peoples of the Americas were weak savages who had to be conquered to make way for a superior civilisation. The scholars and scientists of Europe could hardly have attitudes towards these peoples or make judgements about them that were uninfluenced by these social and political realities.

Some Enlightenment philosophers were staunchly opposed to the exploitation of other nations, but even those, such as Baron de Montesquieu (1689–1755), showed signs of ambivalence: 'It is impossible for us to suppose these creatures to be men, because, allowing them to be men, a suspicion would follow, that we ourselves are not Christian'. Montesquieu, an ardent opponent of the evils of despotism, highlights here the thinking of the age; and this type of sophistry stems from guilt at not having opposed such a pernicious trade. Despite this example of expedient reasoning, he launched bitter attacks against slavery in his writings. However, to permit those subjugated as slaves to live as fully human presents a threat, an anomaly that overturns the certitude of the time. Despite the high ideals of reason and liberty, the Atlantic slave trade was in full swing at the time of the Enlightenment and some philosophers and thinkers were slave owners or profited from slavery (John Locke, for example, was Secretary of the Board of Trade and Plantations). The fact is that the scholars associated with Enlightenment thought were working in the eighteenth century, a time when the African Atlantic slave trade was reaching its peak. Hence the perception many had of Africans was as the most valuable slaves, the commodities whereby enterprising colonists could turn enormous profits in a very short time.

However, the introduction of plantation slavery did not originate, as Hall (2002: 58) reminds us, in notions of racial superiority. Rather, it is more useful to consider 'how slavery (the product of specific problems of labor shortage and the organization of plantation agriculture – supplied, in the first instance, by nonblack, indigenous labor, and then by white indentured labor) produced those forms of juridical racism which distinguish the epoch of plantation slavery.'

It could be argued that the use of racial divisions emerged as a way of resolving the conflict between, on the one hand, the ideology of equality for all and universal reason and, on the other, facts of social inequality.

To their credit, most of the classifiers accepted the principle of the unity of the human species, if for no other reason than adherence to scriptures. Most also expressed a belief in the potential improvement of so called 'savage' peoples in accord with Enlightenment ideas about environmentally induced change and human progress. Differences were explained as the result of environmental factors that had led to degeneration into savagery.

However, this state could be risen above, as is clear from one of the first novels, Daniel Defoe's *Robinson Crusoe* (1719), which examines the trials of the castaway Crusoe; restored to a state of nature yet retaining his cultural training and the tools of civilised endeavour salvaged from the wreck. Despite being stripped of the external trappings of culture, he is able to construct a microcosm of western culture based on his reasoning. His meeting with the 'savage' he names Friday is a confrontation between the bearer of western culture and one living in 'a state of nature'. However, Crusoe acknowledges that God 'has bestow'd upon them the same Powers, the same Reason, the same Affections [. . .] and all the Capacities of doing Good [. . .] that he has given to us' (*Robinson Crusoe*, chapter 6). Indeed the thrust of Enlightenment thinking embraced the universality of reason and sociability and the existence of a common human nature. There was a notion that due to local conditions these finer sensibilities had 'degenerated'. Yet at the same time the novel is a blueprint for the colonial spirit as Crusoe creates the island as his own personal fiefdom and a working economic system (see Said 1993).

So, while there was both vehement resistance and collusion with slavery, it was one of the biggest and most significant movements of people ever experienced in which over 15 million people were transported to the New World colonies (a conservative estimate) of whom some 5 million died during the journey there. What is much less well known is the effect that this wealth had on the economic prosperity of the western countries, making the Industrial Revolution possible.

RATIONALISATION OF COLONIAL EXPLOITATION

One of the most striking events in the recent history of mankind is the expansion throughout the entire world of most European peoples. It has brought about the subjugation and, in some instances, the disappearance of virtually every people regarded as backward, archaic, or primitive. The colonial movement of the nineteenth century was the most important in magnitude, the most fraught with consequences, resulting from this European expansion. It overturned in a brutal manner the history of the peoples it subjugated.

(Balandier 1974: 34)

Yet this brutal exploitation was by no means the only example of empire building. Wallerstein's world-systems theory suggested that, despite the difficulty in establishing the scope and nature of global systems, there have certainly been capitalist-type colonial powers from the earliest period of human civilisation. The ancient empires of Egypt, Rome, China and Mughal India, feudal Russia and Ottoman Turkey predate the modern colonial period. The scale of upheaval that occurred between 1500 and 1850, however, was unprecedented. Nearly 10 million slaves were moved from Africa to the Americas. The scale of colonisation reached its apogee in the nineteenth century, when the 'Great Migration' took place: over 40 million people moved to the new colonies.

The so-called 'New Imperialism', 1870 to 1918, was brought about by the Industrial Revolution, which created large surpluses of European capital and heavy demands for raw materials. Nationalism and Social Darwinist thought provided a powerful rationale for this expansionist movement. The scientific evidence for the concept of natural selection appeared to give credence to the earlier and less empirically based notion of 'survival of the fittest'. There was an emphasis placed on the moral superiority of the exploiters, and the obligations of the 'white mans burden' as popularised by Kipling. These fuelled the spirit of nationalism. It was also politically prestigious to have colonies. England, France, Germany, Belgium, Portugal and the Netherlands made the largest additions to their colonial domains during this period of the New Imperialism. Chineweizu makes the point forcefully that the success of the western nations has been at a very high price for the rest of the world:

> In the case of the West, the human price of western industrial prosperity was paid by other peoples over several centuries. Among these other peoples must be reckoned the aboriginal peoples of the Americas, Australia, and New Zealand, who were exterminated to make room for European immigrants; the millions of black Africans who slaved for over three centuries in the Americas, furnishing forced labour for the capital formation that powered the rise of British, French and United States industrialism; and the millions of peasant immigrants from Eastern Europe whose cheap labour paid for American industrialization after her civil war.
>
> (Chinweizu 1987: 425)

Kenan Malik has argued that the change in inclusive Enlightenment thought – ideas of universal human kind – began with the need for explanatory frameworks for the rapidly growing inequalities at home and abroad. Much of the ethno-political relations today – the stories that confront us in the daily news – are the consequences of historical events in which a few European countries took forcible possession of nine-tenths of the globe and ruled and exploited countries of Africa, Asia, the Americas and Australia for around 500 years. Yet today it is a history that is dimly remembered in the west or actively resisted and contended when it seems likely to paint an inglorious picture of a nation's history. One of the features of this possession is the erasure of histories and the forced transportation of millions of people as a labour force to power the empire's industrial age (through slavery and later indentured labour) and to provide wealth for European elites.

The colonising of America and Australia was achieved partly through the use of convict labour to build the infrastructure of the new colonies: railway systems in America, timber and agriculture in Australia. The impetus to colonise new lands and passivise the indigenous peoples was powerful and rationalised through several dominant discourses. The influential writings of John Knox, Comte Arthur de Gobineau and Thomas Arnold claimed to prove the inherent superiority of the 'white races'. This superiority was the reason for European technological advances and colonial domination. Such views predated but helped set the agenda for later Social Darwinist thought, which accorded with a popular view of the inherent morality and civilised virtue of the 'white race' attained through evolutionary struggle. There was a proliferation of popular pseudo-scientific treatises on the evolution of human types.

A variety of uses have been made of biological evolution. Some simplified the idea to 'survival of the fittest'. Others believed that what occured among species in the animal kingdom was identical to the process which took place in humans.

They believed that white Protestant Europeans had evolved much further and faster than other 'races'.

Herbert Spencer (whose notion of 'survival of the fittest' was discussed previously) had suggested that human society is in constant evolutionary struggle in which the fittest – which happened to be the most affluent – were chosen to dominate. There were armies of the unfit and the poor, who simply could not compete, and just as nature weeds out the unfit, an enlightened society ought to weed out its unfit and permit them to die off so as not to weaken the racial stock. Human society is always in a kind of evolutionary process in which the fittest – which happened to be those who can make lots of money – were chosen to dominate. There were armies of unfit, the poor, who simply could not compete. And, just as nature weeds out the unfit, an enlightened society ought to weed out its unfit and permit them to die off so as not to weaken the racial stock. This idea eventually led to a variety of practices and beliefs. For example, 'Nordic racism' based on eugenic principles became very influential in the USA as well as in Europe. The American Breeders Association, a lobbying organisation, published an influential journal sent to thousands of homes. 'The magazine contained a mixture of short, readable articles and reviews on a variety of topics, from plant and animal breeding to calls for sterilization of delinquents and racist immigration laws' (McCaskell 1994: 14). Largely due to pressure from this association, the US immigration policy was changed in 1924 to only allow northern Europeans, or so-called 'Nordics'. American eugenic ideas, based upon ideas of the Nordic type, were widely influential and there is evidence that Hitler himself held the US programme in high esteem. Eugenics promulgated the belief that the unfit transmit their undesirable characteristics. Through a controlled breeding programme, the racial stock could be protected from degeneration via the transmission of these 'undesirable' characteristics.

As a consequence of these (still tenacious) myths, the early settlers frequently discounted the indigenous populations as less than human, as part of nature to be vanquished. In the early maps of the Antipodes, Australia was labelled '*terra nullius*' meaning 'the empty land', indicating that Aboriginal people were seen as having no prior claim over the land. When indigenous groups were not systematically slaughtered, they were removed from their lands and taken into the custody of missionaries (these regimes often had the same effects as active genocide). A mixture of paternalism and evangelism has meant that up until the 1960s, Aboriginal people were denied the right to vote and have only been granted recognition as being the prior inhabitants of Australia since the Mabo High Court ruling.

In 1992, a landmark court case, the famous Mabo Ruling, overturned centuries of legal refusal to grant this recognition. After a protracted legal struggle of nearly ten years, Eddie Mabo and four other Torres Strait Islanders were able to establish ownership of their land prior to annexation by the state of Queensland. The implications of this ruling shattered the legal fiction of *terra nullius* – the idea that Australia had been an empty land before white colonists arrived.

Despite this affirmation, recent legal constraints have placed a heavy onus on Aboriginal people to give exhaustive evidence in court of their prior ownership of land.

As Geoff Clark said, reflecting on another land-ownership case that had been lost, 'In addition, the test of a continuous connection to land since occupation is onerous and unjust. The effects of the forced removal of our people from traditional country make it impossible for us to have their rights recognised. The mere closing of a pastoralist's gate can sever the connection with traditional lands, as we saw in the De Rose Hill claim (http://www.eniar.org/news/ yortayorta1.html).

There is also a very prevalent romanticism regarding native peoples. It is a notion of their closeness to nature and their being untainted by the artifices of civilisation. The 'romantic' has the same paternalistic passivising effect as the directly racist, but under the guise of extolling their innocence as childlike or closer to nature. Romanticism from Rousseau and through the Romantic literature of the nineteenth century has exerted an influence that is still prevalent today in beliefs of romantic and primordial ethnic stereotypes. It is a small step to argue for genetic inferiority if one believes in a primordial theory of ethnicity or race.

Anthropology seems to present an objective account of people, yet frequently functions, unwittingly perhaps, to reinforce attitudes of romantic or directly racist discourses. Early anthropology served merely to catalogue the primitive rituals and to collect artefacts and could be seen as another link in the chain of colonial domination. The discourse of the popular television documentary about these 'Others' very clearly serves as a kind of armchair museum of exotic, primitive and colourful (*National Geographic* style) imagery.

Religious missions to the colonies probably helped to convince the colonists that they had God and virtue on their side and further rationalised a paternalistic or aggressive and vengeful approach to indigenous peoples.

There was (and still is) a scramble for the Earth's resources, which were needed for the growing industrialisation that required raw materials, particularly plantation crops such as rubber, sugar, coffee, cotton, tobacco, cassava, etc., and of course for the labour to produce these crops: slaves. When slavery was abolished in the British Empire in 1838 (not until 1865 in America), the era of the indentured labourer began. Colonial masters required cheap labour so they sought migrant workers from India and other colonies. The situation in the Caribbean, Malaysia and in Pacific islands such as Fiji reflect this pattern of employment, which in practice was not unlike slavery. Colonial overseers were still known to have flogged workers in the Caribbean up until the 1940s.

One of the features associated with colonial rule has been a tendency to play on divisions between subject groups within the colony to seed internal dissent and to weaken unified resistance to the colonial regime. 'After all, it is now widely accepted that colonial regimes and their successor states invented, promoted, and exploited "tribal" differences and traditions' (Comaroff 1995: 246).

The internalised divisions that are part of the impact of colonialism create an active divestment of original culture and emulation of the colonial values. The divisions were not just external through segregation and divisions of labour but were part of the mind of the colonial subject. Fanon's contribution has been to demonstrate this, and his work *The Wretched of the Earth* (1961) embodied the spirit of resistance taken up by the anti-colonialist movement. He believed that only through physically expelling the invader from the nations would the psychic wounds be salved.

EFFECTS OF COLONIALISM

Vulnerability of new lands and peoples in some cases destroyed existing ecosystems. Peoples had little resistance to diseases brought in by Europeans and, in some cases, succumbed in their thousands. Indigenous peoples were systematically slaughtered by new settlers or forced to move to new environments. The Tasmanian Aborigines were almost wiped out or relocated to the remote Flinders Island by 1835, just thirty-two years after the arrival of the first British settlers. Some textbooks simply list the Tasmanians as being extinct or as having died out, with no explanation given. There are scarce records of the full horror of the hunting down and killing that was perpetrated with extreme brutality. John Pilger, in his book *Heroes*, recounted one surviving account from an Aborigine known as Old Mr Birt of a story told him by his mother:

> The buried our babies with only their heads above the ground. All in a row they were. Then they had a test to see who could kick the babies' heads off the furthest. One man clubbed a babies head off from horseback. They then spent the day raping the women; most of them [the women] were then tortured to death by sticking sharp things like spears up their vaginas until they died. They tied the men's hands behind their backs, then cut off their penises and testicles and watched them run around screaming until they died. I lived because I was young and pretty and one of the men kept me for himself, but I was always tied up until I escaped into another land to the west.
>
> (Pilger 1986: 580)

Recently, historian Keith Windschuttle (2003) claimed that the numbers murdered were inaccurate and most died from natural causes; that, in fact, the colonial experience in Tasmania was one of the most benign, and that full-blood Aborigines in Tasmania died out due to their isolation and vulnerability to diseases like pneumonia and tuberculosis.

The claim that many revisionists make concerning atrocities in Germany, Japan, Ireland (and probably now in Iraq) is that as there are no eye witnesses it could be a fiction. It appears that Windschuttle felt a desperation about the stain on the nation, the legacy of guilt that he (along with the Prime Minister John Howard) so wanted to be rid of. Indeed, Howard made clear his sympathy for Windschuttle by awarding him a centenary medal for services to history. This must have seemed a godsend to Howard who has dubbed the more negative view of Australia's past as 'the black arm band view' of history (see case study in Chapter 6). However, these revisionist claims have been fiercely disputed. Robert Manne of La Trobe University responded to Windschuttle by commissioning eighteen historians to address and firmly refute his claims (2003).

It is important that such revisionism does not succeed. The genocidal colonialism was not restricted to the British in Australia. The Belgian Congo was one of the most extreme cases, with possibly 10 million people being slaughtered. Rom, a minor official who became a commissioner, is said to have used Africans' heads for his garden borders and may be the real-life model for the shadowy figure of Mr Kurtz, Conrad's ruthless colonial administrator. America's genocidal destruction of indigenous peoples at home and the brutal repressive war waged in the Philippines where at least 20,000 were slaughtered are hardly ever cited. The scale of these atrocities and the lack of remorse reflect the perception of the colonial Other as not fully human. These are bodies without rights, 'unpeople' (a term Curtis (2004) uses to describe the civilian deaths in Iraq).

As Gilroy suggests, 'The countless tales of colonial brutality are too important to be lightly or prematurely disposed of. They cannot capture the whole complexity of imperial affairs, but these days they tend to get overlooked because a sanitized history of the imperial project is required by those who wish to bring it back to life' (2004: 52).

Through his psychoanalytic insights into the depersonalisation of the dis-possessed, Frantz Fanon captured the plight of the black colonial subject as one of a shattered self-image, the colonial 'look' creates the mirror, and in it the black person sees himself as nothing human as a mere object. 'The black man has two dimensions. One with his fellows, the other with the white man. A Negro behaves differently with a white man and with another Negro. That this self-division is a direct result of colonialist subjugation is beyond question' (Fanon 1967a: 17). This internalised image of self may be considered one of self-contempt. Over 100 years ago, the great writer W. E. B. Du Bois eloquently wrote about the duality of the black persona as a result of this internalised divide:

It is a peculiar sensation, this double-consciousness, this sense of always looking at one's self through the eyes of others, of measuring one's soul by the tape of a world that looks on in amused contempt and pity. One ever feels his two-ness – an American, a Negro; two souls, two thoughts, two unreconciled strivings; two warring ideals in one dark body, whose dogged strength alone keeps it from being torn asunder. The history of the American Negro is the history of this strife – this longing to attain self-conscious manhood, to merge his double self into a better and truer self. In this merging he wishes neither of the older selves to be lost.

(Du Bois 1897: 194–8)

These aspects of colonialism are important to comprehend. The distortion that has relegated black and Asian cultures to the periphery of world events has shaped our modern/postmodern societies. However, it is unrealistic to portray colonialism as a one-way process imposed on passive victims. There were effects on the colonisers by those subjected to their domination, but, more than this, the actions of British imperialists had marked impacts on how domestic 'Others' were constructed. They were actively engaged in transforming their own society . . . the nether reaches of urban society were directly linked to colonies, to undomesticated primitive lands. Cultural colonialism in short, was also a reflexive process whereby 'others' abroad, the objects of the civilizing mission, were put to the purposes of reconstructing the 'other' back home (Comaroff and Comaroff 1992: 293). Colonialism has a major impact on the structure of our contemporary societies. It is a particularly significant factor in the historical roots of diaspora, and the fractured and hybrid identities which are so much a part of our cities today.

The black diaspora: people imported as labour around the world. People taken by force from their homelands as slaves or as indentured labourers from India, China and Portugal, amongst other countries. These diasporas are the basis for multicultural or multi-ethnic nations: for example, Brazil, Australia, America, France, the United Kingdom and Canada, reflecting the social history of colonialism. People imported or transported to the New World or Australasia as convicts, slaves or, in the modern post-war era, as cheap labour (for example, in the United Kingdom and France, there are members of colonial countries, India, Pakistan, the West Indies, or North African countries). Multiculturalism, as we will see in later chapters, can be seen as a progressive force for world unity or as a form of tokenism that really means assimilation and integration.

REPARATION MOVEMENT

A point made by the reparation movement is that transatlantic slavery constitutes the biggest crime against humanity from which the colonial nations were able – due to their plunder and at the expense of Africa – to accede to the high ground of economic development while Africa remains impoverished and peripheral (and, indeed, still prey to the descendant forms of colonialism). In 1997, Lord Gifford made the following comment in a speech before the House of Lords:

My Lords, the Question raises an issue which is being debated with increasing vigour and intensity by African people around the world; and by African people I mean people of African descent, wherever they live, whether in Africa itself, in the United States, in Great Britain or in the Caribbean, where I now live and practise law.

The issue is this. The under-development and poverty which affect the majority of countries in Africa and in the Caribbean, as well as the ghetto conditions in which many black people live in the United States and elsewhere, are not, speaking in general terms, the result of laziness, incompetence or corruption of African people or their governments. They are in a very large measure the consequences the legacy – of one of the most massive and terrible criminal enterprises in recorded human history; that is, the transatlantic slave trade and the institution of slavery.

> (African Reparation Movement from Lords' Hansard
> (1997) http://www.arm.arc.co.uk/LordsHansard.html)

The scale of the depopulation of Africa was enormous. Some black scholars estimate a holocaust of between 50 and 100 million; rather more than conservative white researchers have suggested – around 10 million. What is certain is that five centuries of exploitation left Africa weakened – and it could be argued the frequent geopolitical problems, droughts, famines, civil wars, etc., are part of the West's legacy to Africa, Asia and South America.

The scarring of colonialism has left its imprint on peoples across the world. Gilroy (2004) in his examination of post-empire melancholia makes the point that for nations to shake off the lingering effects of colonialism they need to come to terms with some culpability at a national level:

> before the British people can adjust to the horrors of their own modern history and start to build a new national identity from the debris of their broken narcissism, they will have to learn to appreciate the brutalities of colonial rule enacted in their name and to their benefit, to understand the damage it did to their political culture at home and abroad, and to consider the extent of their country's complex investments in ethnic absolutism that has sustained it.
>
> (Gilroy 2004: 108)

NEO-COLONIALISM AND AUTO-COLONIALISM

A landmark meeting of UNESCO at the end of the Second World War brought together prominent scientists from around the world to make a definitive statement about 'race'. The Florence Declaration of 1950 states unequivocally that based on the latest findings of scientific research at the time they rejected the idea that there were fundamental differences due to race in the human species and unequivocally condemned the theories based on the superiority of one or more races. Those two statements were chiefly concerned with the biological and anthropological aspects of the problem.

(UN Economic and Social Council 1999: 7–8)

However, despite this, racism functions to maintain the powerful elite through hierarchical formulations of race that make racism a pernicious weapon. Even as these tenets of a world free from systematic racism were being laid down, apparently drawing a line under the evils of colonialism and the Nazi holocaust, the spurious reasoning that had permitted them was being promulgated elsewhere in the western world. Indeed there is evidence that US eugenics movement had been something of an inspiration to the Third Reich. Forced sterilisation was still being carried out in Puerto Rico (estimates of up to 35 per cent of working-class women), in Sweden up until the 1950s pursued the largest per-capita eugenic programme targeting 'deviant' groups, for sterilisation. In addition to America and Europe, Asian countries too have made clear attempts at ethnic cleansing, notably Tibet under the Chinese (but also East Timor and Irian Jia under Indonesia). In addition, immigration policies and the treatment of refugees have frequently been viewed as either directly racist or else inspired by labour movements to protect the nation from an influx of labour that might undercut domestic work rates (for example, the White Australia Policy).[2]

Ostensibly 'white' rule was at an end but, by exposing the true politics of global power, Kwame Nkrumah's in his 1965 study of neo-colonialism (another landmark text) *Neo-colonialism: The Last Stage of Capitalism*, gave this definition of neo-colonialism:

The essence of neo-colonialism is that the state which is subject to it is, in theory, independent and has all the outward trappings of international sovereignty. In reality its economic system and thus its political policy is directed from outside [. . .] The neo-colonialism of today represents imperialism in its final and perhaps its most dangerous state.

(1965: 1)

Forms of colonialism then seem to be prevalent still today – although the forms of exploitation are now linked to the dramatic changes wrought by political,

---

2 From time of federation in 1901 until the 1970s, Australia actively discouraged the migration of people considered undesirable. This policy is widely known as the White Australia Policy. Undesirable people included 'coloured' people as well as prostitutes, criminals, the insane and any person suffering from a contagious disease.

economic and cultural globalisation. Evidence from the UN Human Development Index shows that the gap between the wealthy western countries and the poorest areas (Africa, Asia, South America) has increased steeply in the past forty years.

> [T]he richest 20% of people have seen the differential between themselves and the poorest 20% double: where in the 1950s the richest one-fifth of humanity received 30 times as much as the poorest fifth, this has now increased to 60 times as much. And this outcome occurred even while a potential alternative – however malign – still to some degree inhibited a capitalism as yet unsure of its ultimate triumph.
>
> (Seabrook 1996: 1)

The 'winners' and the 'losers' in this accelerating process are quite clear. Transnational corporations originating in the West have sales figures that are greater than the gross domestic product (GDP) of many countries combined. 'For example, 50% of the world's population survive on 6% of the world's income. The assets of the 3 richest people exceed the GDP of 48 less developed countries' (*Guardian*, 6 September 2000).

> Total sales by General Motors in 1998 were greater than the GDP of countries like Thailand or Norway. Sales by Sumitomo, Exxon and Toyota were higher than the GDPs of Malaysia, Colombia or Venezuela.
>
> (Third World Network 2004, online document)

> Of the 100 largest economies in the world, 51 are now corporations. Wal-Mart, No. 12 on the list – Canada ranks No. 8 – is larger than 161 countries; in other words, its gross revenue is greater than the total wealth, or gross domestic product (GDP), of any of these 161 countries. General Motors is larger than Denmark, Ford is bigger than South Africa, and Toyota surpasses Norway. The largest 10 corporations had revenues in 1991 exceeding the combined GDPs of the 100 smallest countries. Put another way, the 200 largest corporations have more economic clout than the poorest four-fifths of humanity.
>
> (Dobbin 1998: 3)

All this suggests a picture of the world in which power has followed the development of enormously powerful global trading blocs with vast resources in the hands of a small elite. The governance of the poor countries has ceased to rest with their nominal leaders and has increasingly been passed over to western financial institutions and those transnational entities for which the preservation of western dominance is axiomatic. 'Their talk of poverty abatement, structural adjustment, their touting of economic success stories – once Brazil, now New Zealand, once even Nigeria, now Thailand – are calculated to conceal the real purpose of the integrated world economy, which is the supranational management of worsening inequality' (Seabrook 1996: 1).

Without wishing to present any overly polemic case, two events can be compared here, one virtually forgotten, the other still ringing in our ears. Bhopal in 1984, where 'toxic gas from a Union Carbide plant may have killed 20,000 people, with the toll still growing, a legacy of cancers, and genetic defects, and the fight for compensation not yet over' (*Guardian*, Monday, 29 November 2004) and the attack on the World Trade Center in New York in which 2,823 people died in the buildings and in the aircraft that crashed into them.

These are obviously not commensurable cases: 9/11 was not an industrial accident, it was an intentional attack calculated to cause maximum impact and hurt. However, the lack of social justice in the first case, where apparently many times more people were affected and continue to be so (Union Carbide, it was reported, have not cleaned up the area in which lethal chemicals are still a danger to people) arguably indicates the prevalence of core and peripheral values ('wedom' and 'theydom' written large). Similarly, the number of Iraqi civilians who have died in the military invasion number – at best estimates, about 24,865 civilians were killed up to 19 March 2005 and 45,000 Iraqis have been wounded (see *Guardian Unlimited*, July 2005). There were attempts to persuade the public that Iraq was involved in 9/11, but there is no firm evidence that this is true.

What relevance do these cases have to issues of race and ethnicity? Quite clearly, the clash of belief systems is central to such actions, as is the impact of neo-colonialism. Decentralised industrial operations in developing countries has become the normal pattern. There are also firm precedents for invading oil-rich countries; the Twin Towers were for some a symbol of western affluence and neo-colonial domination. 'Religious fundamentalists do not single out the United States for any other reason than its hegemonic power' (Ali 2003: 282).

CHAPTER SUMMARY

The western world has been defined through its colonialist enterprises (and continues to be so). The expedient use of concepts of 'race' in the seventeenth century have become a defining divide in the project of modernity. Slavery is an ancient institution stretching from pre-history to the present day and, at the time of writing, slaves in Niger had only just been freed (part of the ancient African trade that had survived). Yet racial slavery was a unique and relatively recent movement in associated with colonialism. The consequences of slavery and other forms of booty capitalism have been two centuries of relative affluence and dominance for western countries while simultaneously underdeveloping countries in Asia, Africa and South America. However, the pace of change has increased markedly in the past twenty-five years and the scale of disadvantage and division has reached unprecedented size, as neo-colonialism and auto-colonialism have widened the gap. Structural economic plans brokered by the World Bank and the International Monetary Fund (IMF) have enabled the West to exploit the lack of infrastructure of the world's poorest nations. Apart from the material affects of colonialism, Du Bois and Fanon have expressed the troubling duality of the post-colonial psyche but, although it is less apparent, the effects of colonialism are manifest in the white populations in their lingering post-empire melancholia.

EXERCISE 3.1 GUYANA: LOOK WHAT THEY DONE TO THE MOTHER

1   How might we account for the apparent reverence which the Guyanese speaker has for the 'mother' Queen Victoria?
2   Are there elements of the exchange that reflect an inaccurate or overly nostalgic view of colonial history?
3   What signs of persistent hegemony of colonial values could you detect from the exchange?
4   What are the signs of ethnic tension in the exchange?
5   Why do you think rice could be such a grievously felt issue?
6   How might Goffman's dramaturgical theory be applied to the above extract?
7   Discuss the defacement of the statue and its resurrection and the meaning of such cultural icons in post-colonial societies. You might consider other fallen statues and their meaning, for example, Saddam Hussein's in Iraq or Stalin's and Lenin's statues in eastern Europe.

EXERCISE 3.2

1   The scale of depopulation of Africa was enormous. What are the implications and consequences of this history of exploitation?
2   Colonialism and slavery are more about capitalism than racism. Discuss.
3   The colonial exploitation of people as slaves; as mere commodities in the production process, did become inextricably linked to skin colour. What arguments were used in the defence of slavery?
4   How much credence was given to 'race sciences' that attempted to justify slavery as natural domination of inferior races?
5   How persuasive were arguments about the protection of private property and livelihood of colonists and slave owners?

6   Colonialism has left its imprint on vast areas of the world: South America, Africa, and much of Asia. What are the consequences for the post-colonial subject in these areas?

7   Should reparations be made to the countries and peoples who were subjected to such treatment, or to indigenous peoples such as the Maoris and Australian Aborigines who claim their countries were stolen by colonists?

8   Consider the world events mentioned in the last section. How are global trade and terrorism involved in the construction of ethnic/religious otherness?

CHAPTER 4

Theories of Race and Ethnicity

PRIMORDIAL OR INSTRUMENTAL ETHNICITY

Are 'race' and ethnicity part of our 'natural' makeup or are they features which can be exploited for social and economic advantage? In crude terms this is the thrust of these two influential trends in theory. Can ethnic groups and the apparently universal experience of ethnocentrism be understood as primordial or instrumental phenomena? Definitions of primordialism can range from simply the force and strength of traditions and cultural ties to ideas of genetically inherited features and characteristics. At the most biologically determined end of the spectrum, sociobiologists have argued that there is a biological aspect to the formation of ethnic bonds. They believe that social behaviour is guided by evolutionary strategies and motivated towards securing long-term survival of the group. Theories such as 'inclusive fitness' (Hamilton 1964) and 'kin selection', which operate amongst animals, are therefore suggested to be relevant to human behaviour. 'A person's inclusive fitness is his or her personal fitness plus the increased fitness of relatives that he or she has in some way caused by his or her actions' (Reynolds et al. 1987: xvii). These concepts operate together; inclusive fitness is achieved through kin selection. These biological imperatives (which posit an invisible guiding force of biology) are considered by sociobiologists to explain altruism. The individual is a vehicle for the genes that must be passed on – however, in examples of self-sacrifice to save or defend a kinship group, the argument is that the gene stock will still survive even if the individual dies. Such explanations are reasonable when applied to the animal world – bees, ants or birds for example

– but sociobiologists extrapolate these ideas of the 'selfish gene' (Dawkins 1989) and inclusive fitness to human society. To consider a person as little more than a gene's 'survival machine' (Dawkins 1989: 132) entirely ignores the enormous evidence for social and cultural forces that shape behaviour. Furthermore, to conjecture that ethnic identification and acts of loyalty and sacrifice can be reduced to genetic determinism seems extreme. Sociobiology has met with resistance in the past thirty years, which is not surprising as it has certain features in common with Social Darwinism – in particular the notion of biological predestination. The successor to sociobiology, evolutionary psychology, seems also to depend on similar reductionist and adaptionist[1] arguments.

More reasonable forms of primordial explanation exist however. Traditional ties are passed along to members of a defined group. These attachments of kinship and heritage are clearly part of many if not most people's upbringing. However, the concept may be extended further to include a harder primordial boundary in which ties of blood, religion, custom and belief become ineffable and have a deeper psychological effect on members of the group. Notions of primordial ethnicity such as those developed by Clifford Geertz (1973) suggest that ethnic identity developed from certain 'givens' of social existence, including blood and kin connections, religion, language (even dialect), region and custom.

Geertz suggests that these form 'ineffable', 'affective' and 'a-priori' bonds. Similarly it is apparent that these bonds are also considered to be (via more irrational criteria of blood inheritance) the basis of character and the cause of long-standing ethnic rivalry and even hatreds. Primordialism (in its most extreme form) suggests that cultures are fixed and unchanging – almost genetic blueprints – indeed, sociobiology would suggest that there is a biological imperative to preserve the genetic stock. Such viewpoints may be ideologically employed when complex situations occur that require a careful analysis of social histories. Attributing them to some irrational primordial core may fit with the dominant prejudices of the public. For example, during media coverage of the conflict in Rwanda, explanations tended to centre on descriptions of primordial tribalism leading to some sort of blood lust. The true complexity of the situation became lost in a media blitz on brutal tribal atrocities. The underlying causes were typically not sought; rather, journalists merely focused on irrational tribalism.

The background to these conflicts often stems from a history of invasion and reprisal over many decades or even centuries. Tutsis massacred Hutus in 1972 (see Kuper 1996); the ongoing ethnic conflict between Russia and Chechnya can be traced back at least 400 years; the conflict in Northern Ireland can be traced back to the twelfth century (see Curtis et al. 1984). As has already been discussed,

---

1 i.e. explanations for human attributes as developed to meet the needs of their environment.

the colonial practice of seeding derogatory stereotypes and manipulating group boundaries between the colonial subjects clearly has a long history and can be shown in some cases to have led to factionalism that has occasionally led to genocidal conflicts. Kuper comments that:

> Where there were two tiers of domination in the colonial structure, decolonization was particularly charged with genocidal potential. Plural societies preceded colonial imperialism, and in some cases capitalist colonization of a plural society resulted in the superimposition of an additional layer of domination on an earlier domination. In a number of these societies, decolonization detonated explosive genocidal conflicts, as the earlier rulers and their one-time subjects engaged in violent struggle under the impetus of electoral contests in a democratic idiom, introduced by the colonial powers in the movement to independence.
>
> (Kuper 1996: 266)

CRITICISMS OF PRIMORDIALISM

The concept of **apriority** is problematic when it is considered that most ethnic identities seem to undergo renewal, modification and remaking in each generation. Second, the notion of **ineffability** can be easily criticised because in practice such supposedly primordial attachments are tied to circumstances. **Affectivity** is a concept that implies a mystification of emotion or belief in sociobiological worldviews; this is a very weak argument and a genetic dead end for analysis. While a moderate form of primordialism seems realistic, the extension of such notions allow the conventional racist views of the materiality of difference to intercede. Such hard-line definitions are unable to adequately account for ethnic change and dissolution or for effects of immigration or intermarriage.

INSTRUMENTALISM

The other axis of explanation is presented in various forms of instrumentalism in which ethnicity indicates that there is some intentional or conscious strategies behind identity formation a type of political resource for competing interest groups. Ethnic groups and ties are strategically employed for attaining individual or collective goals. One form of this is the rational-choice approach advocated by Hechter (1995) and Banton (1987). In this approach, any action can be seen as determined by a rational motive as the basis for the pursuit of scarce resources: public goods such as housing, benefits, political power or competition for employment. In contradistinction to primordial theories here the basis for ethnicity is superficial and strategically employed. The model is that of an essentially individualistic and somewhat aggressive actor, self-interested, rational, pragmatic and, perhaps, with a maximising orientation as well. What actors do, it is assumed, is rationally to go after what they want, and what they want is what is materially and politically useful for them within the context of their cultural and historical situations (Ortner 1984: 151).

Perhaps the most significant words here are 'rational' and 'rationality'. Theories of rational choice seek to predict the conditions under which collective action emerges. How is social conformity and cohesion maintained in society? The Durkheimian – Parsonian answer is that people obey because they share certain common values and beliefs. In sociological terms, people internalise certain values and norms that induce them to participate in, accept and reproduce relations of production. However, rational-choice theories seem to derive from the materialistic premises alluded to by Ortner, in which a pragmatic behaviouristic view of human nature, to maximise gains and avoid losses, governs action.

CRITICISMS OF INSTRUMENTALISM

The criticisms of instrumentalist views of ethnicity are, first, that such views are unable to cope with ethnic 'durability'; second, they ignore mass passions evoked by ethnic ties and cultural symbols; and, third, they assume the ethnic nature of organisations.

Ethnic identity and aspects of belief and cultural practice are relatively long lived in many cultures. This is witnessed acutely in the way Muslims have been treated since the 9/11 attacks on the World Trade Center. Any distinctive features of dress, especially headscarves, hijab, or other traditional Muslim coverings have been seen to mark out Muslims. Indeed, the assaults on minority ethnic groups who maintain traditional dress have multiplied.

> Ethnic identity undoubtedly is formed around real shared social space, commonalities of socialization, and communities of language and culture. Simultaneously these identities have a public presence; they are socially defined in a series of presentations (public statements, assertions, images) by ethnic group members and non-members alike.
>
> (Fenton 2003: 194)

So can ethnicity be understood as a primordial or an instrumental phenomenon? Neither primordialists nor instrumentalists seem able to account for the long-term changes and movements of ethnic communities. It would appear that there are elements of both to be recognised in practice. To reduce, complex human behaviour to mere biology, on the one hand, or mere pragmatism, at the other extreme, appears to ignore human capacity to operate at the level of the symbolic and denies the importance of culture in its broadest sense.

When considering plural societies this tension between durable ethnicity and expressions of shared identity and desires for political and economic power are very significant. When colonial regimes have operated, the struggles between the post-colonial subjects can be intense. It is to these so called 'plural societies' that we now turn.

PLURAL SOCIETY THEORIES

Theories that seek to explain the ways in which race and ethnicity operate as loci of power within society are relatively recent. The phenomena associated with plural societies themselves are fairly recent and were previously, as we have seen, explained away through crude racial theorising that has been shown to have little foundation in scientific fact as well as associations with the Nazi pseudo-science of race.

The concept of a 'plural society' first emerged through anthropological analyses of colonial societies at the turn of the twentieth century. Anthropologist J. S. Furnivall, who studied Indonesia and Burma, wrote that 'the first thing that strikes the visitor is the medley of peoples – European, Chinese, Indian and native' (1948: 304) that constitute the society. The different groups, Furnivall wrote, 'mix but do not combine'. Each group 'holds by its own religion, its own culture and language, its ideas and ways'. The result was a 'plural society, with different sections of the society living side by side but separately within the same political unit' (Malik 1998).

Furnivall's belief that plural societies are composed of essentially antagonistic ethnic groups prevented from all-out conflict by the coercive force wielded by colonial powers could certainly be seen as anthropology providing support to paternalistic colonialism. M. G. Smith elaborated theoretically on Furnivall's view of structurally segmented enclaves. The extension he proposed defined pluralism in terms of differences in compulsory institutions (for example, kinship, education, property, economy, recreation) and minority control of intersectional relations in most examples of colonial government. Such plural societies can be characterised, in Smith's view, as, 'defined by dissensus and pregnant with conflict' (Smith 1974: xiii).

The situation in Guyana seems to fit with this dormant sense of ethnic antagonism. During an interview, Guyanese academic Berkeley Stewart suggested a diagram of a 'progressive' model of race relations (see Figure 4.1).

In Figure 4.1.a, if 'A' is the colonial force that governs the country, they have obvious political motives for exploiting any racial divisions and often would seed dissent in the form of slurs and scares about each of the enclaves. So the subject groups are divided. However, with time and the fluctuating influence and

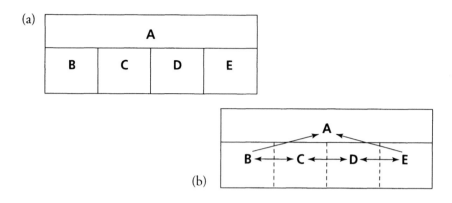

Figure 4.1 Dynamics of plural society

support for the colony, the subjugated groups will begin to unite beneath the banner of resistance against a common oppressor, 4.1.b and there will be increasing mobility between the groups as the pressure increases and the position of 'A' becomes more uneasy. If 'B' were African-Guyanese and 'C' Indian-Guyanese, certain cultural/ethnic dimensions will operate to allow or delay this ascent to higher levels of administration and responsibility. In Guyana, the Africans had the advantage of being more acculturated than the Indians – their original culture being largely destroyed or lost and therefore embracing the language and social mores of the dominant group. The Indian-Guyanese, having stronger cultural/ language bonds to their origins, would be held back by religious considerations from participating in the education system. Stewart was, however, optimistic that the eventual outcome would be a levelling of boundaries and a thorough acculturation, which he believed was actively in process at the time.

This model has several useful descriptive aspects and does account for the shifting identities within colonial and post-colonial plural societies. It places the traditionally conservative anthropology of Furnivall into a more dynamic model of change and ultimately of competition and ethnic rivalry. However, Stewart seemed to pursue a Durkheimian optimism about the ultimate levelling and acculturation in a society that was, and continues to be, polarised ethnically. There is an inherent ambivalence in pluralist arguments. They underline the negative aspects of colonialism but at the same time can be seen as presenting a defence of colonial leadership to maintain order and stability to the society. Plural-society theorists such as Furnivall (studies of Indonesia) and M. G. Smith (studies of the Caribbean) attempt to account for the manner in which separate ethnic groups or cultural enclaves are related to each other. For Furnivall, the central agency that holds groups together is 'the marketplace', emphasising economic and commercial relations albeit as a metaphor for the society as a whole. Smith, however, focuses upon political institutions. Both would consider their perspective to include relationships of production, yet do not spell out these distinctions. Recognising the complex interplay of ethnic enclaves under colonial regimes may benefit from a closer examination of varieties of Marxist and Weberian theory which offer analyses of race and ethnicity and their interweaving with class, status and power.

MARXIST THEORIES

Although Marx made little mention of 'race', the legacy of his conception of society as a struggle between the exploited and the exploiters has remained an influential discourse and one that many social commentators see as increasingly more relevant as the global forces of capitalism expand, as they consolidate their grip on resources and as divisions between economic classes reach unprecedented distances. Class is significant for all major social divisions as social standing and status, centrality or marginality have demonstrable economic consequences. This is true whether the social meaning or subjective identity of difference is taken into account, whether it be division based on gender, sexuality, race/ethnicity or disability. For this reason, the issue with assessing Marxist thought and its influence is not whether it is important but how the complex social and economic factors interrelate with complex aspects of ethnic identity, citizenship and historical legacy.

In the traditional Marxist approach, 'race' was (and still frequently is) seen as illusionary, a mere element to be exploited by capitalism. Traditional Marxist thinkers clearly see colonialism as a vital stage in the ultimate structural change that societies must undergo to evolve towards socialism. 'Marx himself recognised colonialism as a brutal precondition for the liberation of these societies' (Loomba 1998: 21). The historical dialectical process that ground on from primitive communism of small tribal communities through the barbarity of slavery to other forms of colonialism (only marginally less barbaric forms like indentureship for example) to industrial capitalism (where the formally free labour force begins to gain consciousness of the vulnerability of the oppressor) and ultimately through collective action of the proletariat to socialism. So each stage in this inevitable historical evolution was a necessary precursor of the next.

Race/ethnicity are seen as a part of a superstructure and hence are considered secondary or epiphenomenal to the economic base and relations of production. The organisation of production creates class differences in each society. Traditional Marxist views such as those of R. T. Smith are typical of this viewpoint. Actively playing down ethnic differences, Smith calls them: 'the residue of cultural peculiarities' (Smith 1962: 198). Moreover, he stresses that should the source of inequality be removed and equality of opportunity be restored, any ethnic differences would dissolve.

So, traditional Marxists still maintain that race and ethnicity are a mask that serves to obscure true relations of power in a society, which are, in fact, class based.

> In British Guiana [. . .] there are forces tending to create different groupings, different occupations and different social classes, and there are forces tending to bind the members of these differentiated groups into some kind of unity and interdependence. Race, cultural differences, and even slight differences of colour are used to some extent as the basis for differentiation and the conflicts which could arise within a frustrated and dissatisfied society could easily crystallise around these factors.
>
> (Smith 1962: 143)

Certainly, differences in ethnicity are frequently channelled, amplified and strengthened through political allegiances. The ideological shaping of ethnic identities has been well documented in situations like this. Premdas, focusing on links between voluntary associations and political campaigns in Guyana (1972), has shown the way political and economic imperatives have led to mutually opposed ethnic enclaves.

However, the suggestion that ethnicity simply lies dormant, to be utilised as the most visible rationale or expression of deeper divisions inherent in economic structures and the state, is not wholly convincing. There are class distinctions, but these do not correspond simply with those of ethnic background. Why should ethnic boundaries persist when such boundaries do not correspond to the boundaries defining class interest groups? It is unnecessary for class and ethnicity to be seen as discrete independent variables in a competition for primacy. Rather it may be possible for both to be viewed as interacting elements in a systematic theory of boundary formation in a society.

As Rex has suggested 'it is not necessary to exclude from consideration the possibility of a situation in which either ethnicity or class, or both together operate as the main means of boundary marking' (Rex and Mason 1986: 6). Generally, however, the role of racism is seen to have its origins 'in the ideologies and racial typologies that were often invoked to justify the open exploitation of colonial times' (Cashmore 1989: 127). Examples of this tactical racism are plentiful. Walter Rodney writes of the divisive use of stereotypes on the plantations of British Guiana to maintain control and exploit labourers even after slavery had ended: 'Early in the history of indentureship, planters recognised the value of having a working population segmented racially; and they never lost sight of the opportunity of playing off the two principal races – by using one to put down any overt resistance by the other' (Rodney 1981: 188). Rodney also quotes evidence given at the West Indian Royal Commission, clearly showing that this manipulative attitude was commonplace in the colony:

The two people do not mix. That is, of course, one of our great safeties in the colony when there has been any rioting. If the negroes were troublesome every coolie on the estate would stand by one. If the coolies attacked me, I could with confidence trust my negro friends for keeping me from injury.

(Rodney 1981: 188)

Marx's materialist vision of evolving eras of historical struggle, while it may regard other issues of identity to be part of the illusion of false consciousness, a veil that would be lifted after radical consciousness is achieved, does, nevertheless, clearly recognise the importance of abolishing slavery. Marx and Engels recognised the pivotal importance of the struggle for emancipation and organised workers in textile mills in the north of England to block purchases of Confederacy cotton. After 1790, as Steven Marcus reports, 'it was the slave states of the American South that became the major suppliers for Lancashire mills' (1974: 8).

Writing about slavery just after the Civil War, Marx (1982) made the following comment, which clearly shows that he recognised that racial divisions were crucial to the success of the exploiters: 'In the United States of North America every independent movement of the workers was paralyzed so long as slavery disfigured a part of the republic. Labour cannot emancipate itself in the white skin where in the black it is branded.' Furthermore, Marx realised that the conditions amongst the industrial working class in Britain were not dissimilar to the racist divisions between black and white people in the USA.

The following passage comes from a letter that Marx wrote from London to Sigfrid Meyer and August Vogt in New York on 9 April 1870:

Every industrial and commercial centre in England now possesses a working class divided into two hostile camps, English proletarians and Irish proletarians. The ordinary English worker hates the Irish worker as a competitor who lowers his standard of life. In relation to the Irish worker he regards himself as a member of the ruling nation and consequently he becomes a tool of the English aristocrats and capitalists against Ireland, thus strengthening their domination over himself. He cherishes religious, social, and national prejudices against the Irish worker. His attitude towards him is much the same as that of the 'poor whites' to the Negroes in the former slave states of the U.S.A. The Irishman pays him back with interest in his own money. He sees in the English worker both the accomplice and the stupid tool of the English rulers in Ireland. This antagonism is artificially kept alive and intensified by the press, the pulpit, the comic papers, in short, by all the means at the disposal of the ruling classes. This antagonism is the secret of the impotence of the English working class, despite its organization. It is the secret by which the capitalist class maintains its power. And the latter is quite aware of this.

(Marx and Engels 1982: 222)

The contention contained in Marx's letter is certainly a valid assessment of the instrumental use of race as a strategic tool to enable the divide and rule of workers by the elite, whether they are factory and mill owners, colonists in the New World or, perhaps, a government that wants to draw attention away from the numbers of unemployed under stringent economic policies (for example, the neo-conservatism of Margaret Thatcher in the United Kingdom, Reagan in the USA during the late 1970s and early 1980s) and in the 2000s Bush and Blair's 'war on terror' and its concurrent concerns about 'asylum seekers' and refugees. Critics of Marxist views might do well to consider the enduring relevance of the view that race is not an inherent identity based on biological or cultural characteristics but is used expediently – as a fluid set of rationalisations, continuously shifting to respond to considerations related to the demands of industry, military needs in times of war and calls for national unity in the face of economic global threat.

Racism is not a universal and transcendental phenomenon but rather socially constructed, historically specific policies shaped by the labour market, ideology, government intervention and political resistance. The efforts to create ethnic antagonism have been well documented during the period of European imperial power (see the case study of Guyana in Chapter 7) through the use of derogatory stereotypes and divisive policies that pitch the different groups into competitive relationships, thus effectively dividing workers and creating obstacles for collective resistance to colonialism. In the post-war era there is evidence that more subtle ideological forces are employed in addition to the coercive apparatus of the state. More progressive Marxist forms recognise the influence of the media and cultural reproduction through the agency of education. (The case study in Chapter 6 illustrates the way media can crystallise public concerns and channel the flow of collective anxiety.)

Marxism suggests that racism serves the ruling class in several ways. First, to legitimise domination and exploitation. If racial hierarchies are accepted, this inequity is neutralised. For example, colonial attitudes expressed colonial relations as a 'natural' hierarchy:

> Nature has made a race of workers, the Chinese race, who have wonderful manual dexterity and almost no sense of humour; . . . a race of tillers of the soil, the Negro . . .; a race of masters and soldiers, the European race. Reduce this noble race to working . . . like Negros or Chinese and they rebel.
>
> (Quoted in Loomba 1998: 126)

Second, the above quote (and Marx's own example of Irish racism in the textile mills) illustrate that racism provides a method of dividing and ruling the workforce. Not only does this prevent a collective working-class consciousness from emerging but it also develops functional divisions of labour.

A third key use of racism is to distract attention away from the divisive actions of the elite by effectively scapegoating a vulnerable group. The argument used within the Third Reich that the Jews had been the reason for Germany's defeat in the First World War, rallied collective support and a wave of revulsion that made the Final Solution possible.

The roots of racism could be argued to always have been grounded in labour relations. Race was a constructed concept which, as we have seen, enabled colonialists to justify an expendable workforce of slaves. In contemporary society, it could equally be argued that the focus on difference (ethnicisation or racialisation) between workers is still maintained and serves a similar function. In recent years there has been considerable work around the dynamic intersection of race and class in specific contemporary situations, and especially postwar Britain. Race is fundamental to the formation of the working classes in general and to the experience of black labour in particular. It has been suggested that class relations within communities of black working-class people 'function as *race-relations*. The two are inseparable. Race is the modality in which class is lived' (Hall et al. 1978: 394). Similarly, race provides the lived reality of class relations. Hence, race has consequences for all within that class, it moulds and shapes their conditions of existence, it has transformative power, bringing about changes in opportunities and the relative open or closed conditions between black people and their economic relationships with the greater society.

In assessing the connection between race/ethnicity and class, the starting point is often the relative economic positions of ethnic groups, extrapolating from economic processes to class. The view that immigrants or migrants are part of an underclass is a frequently used one. Marxist theorising argues that migration provides a reserve army of labour which functions to keep wages low and maximise profits (see Castles and Kossack 1985). However, the post-Fordist restructure of the labour force and the recognition that the other forms of social division such as ethnicity and gender are not merely the result of class structures render any simple views of race as class as highly problematic.

While notions of race and racism have been shown to have complex origins associated with the beginnings of capitalism in the USA and Europe, can racism be shown to have grown out of capitalism (as Oliver Cox, the black Marxist writer claims (1976)) or does the structuration of racial boundaries have influence on the formation of class (a view supported by John Rex (1980) and Stuart Hall (1980))? Some, such as Anthias, suggest that Marxist theories are not fully adequate, arguing that ethnicity has much more to say about the ways people live and communicate and interact with one another, that historically, racial divisions pre-date capitalism and indeed have had a powerful formative influence on the formation of capitalism: 'Since the three hundred years of slave labour are central to the development of capitalism, the Marxist interpretation of history in terms of the dialectic of capitalist class struggle is inadequate' (Anthias and Yuval-Davis 1992: 134).

Sivanandan's view, based on UK studies (1986), gives support to the position that racism is fundamental to capitalism. Colonialism formalised racism as a means of rationalisation or economic justification that sowed the seeds for racist ideologies. Wallerstein (Balibar and Wallerstein 1991: 33) observes that racial hierarchies operate as a 'magic formula' for capitalism, allowing very low wages for some sections of the work force and stifling protest through a process of 'ethnicisation' of the workforce.

Robert Miles produced a critique of the sociology of race. In his view, the object of the study should be racism, 'which he perceived as integral to the process of capital accumulation' (Solomos and Back 1996: 8). In this view, race and the process of racialisation are masks that disguise the real economic relations: 'racism is mostly conceived as ideological, a set of rationalizations for sustaining exploitative economic practices and exclusionary political relations' (Goldberg 1993: 93).

The migrant-labour model developed by Robert Miles and Annie Phizacklea prioritises the political economy of migrant labour and avoids any reference to 'race relations', which they feel add status to a divisive social and political construct. In other words by attributing meaning to the term 'race' the term is reified and 'leads to a commonsense acceptance that "race" is an objective determinant of the behaviour of black workers or other racially defined social categories' (Goldberg 1993: 99).

To Miles, race is only a political category, but the process of racialisation is 'a dialectical process of signification' (1989: 75), that goes hand in hand with exploitation of 'migrant labour'. Racialisation can be used, Miles says, in 'those instances where social relations between people have been structured by the signification of human biological characteristics in such a way as to define and construct differentiated social collectivities' (Miles 1989: 75).

Miles gives an illustration of this process at work in colonial Kenya of the 1920s. Like many colonial outposts, the African population was prevented from planting coffee, but not because they would pose a threat to the colonists, but rather because the relative independence and contentment that this might bring to Africans who were forced to live on reserves was seen as likely to reduce the necessity of working for the colonial landowners. The imposition of a number of taxes levied forced Africans to work to manage to pay them (see Miles 1989: 109–10).

The reification of 'race' and the use of terms like 'race relations' and 'racism' run a significant danger, Miles warns, of giving reality to a spurious and ideological term: 'Race is an idea which should be explicitly and consistently confined to the dustbin of analytically useless terms' (Miles 1989: 42). Certainly this was a timely warning that some of the most prominent analyses, by implicitly accepting the term 'race' in sociological studies and by losing sight of the political meanings of such a dubious term, had inadvertently lent the concept some theoretical credence. 'His [Miles's] work constitutes an attempt to reclaim the study of racism from an apoliticised sociological framework and locate it squarely in a Marxist theorisation of social conflict' (Solomos and Back 1996: 10).

In post-colonial societies such as Britain, many countries in western Europe and America, the exploitation of 'asylum seekers', 'guest workers', workers who are living in often desperately poor conditions and with the threat of exposure to the immigration authorities, seem to bear out Miles's migrant labour thesis. While governments are not averse to employing public fears and xenophobia to take a strong platform on immigration before elections, the media has employed the most lurid stories about the threat from 'scroungers'. However, basic services in our inner cities are staffed largely by migrant workers of one sort or another. A recent estimate asserts that that nearly a third of America's full-time farm workers are 'unauthorized' (Reason 1999). Similarly, against a backdrop of accusations of asylum seekers and other migrants travelling to Britain solely to exploit the National Health System, figures suggested that

> there are around 90,000 vacancies in the UK health and social care sectors, when there could be thousands of refugees with the appropriate skills without permission to work, or facing numerous other barriers to work. The NHS already relies heavily on foreign labour: according to the Greater London Authority, 23% of doctors and 47% of nurses working within the NHS were born outside the UK.
>
> (Refugee Council online, July 2004)

It becomes clear that these attempts to exclude migrants have the ironic consequence of constituting them as an ideal labour force that can be exploited, coerced and paid the very minimum (in some cases not paid at all). In fact, the situation for many refugees who wish to leave their countries has been recognised as not much better than slavery.

> The economic position of black people is often a starting point when examining the connection between race and class. There can be said to be two strata within the working class: indigenous workers forming the upper, more privileged group and, beneath that, the immigrants who are (even in times of relative prosperity) the most exploited and underprivileged group in society.
>
> (Anthias and Yuval-Davis 1992: 62)

The black Marxist writer Oliver Cox perceived racism as developing out of capitalism 'and provided a means for furthering the use of labour as a commodity, pure and simple, resulting in a greater exploitation' (Anthias and Yuval Davis 1992: 63). Miles indicates that 'there are a range of exclusionary practices in society that are not merely coterminous with racism but are "a component of a wider structure of class disadvantage"' (1989: 9).

Certainly Marxist perspectives offer powerful insights into the use of racism as a means to an end. However, the weakness of traditional Marxist analyses for issues of race and gender was an over-emphasis on economic bases as primary and a blind spot where other instrumental intersections with the institutions of capitalism were concerned. The role of the family, culture, sexuality and ethnic identity were not given serious analysis. Marxist theory, through which the relations of the means of production are operationalised through human subjects caught up in the struggle for survival, has been criticised as economistic and reductionist, allowing very little recognition for human agency. Yet, by contrast, Marx's beliefs in social change through conscious and collective action partly mitigate such a conclusion.

STRUCTURALIST CRITICISM OF MARXISM

Stuart Hall and other scholars at the Centre for Contemporary Cultural Studies have been influential in the work of many post-colonial critics. Hall has made interesting use of concepts developed by the Italian Marxist Antonio Gramsci to allow a more sophisticated Marxism to be brought to bear on the discourses that compose racism. Gramsci's concept of 'hegemony', based on the suggestion by Machiavelli that political domination of the masses is achieved by a combination of force and fraud, led Gramsci to consider the manner in which elites were able to create willing submission to colonial rule. This view was quite different to the notion of direct repression and coercion, but does not deny the existence of brutal repressive force as well. However, 'hegemony is achieved not only by direct manipulation or indoctrination, but by playing upon the commonsense of people, upon what Raymond Williams calls their "lived system of meaning and values"' (1977: 110). A similar argument has been advanced by Herman and Chomsky in *Manufacturing Consent* (1995) in their thesis on the propaganda model. They argue that there is a subtle and covert process of control which is achieved through the logic of market forces and the complacency of consumer society. These operations are much less visible than the aggressive censorship exercised by more dictatorial governments.

Hall perceptively draws out the importance of these ideas for thinking about the relationship between race, ethnicity and colonialism on the one hand and capital and class on the other (see Hall 1996). Gramsci's work in the ideological field has proved very fruitful when applied to the complex interrelation between capitalism and racism. Hall comments that:

he altogether refuses any idea of a pre-given ideological subject – for example, the proletarian with its 'correct' revolutionary thoughts or blacks with their already guaranteed current anti-racist consciousness. He recognises the 'plurality' of the selves or identities of which the so called 'subject' is composed.

He argues that this multi-faceted nature of consciousness is not an individual but a collective phenomenon, a consequence of the relationship between 'the self' and the ideological discourses which compose the cultural terrain of a society.

(Hall 1996a: 433)

Like Gramsci, Althusser (1971) argued against any ultimate reduction to the economic base and, further, that ideology has a material existence as it can always be found to be implicit in the apparatus of social control. Ideological apparatus could therefore exert influence on the economic base. He proposed the terms 'repressive state apparatuses' (RSAs) and 'ideological state apparatuses' (ISAs) to explain the dual nature of control articulated by Gramsci. The coercive effects achieved by RSAs are less noticeable in advanced capitalism, but when direct dissent and threat to the state occurs they will be used, for example in the 1980s UK miners' strike or the violent suppression used in the poll-tax demonstrations. In this view, when policies and the state's hegemony is under threat, RSAs in the form of the army and the police are typically employed. ISAs include church, family, media and schools and both achieve consent more effectively and ensure the state is not exposed as coercive (it can maintain the aura of what Mark Curtis calls 'basic benevolence'). The media is especially influential in undermining opposition (again see Herman and Chomsky 1995). Media representation of black and Asian people is a case in point. The media moral panic surrounding asylum seekers and refugees can be shown to present a distorted focus on an issue that is high on the political agenda partly perhaps from pressure from media sources. Media Lens recently reported that there is a high degree of uniformity in the 'quality press' in the United Kingdom when it comes to covering issues of asylum seekers. These papers (the *Daily Telegraph*, the *Independent* and the *Guardian*) showed a 'consistent unity of themes' with focus on: 'bogus' asylum applicants, crime/terrorism perpetrated by asylum seekers, accommodation/ detention issues. However, Matthew Randall (2003) argues that to be a truly independent and honest 'quality' press, other 'macro-stories' should be given coverage, for example:

- The fact that the NHS would cease to function without overseas nurses. The Royal College of Nursing reported in February 2003 that a quarter of all nurses working in the NHS (42,000) come from overseas.
- The fact that the declining UK population is a cause for concern.
- A UN report recommended 'replacement migration' as a solution.
- This recommendation was rejected by the European Commission on the grounds that the impact of immigration on population was insignificant.
- British arms trade to countries that top the asylum-seekers countries of origin: a coincidence?

- Conditions in countries of origin: poverty, human-rights abuses, global income disparity, conflict and torture.
- US and UK involvement in Iraq, Afghanistan, the Balkans and Somalia has led to increased violence and uncertainty for millions of the citizens of these nations who make up the largest percentage of the world's refugees.

The manner by which this and other issues are covered in the press illustrates our potential to be exposed to a very narrow selection of possible news, while inoculated to bias by the belief that our press has a liberal bias and covers a broad spectrum of political viewpoints. It has been argued that, as the media is market driven and conforms to the will of the political elites, a hidden agenda operates by which other stories are filtered out and papers with very different readerships and ideological biases in practice operate within a very narrow field tending to fall into line with dominant political agendas of the time.

This could be seen as a vindication of a central theme in Althusser's work, the manner in which human subjectivity is shaped by external forces. 'In fact subjectivity, or personhood, Althusser suggested, is itself formed in and through ideology' (Loomba 1998: 32). This formative impact of ideology is particularly noticeable in the colonial situation where ethnically distinct occupational boundaries, residential patterns and other social divisions were often encouraged and maintained by colonial administrators. This occurred either because of the pragmatic circumstances in which different groups were brought to the colony – for example, indentured labourers to replace slaves – or because of intentional planning to foster separate and easily manipulated enclaves.

In addition, Althusser attempted to explain the internal process by which the subject was influenced by ideological means. He describes *interpellation* (discussed in Chapter 1) as a process of identification, by which a subject (mis)recognises him or herself in an 'identity' or role which is offered them in society. The agent addressing me might be an authority figure but, equally, could be a representation in a cultural text. Althusser hopes to show how ideologies either 'recruit' people to particular, acceptable subject positions in society or else transform individuals into subjects who learn to identify with certain representations. Thus the agent addressing me might equally be a representation in a cultural text. Books, advertisements, TV programmes and films all contain representations of characters and situations with which we might identify. And bound up with such representations are certain societal norms, gender roles, attitudes towards certain groups, etc., which may be disseminated and normalised or satirised. Ethnic identification could at times be seen to be a process of interpellation.

These heterogeneous Marxist approaches indicate that racism and race identities are not merely determined by class but represent a social construction which is a complex interrelation of social, political, economic and cultural structures within capitalism. The cultural-studies approach, which recognises the material effects of the production and circulation of cultural meanings, has drawn on both Althusser and Gramsci. This allows subtle studies of the production and dissemination of ideas about race. Each context has a unique interplay of ideological forces which serve to form the identity of ethnic groups both in relation to one another as potential rivals and to the dominant group (which may not always be the majority culture, but which holds the position of dominant elite).

WEBERIAN/NEO-WEBERIAN THEORIES

Weber's work has been viewed as an extension and refinement of Marx's. Indeed, some feel that Weber 'spent his life having a posthumous dialogue with the ghost of Karl Marx' (Cuff et al. 1992: 97). This is a view which has some credibility, and differences between the two should not be overstated. However, for many Marxists, Weber's idealism and specificity of approach (methodological individualism) illustrates the tendency of sociological analysis to avoid the broad political question (the overt realpolitik of inequality and exploitation) and shows acquiescence to the power of the marketplace. Weber was passionate in defence not of the underprivileged and exploited but of the individual's right to self-determination and freedom from being pigeon-holed. His bleakest vision was the ascendancy of bureaucracy and rationalisation, either in the interests of global capitalism *or* of communism, whereby the individual is trapped in a dehumanising 'iron cage'. Perhaps in relation to ethnocentrism and racism the Nazi holocaust is the paradigm case of this process that Weber saw inexorably reducing individual integrity. Only a cold and calculating bureaucratic machine could manage the slaughter of millions of people in death camps and the efficiency with which this was achieved, by the use of numerical codes converting people into numbers. (A cataloguing system provided by IBM tabulating machines is alleged to have had a hand in expediting the final solution, see Black 2001.)

John Rex and David Mason (1986) brought a Weberian emphasis to their studies of ethnic relations, broadening the scope of sociological analysis of this neglected field to allow other factors of the individual psyche to be taken into account in the study of race, which traditional Marxism would see as a distraction. For Weber, who had given more thought to ethnic relations, the ethnic boundary making could be seen as a method of closing rank against outsiders, of creating monopolistic social closure. For traditional Marxists, social divisions other than those based on relations and forces of production are nothing other than false consciousness that allows the persistence of an elite that will encourage such divisions and profit from them (whether they are delusory or not). According to Weber:

An ethnic group is based, in this view, on the *belief* shared by its members that, however distantly, they are of common descent. [. . .] race creates a 'group' only when it is subjectively perceived as a common trait: this happens only when a neighbourhood or the mere proximity of racially different persons is the basis of joint (mostly political) action, or conversely, when some common experiences of members of the same race are linked to some antagonism against members of an *obviously* different group.

(Weber 1978: 35)

Further he suggests that: 'ethnic membership does not constitute a group; it only facilitates group formation of any kind, particularly in the political sphere. On the other hand, it is primarily the political community, no matter how artificially organized that inspires the belief in common ethnicity' (Weber 1978: 35).

Weber therefore considers that the belief in common ancestry is a consequence of collective political activity rather than its cause. So, far from some primordial view of ethnic roots, people begin to see themselves as belonging together as a consequence of this collective action. Therefore, the pursuit of collective interests can be seen to encourage ethnic identification.

John Rex's unique contribution has been to offer an analysis which takes account of the interwoven nature of class, race and ethnicity. Rex describes the dynamic relationship between ethnicity and class in terms of the structures of dominance operating in society and: 'Those structures are classes and groups in conflict, which define themselves and are defined in ethnic and racial terms, but which also engage in a kind of class struggle resulting from their immediate relation to the means of production and its supporting political apparatus' (Rex in Rex and Mason 1986: 77). Further, Rex sees different theoretical frameworks as useful contributions to the understanding of ethnic identities and relations. He argues that a more useful approach would be to look specifically 'at the point at which conflict most usually arises, namely in the business of employment relations and production' (Rex 1986: 70). This shows the important unifying significance of Rex's approach.

Guyana is a good example of the way in which employment relations and ethnicity have created a division which corresponds to class relations. The East Indians were brought in as indentured labourers and the African-Guyanese are the descendants of freed slaves. It can be argued that the two groups have, since their first encounters, been in a frequently antagonistic relationship due to the competition for labour and the resentment of one for the other, which was also exploited actively by colonists.

Rex (1980) suggests that in South Africa capitalism was installed through the enforced labour of the Bantu peoples. Thus race relations were crucial in making available a labour force. In *Capital*, Marx had suggested that capitalism depends upon 'the free laborer selling his labour power' to the owners of the means of production (1961: 170). But in South Africa, as in a variety of other colonial situations, the labour of colonised peoples was commissioned through a variety of coercive measures. It was not free labour at all. Rex quotes an East African settler to make his point: 'We have stolen his country now we must steal his limbs . . . Compulsory labour is the corollary of our occupation of the country' (1980: 129).

Rex refers to Weber's dual concept of capitalism which involves a form of capitalism peacefully oriented to market opportunity (free labour markets) and 'adventurer' or 'booty' capitalism which was characteristic of imperialism (for example, South Africa under Apartheid).

> I find these notions useful in that what seems to me to be involved in South Africa is not so much a society which articulates two modes of production as one in which a modern capitalist state is marked by strong elements of surviving booty capitalism. So far as the status of relatively unfree black labour is concerned I believe that it is best understood in terms of a typology of labour which can be derived from Weber's *General Economic History* (1961) and from his writings on agrarian institutions in the ancient world.
>
> (Rex 1986: 68)

This is at odds with classical Marxism which attributes capitalism's efficiency to having replaced the oppressive forms of coercion and slavery with the idea of the 'free' labour market. Capitalism then – contrary to traditional Marxism – does not always mark an end to coercive use of racial hierarchies, but uses them fully and intensifies them to produce the most efficient labour power to power its enterprises. Indeed, as Miles reports on Kenya and Rex comments about South Africa, the capitalist systems there have exploited the resources very much following the principles of rationalisation. 'The South African labour system is the most efficient system of labour exploitation yet devised, resting as it does on the three institutions of the rural reserve, the mining compound and the controlled urban "location"' (Rex 1980: 129).

Rex and others suggest that racism helps to structure capitalist expansion. It is especially important

> in maintaining certain hierarchies when the state and legal systems can no longer be blatantly partisan. [. . .] When the social order could no longer be buttressed by legal sanctions it had to depend upon the inculcation in the minds of both exploiters and exploited of a belief in the superiority of the exploiters and inferiority of the exploited. Thus it can be argued that the doctrine of equality of economic opportunity and that of racial superiority and inferiority are complements of one another. Racism serves to bridge the gap between theory and practice.
>
> (Rex 1980: 131)

Interpretative approaches to social phenomena place much more emphasis upon analyses of individual behaviours and the motives behind these in contrast to Marxian notions, which are structuralist approaches to society and seek underlying laws of mass social change. Belief systems underpin much of our behaviour and thus Rex makes the point that 'the sociology of race relations must take account of subjective definitions, stereotypes, typifications and belief systems in the business of defining its field. And we would emphasize that patterns of social relations may be considerably changed through the causal agency of such belief systems' (Rex 1970: 9). Belief systems are associated with a restricted range of structures; Rex therefore believes the task is to uncover these.

Some sociologists have tried to develop a more theoretical approach to explaining the position of ethnic minorities in the labour market and in society as a whole. From one point of view, ethnic minorities form an 'underclass'. The concept of an underclass is based upon a Weberian analysis of stratification. The concept of a racialised underclass has been put forward by several researchers. Rex and Tomlinson (1979) argue that the position of many black people in UK can be better understood in terms of a systematically disadvantaged underclass in stark contrast to the majority of the white working class. Recent (UK) figures suggest that ethnic minorities are consistently discriminated against in terms of job opportunities, and three or four times less likely to be employed regardless of the prevailing economic circumstances than the white community. So as a result it is hardly surprising that 'instead of associating with working-class culture, community and politics, they formed their own organisations and became in effect a separate underprivileged class. In short they formed an underclass which was perpetuated by the predominance of ethnic minorities in the secondary labour market' (Rex and Tomlinson 1979: 390).

Ethnic identity then is a construct which is at times negotiable and unfixed, but at other times, has relatively firm boundaries set (especially where political movements reflect ethnic identity).

It is unnecessary for class and ethnicity to be seen as discrete independent variables in a competition for primacy. Rather it may be possible for both to be viewed as interacting elements in a systematic theory of boundary formation in a society. As Rex has suggested, 'it is not necessary to exclude from consideration the possibility of a situation in which either ethnicity or class, or both together operate as the main means of boundary marking' (1986: 6).

It can be seen from this discussion that Weber's methodology and his emphases on meaning and verstehen have added depth and complexity to conceptions of race and ethnicity. Weber used the term *verstehen* in reference to the sociologist's attempt to understand both the motives and the context of human action. It becomes apparent that human cultures are complex structures that we simultaneously create and are created by or, as Clifford Geertz writes, 'Believing, with Max Weber, that man is an animal suspended in webs of significance he himself has spun, I take culture to be those webs, and the analysis of it to be therefore not an experimental science in search of law but an interpretive one in search of meaning' (1973: 5).

SYMBOLIC INTERACTIONISM

One such interpretative science in search of meaning is symbolic interactionism, stemming from American social psychology, the work of the Chicago School of Sociology and the philosophical thought of George Herbert Mead. The term, which was first used by Herbert Blumer in 1937, was founded on the basic tenet that human beings construct and transmit culture through complex symbols. The key concern is with the way in which meanings are expressed about the self, human relations, feelings and bodies. There is a clear affinity to the structuralist and semiotic project (explained in Chapter 1) whereby people encode and decode conventional codes by which they mediate their existence. In addition, the inter-actionist approach seems well suited to the study of dynamic situations such as ethnic relations where there are constant changes and negotiations of identity.

One advocate of this approach is Richard Jenkins (2003). Drawing on anthro-pological approaches to ethnicity by Barth (1969) and Geertz (1973), Jenkins highlights the key areas of a consensual anthropology of ethnicity: ethnicity is primarily 'about collective identification based in perceived cultural differentiation' (2003: 7) and shared cultural meanings, but ethnicity is produced by communi-cation and interaction across boundaries. Further, based on his work *Social Identity* (1996) and *Rethinking Ethnicity* (1997) Jenkins suggests that ethnicity is relatively flexible and that, although anthropologists have focused on boundary formation and maintenance, the content within the boundaries is equally important. The individual (and collective) sense of identity is constituted by a process of iden-tification through constant interaction between others and self. Jenkins has called this 'the internal-external dialectic of identification' (1996: 20).

For interactionists, social contexts are always encounters that have shifting and unstable outcomes, similar to Stuart Hall's description of ethnic identity as always incomplete, always in the process of becoming. This approach, which certainly appears theoretically strong in interpreting the local dynamics of ethnic identities, has been criticised for emphasising the agent 'at the expense of the social structure' (Malesevic 2004: 72–3). It is hence less likely to recognise the impact of macro-structural and material factors, as the focus is on the social actor's negotiated response to social contexts encountered.

Erving Goffman's dramaturgical theory of social relations has some useful features too (see Goffman 1984), such as the suggestion that ethnicity (like gender and sexuality) can be performative, obeying certain rituals and rules. The analogy to social interactions occurring in the public arena, like actors on a stage, is a useful one, allowing some recognition of how cross-cultural encounters may be rehearsed as people engage in 'impression management' and differentiate between 'backstage' and 'frontstage' zones. Examples of this abound in ethnically divided nations. In Malaysia, I witnessed an outbreak of conflict in the east coast Malaysian town of Mersing. A Chinese Malay entrepreneur entered a Chinese café where many western travellers typically assembled and was signing up tourists as passengers for a catamaran crossing to a nearby island. Conflict occurred when a Malay with an old fishing boat also tried to sign up passengers. Unable to compete with the faster, more luxurious catamaran, he suddenly exploded with rage, violently cursing and throwing chairs at the Chinese Malay. This certainly was not a context in which 'healthy competition' was acceptable. The Chinese Malay backed off quickly before the police (who are almost all Malay) had a chance to intervene. The apparent speedy acquiescence of Chinese Malays in this sort of confrontation is a reflection of the political and economic regulations within the country that are designed to benefit Malay Malays through affirmative action (reflecting the Malay dominance of the political system, army and police, and the Chinese power as business people in the country)[2] However, after this incident, when the Chinese café closed for the night, the Chinese owners of the café invited me in for a meal and, as the steel shutters were closed on the street, their previous silence and show of 'business as usual' fell away and gave way to angry invective that had obviously been bottled up most of the day.

In *Interaction Ritual*, Goffman gives the example of 'face work'. 'Face' for Goffman is used to mean 'the positive social value a person effectively claims for himself by the line others assume he has taken during a particular contact' (1972: 5). One basic type of face work is avoidance. In other words, the actor will avoid social contexts that present the possibility of 'losing face'. Goffman gives the example of the 'middle- and upper-class Negro who avoids certain face-to-face contacts with whites in order to protect the self-evaluation projected by his clothes and manner' (1972: 15).

Goffman's analysis adds another level of analysis to the internal landscape of racism, this constant negotiation of internalised self-identity, negotiated between one's own community and the negative public image generalised by the wider society. It may also be used to show the phenomenon of self-contempt where the stigmatised identity is internalised or projected onto others in whom the hated features are perceived. A consequence of structural injustice, it could be suggested, is a dehumanising self-contempt formed as the socially stigmatised identity is internalised. This self-contempt indicates the hegemonic power of racialised divisions.

---

2 See Chapter 7 for more illustrations of these divisions in Malaysia.

FOUCAULT AND DISCOURSE THEORY

Michel Foucault's major contribution to our thinking within the social sciences has been his analysis of a particular form of power that had been relatively over-looked in sociology, where there has been a tendency to talk about power being vested in the state, or to talk about the power of the bourgeoisie or the ruling class and to present a picture of society as being one in which there are good and bad, the power holders and those without power.

Foucault's analyses are quite effective in showing that if there are those centralised forms of power, that doesn't exhaust what we have to say about power. Power also has other qualities, and even if we take the formal position, we have to try and explain how it might come about that power can be centralised in the form of the state. The work of Poulantzas (1973) makes reference to the importance of force and coercion and ultimately insists that this force is vested in the state. While one would want to uphold the notion that most, if not all, centralised states do have at their disposal 'might', force and the power of coercion, that doesn't exhaust power and, more often than not, power is being exercised without any recourse to force – and that is the most effective type of power. Foucault's notion of **biopower** indicates how these discursive forms of power vested in scientific and medical practices can have material effects on certain populations. Foucault makes the point that a primordial discourse of blood could be invoked to validate ideas of race and sexuality. The supposed purity of a bloodline was the basis of a number of definitions of nationality, in Germany and Japan for example.

> Beginning in the second half of the nineteenth century, the thematics of blood was sometimes called upon to lend their entire historical weight towards revitalising the political power that was exercised through the devices of sexuality. Racism took shape at this point (racism in its modern, 'biologising' statist form). It was then that the whole politics of settlement (*peuplement*), family, marriage, education, social hierarchisation and property, accompanied by a long series of permanent interventions at the level of the body, conduct, health and everyday life, received their colour and their justification from the mythical concern with protecting the purity of the blood and ensuring the triumph of the race.
>
> (Foucault 1984: 149)

Foucault is indicating that we must not conflate power with a single source. Power flows have real impacts but may originate from diverse disciplinary areas, shaping and modulating societal action to identify certain groups as deviant and threatening by constituting individual subjectivity. The relationship between language, thought and social action has long been recognised. Foucault's study of discourse has had a marked impact on social sciences as it recognises that our social institutions, policies and structures are organised through 'regimes of truth', dominant disciplinary domains that focus and filter concerns about 'the Other'. Indeed discourse creates 'otherness'. Discourse, as defined by Foucault refers to:

> ways of constituting knowledge, together with the social practices, forms of subjectivity and power relations which inhere in such knowledges and relations between them. Discourses are more than ways of thinking and producing meaning. They constitute the 'nature' of the body, unconscious and conscious mind and emotional life of the subjects they seek to govern.
>
> (Weedon 1987: 108)

Discourse is the constituent of power, the conduit through which power flows. In Foucault's conception of power it is not possessed but rather it is created by inter-relations of knowledge that construct positions for those who are subject to certain practices. For example, the shifting discursive practices of law, psychiatry, anthropology and Social Darwinism 'produce' certain members of society as marginal, criminal, insane, immoral or racially inferior. The effect is never simply the elite imposing ideologically on the masses. In Chapters 2 and 3 we saw the gradual drift from universal ideas of united humanity through complex developments of views of 'the other' as inherently different, affirmed and challenged, never static, despite the attempts to impose laws that dictate new definitions of being (take the 1741 Carolina Laws for example). There is always resistance, never a unitary crushing power (although at times this is hard to accept as the consequences of discourses *can* be crushing and genocidal). 'Truth is not outside of power nor itself lacking in power [. . .] the truth [is] not those true things waiting to be discovered but rather the ensemble of rules according to which we distinguish the true from the false, and attach special effects of power to "the truth"' (Foucault 1980: 131).

Foucault's conception of power is a diffuse one, power is everywhere and it is exercised at innumerable points. One can never be outside of the operation of power. Foucault argues that all discourses produce a discourse of resistance; this omni-presence of power seems to make it hard to imagine resistance being practically or successfully utilised. Foucault did not focus on ethnicity, but it seems clear that this fluid movement of power and resistance could clearly be applied to regimes of colonialism and anti-colonial struggles. His work allows the local intellectual to rally support to various micro-causes. Much of Foucault's work is aimed at giving individuals trapped within a particular discourse a 'voice', universal ideas of human nature or humanity are meaningless. For him, the wider structures that control and create individuals are more important. Foucauldian genealogy has certainly been influential in providing theoretical tools to deconstruct regimes of power and disciplines or regimes of thought, although his denial of ideology has been criticised by Marxist thinkers and his approach has been criticised as lacking rigour.

However, Foucault's unique contribution is to ask how disciplines have imposed their own needs on how we look at the world (for example, the disciplines of sociology or psychology). Foucault deconstructs (takes apart and examines) systems of thought or institutions and their development historically, which has been formative in the way the individual makes sense of the world. He shows the complex institutional and historical relationships between knowledge and power, theorising that stable notions of identity are untenable as individual identity is never immanent but always contingent on social and political discourses which the person both consumes and contributes to.

Discourses that emanate from social, political, historical and cultural sources construct the social world and our identity in negotiation with this world. Discourse is much more than just language. It is also the institutional practices that follow from the partiality of naming and categorisation. For example, the dominant discourses of ethnicity, gender and sexuality entail political and legal definitions of the status of individual subjects. 'Discourses are the practices that systematically form the objects of which they speak' (Foucault 1972: 49).

'One of the slogans of discourse theory is that "discourses create their own object", language itself becomes the material knowledge, since "advances" in knowledge involve reshuffling the classifications made available in discourse' (Muecke 1982: 100).

One application of discourse theory is the way in which whole groups of the world's peoples are categorised and talked about through the discursive practices, for example, through the social sciences, medicine, literature and many others. Stephen Muecke points out the often narrowly ascribed ways of defining and speaking about the 'Other'. The construction of the discourse of race is relatively new and socially imagined – reflecting not essential differences but regimes of thought that are subject to periodic shifts and transformations. Table 1.1 (p. 12) illustrates the social and historical nature of these broad transformations in our recognition of the other. Muecke's seminal (1982) article 'Available Discourses on Aborigines' uses the post-structuralist linguistics of Michel Pecheux to show how Australians marginalise the Aboriginal peoples by a restrictive lexicon of otherness. The case of Aboriginal Australians is not unique: we all use language that embodies categories and cases that can exclude or include and carry a legacy of positive or negative connotations. Muecke suggests that a restricted number of discourses (romantic, anthropological, literary and racist) provide the only means open to white Australians to speak of or construct ideas of aboriginality.

Hall makes the point that while Marxist ideology, Althusserian interpellation and semi-autonomy and Foucauldian discourse have each developed our conception of the forces that operate in producing human subjectivity 'of how individuals are summoned into place in the discursive structures' (Hall and du Gay 1996: 13), they fall short in addressing how the subject is constituted (although Foucault marks the furthest stage in developing this by the description of 'historically specific discursive practices, normative self-regulation and technologies of the self' (Hall and du Gay 1996: 13).

BOURDIEU

Marx conceived of the relationship between human subjectivity and outside forces in the following way:

> Circumstances create people in the same degree as people create circumstances. Both social servitude and the movement towards its abolition have as their condition certain subjective factors. material subjugation; the ideas of the dominant class are dominant ideas; the class which commands material force also commands the means of intellectual coercion, as it produces and propagates the ideas the ideas that express its own supremacy.
>
> (Kolakowski 1985: 158)

This quote shows that Marxian thought is not crude reductionism. Statements like this suggest a more equivocal understanding of the social processes through which power relations operate not merely through structural means but also through internalised value systems. Later theorists, as we have seen, have begun the process of examining how the individual's internal value system is constructed. Pierre Bourdieu's contribution has been to offer a synthesis between the macro-structural processes of the materialist positions and the micro-interactionist and internalised processes of the interpretavists.

Bourdieu has presented a view of power relationships that is similar to Althusser yet maintains some of the original material force of traditional Marxism in his concept of 'habitus'. Habitus is a notion developed in his influential 'theory of practice' (1977) in which the concept as articulated may be useful as a guide to provide an active analytical approach that enables one to address the problem of ethnic identity without the attendant risk of being forced to opt for either instrumentalist or primordialist viewpoints that are seemingly irreconcilable (see Bourdieu 1977, 1990). The habitus is the generative principle that shapes the individual's subjectivity and constrains their behavioural repertoire.

In this view, rather than the pitfalls of Marxian and plural society theories that presuppose some inevitable cycle of ethnic conflict or class-struggle, ethnic relations may be viewed as social and historical codes that, while they shape individual identity and behaviour, are not immutable structures. Rather they are seen as part of a repertoire of strategies that an individual will use, depending on individual as well as communal codes of practice, to make sense of and to negotiate social situations with which they are confronted.

Brackette Williams applies Bourdieu's concept of habitus to the depiction of the struggle for 'symbolic dominance' in Guyana's ethnically polarised situation. In a study of Guyana it became apparent that the attempt to establish hegemony over the rival group was well marked, and everyday interaction in public life was often seen as a battleground for ethnic rivalry and a struggle for symbolic domination. As Bourdieu and Boltanski note, 'symbolic domination really begins when the misrecognition (meconnaissance), implied by recognition (reconnaissance), leads those who are dominated to apply the dominant criteria of evaluation to their own practices' (1976: 4). Bourdieu has explained the reflexive concept of habitus as follows:

> The habitus, a product of history, produces individual and collective practices – more history – in accordance with the themes generated by history. It ensures the active presence of past experiences, which, deposited in each organism in the form of schemes of perception, thought and action, tend to guarantee the 'correctness' of practices and their constancy over time more reliably than all formal rules and explicit norms.
>
> (Bourdieu 1990: 54)

Bourdieu is suggesting that the objective conditions of existence – material events in social history – generate the habitus which, like a grammar of behaviours, in turn generates certain dispositions, attitudes and behaviours; a lexicon from which each individual may choose. This might allow a view of ethnic identity and boundaries that does not treat focus on social class or socio-cultural aspects as either or. All such influences are part of the habitus and have been ultimately derived from the history of an individual, a group, or indeed a population. The habitus is most definitely not an idealist or abstract concept: 'the habitus only exists in, and through and because of the practices of actors and their interaction with each other and with their environment: ways of talking, ways of moving, ways of making things, or whatever' (Jenkins 1992: 27).

The habitus clearly has features in common with a Marxist notion that the material conditions giving rise to a social class will be reproduced in the material practices of those experiencing such conditions. Bourdieu's concept of habitus appears to be a valuable theoretical tool. The following points summarise the advantages as well as possible shortcomings of using Bourdieu's concepts in the study of ethnic identity and relations.

The habitus enables a view of ethnic identity and boundaries that does allow focus on social class and socio-cultural interactions rather than appraising these sets of factors as competing explanatory variables or assigning primacy to one or the other. All acts of ethnic expression can be explained in terms of lived experiences, habitual practices that produce the codes and inscribe meanings onto the body and psyche of the individual. A corollary of this is that the theory of practice allows for analysis of both individual and group. There are differences in each individual's habitus – unique individuals construct their own. However, the individual has also been steeped in the specific traditions of a group, embodying all its social codes. Therefore, while the habitus has a potentially infinite capacity to produce practices, the actual behaviours brought into active practice are 'constrained without violence, art or argument'. The group habitus tends to exclude all 'extravagances' ('not for the likes of us'), that is, all the behaviours that would be negatively sanctioned because they are incompatible with the objective conditions (Bourdieu 1990: 56).

Bourdieu's 'theory of practice' can readily be used to look at cases of inter-ethnic differences, alienation and conflict. The two major groups in Guyana, in many cases, can be seen to share the same language, speak with enthusiasm about the same aspirations, wear similar clothes and display many other similarities. Yet although these superficial similarities are often mentioned, they may be rooted in very different generative structures (see Bentley 1987: 37).

Overlaps in the behavioural repertoire of peoples having characteristically different experiences (and habitus) are likely to give rise to invalid assumptions of mutual understanding, what Jürgen Habermas (1970) calls 'systematically distorted communication' (Bentley 1987: 37).

Furthermore, while it must be recognised that some surface structures appear similar (although derived from different habitus), such congruency of codes may be reserved for those public contexts in which collaboration is a functional necessity. Quite different codes will be exhibited in a more private domain. For example, in Guyana many street traders will take on a friendly attitude and communicate freely with members of the different ethnic groups, playing down any differences; yet with cohorts of their own ethnic group they may actively deride their erstwhile associates, borrowing freely from the available lexicon of stereotypes to describe their encounters. In this way Bourdieu's theory of practice helps us to avoid misreadings of ethnic relations in Guyana.

If differences in habitus can lead to conflict and misunderstanding or selective perception of the 'Other', such differences may occur within a specific group. That is, if members of the same ethnic community are exposed to different objective conditions to those of their fellow members, their habitus will be shaped by the new experiences and thus their ability to relate wholeheartedly to the values of their fellows will be affected. The differences may be connected to age-group differences, which are commonly noted. For example, if an Indian child attends a local school in which the majority of class-mates are African, then their relation to more traditional values will be affected.

In a similar way, new popular idioms gain acceptance in the language, and the gradual accretion of new elements in the lexicon makes possible the discussion of new areas of discourse (the word 'sexist', for example, allowed the opening up of a critical discussion of the treatment of women, which before had little credence).

So within a group, habitus may be developed differently, dependent on such factors as education, occupation, regional differences, exposure to different groups and differences in age group. Bourdieu makes the point however, that the agency of change is the habitus itself rather than the category of experience:

> generation conflicts oppose not age-classes separated by natural properties, but habitus which have been produced by different modes of generation, that is, by conditions of existence which, in imposing different definitions of the impossible, the possible, and the probable, cause one group to experience as natural or reasonable practices or aspirations which another group finds unthinkable or scandalous or vice versa.
>
> (Bourdieu 1977: 78)

Here we see the potential of theory of practice analysis to alert us to processes of change in ethnic relations despite the synchronic appearance of ineluctable polarisation of the ethnic groups.

Another compelling reason for pursuing theory of practice is that the approach allows analysis of the dynamics of the ideological field. In nations such as Guyana and Trinidad, ethnic relations may be usefully seen as a struggle for symbolic dominance, the need for a group to establish hegemony through the dissemination and acceptance of the dominant values. In Guyana, the series of rapid and disruptive changes in socio-political and economic spheres has contributed to 'the loss of coherence between experience and the symbols through which people understand it'. This in turn, 'causes feelings of discomfort and alienation, of rootlessness and anomie. Both powerful goads to action, hence motives for political mobilisation' (Bentley 1987: 44).

However, as Jenkins states in his 1992 critique of Bourdieu, his concept of 'habitus' is uncertain and vacillates between material existence (it purports to embody experiences) and 'as an explanation of practice, something which exists beyond the realms of appearances' (Jenkins 1992: 94). Other problems with methods that attempt a synthesis of theories are highlighted by Malesevic (2004), suggesting that certain synthetic combinations of theory cannot be utilised just to cover possible aspects of a phenomenon, as this would finally by nothing more than 'a mere registrar of events, actions, behaviours and beliefs' (Malesevich 2004: 168). However, on the face of it, Bourdieu, Foucault and other post-structuralist thinkers do seem to have started the groundwork that allows consideration of how both agency and structure can be included in our understanding of how ethnicity is constituted subjectively as well as revealing the manner in which individuals are positioned discursively.

GENDER, SEXUALITY, RACE AND ETHNICITY

Social divisions are emphasised and represented differently in different times and places, whether along the lines of caste, class, status, gender or sexuality, these are the means by which power is articulated and channelled in societies. Furthermore, the means by which a society constructs difference is liable to periodic shifts, as illustrated in Chapter 2. Social divisions are often intrinsically linked, forming a shifting lantern show of oppressions triggered by social economic and political realities of the time. Racist beliefs have always been interwoven with ideas of gender and sexuality. Stereotypes, as we have seen, are an example of this: African-Caribbean men for example were portrayed as possessing 'uncontrolled sexual potency' and a 'potential for violence and criminality', whereas Asian women were 'sexually exotic, passive and unambitious – the docile victims of a traditional culture' (Bilton 1987: 264).

It could be argued that the black body and the female body are at some level connected as prone to objectification by the 'male gaze' – a characteristic of both patriarchy and colonialist values. Popular culture is permeated with ready-made stereotypes and also with the fascination and fear that black sexualities exert in western societies. Paul Gilroy (1993) and Kobena Mercer (1994) make reference to the immense popularity of black musical genres amongst white people. Mercer suggests this is one example of the ways in which 'black men and women have articulated sexual politics' (Mercer 1994: 140) through the candid expression of sexuality and the long tradition of open emotion, sexual politics, loss and longing expressed in the blues and jazz (see also Waddington 2004).

This ambivalence about the sexuality of the other is deep seated and began during early periods of colonisation of the globe. Historically, ethnic divisions and the conception of the racialised Other were frequently presented in gendered terms. The continents were typically portrayed as women, untamed and bared, virgin territory to be colonised.

Profound links exist between the construction of race, ethnicity, gender and sexuality. Slavery and the colonial regime undoubtedly developed an eroticised power relationship between colonial master and subject. This is attested by the legacy of mixed race in the Caribbean and in India. Concubinage and rape were certainly commonplace amongst planters and slave-owners, although the fascination and desire for the Other was always treated with marked ambivalence. The colonial adventure, with its metaphoric and actual rape and plunder, opened up fantasies of sexual domination and the exotic Other, which pervade accounts of colonial life in Africa, Asia and the Caribbean. The racism that combines with this colonial obsession leads to what Young describes as 'the familiar structure of sexual attraction and repulsion' (1995: 150). The fascination with exotic differences is attested in the inordinate interest in anatomical features of African women who were studied, displayed and discoursed upon in inordinate detail. A case in point was the so-called 'Hottentot Venus', a twenty-year-old Quena woman named Sara Baartman who was taken from Cape Town to London in 1810. She was put on public display around Britain and France.

> Contemporary descriptions of her shows at 225 Piccadilly, Bartholomew Fair and Haymarket in London say Baartman was made to parade naked along a 'stage two feet high', along which she was led by her keeper and exhibited like a wild beast, being obliged to walk, stand or sit as he ordered.
>
> (History of Race in Science 1995)

She died in France in 1815. Even after her death she remained the object of imperialist fascination. Baron Cuvier, the eminent social anthropologist and surgeon general to Napoleon had her sexual organs and brain removed and pickled. They were displayed in the Musée de l'Homme until the mid 1980s. This extraordinary interest in her anatomy indicates the function of such displays to European ideas about black female sexuality and European racial superiority.

The same biological reasoning that legitimated slavery and exploitation on the basis of race was also responsible for male tyranny over women. Certainly from the early 1800s to pre- Second World War, a eugenics discourse that borrowed legitimacy from Social Darwinism emphasised a concern with race purity and 'hygiene' and the dangers of descent into moral and genetic decline. Pseudo-scientific ideas were generated by this confluence of racism and sexism. Correlating brain size to race and gender yielded the apparent (although largely spurious) discovery that black people's brains were smaller than white people's, and women's brains smaller than men's. This led to the view that the 'inferior' races were more feminine and that racial mixing would produce children exhibiting increasingly feminine traits. Young articulates this fundamental connection between gender divisions and the development of a racialised discourse as deeply embedded in commonsense views of culture and pre-scientific hierarchical structures:

> Race was defined through the criterion of civilization, with the cultivated white, western European male at the top, and everyone else on a hierarchical scale either in a chain of being, from mollusc to God, or, in the later model, on an evolutionary scale of development from a feminized state of childhood (savagery) up to full (European) manly adulthood. In other words, race was defined in terms cultural, particularly gender difference – carefully gradated and ranked.
>
> (Young 1995: 94)

Tobach and Rosoff cite Pruner's 1866 comment that 'The Negro resembles the female in his love for children and his cabin [. . .] The black man is to the white man what woman is to man in general, a loving being and a being of pleasure' (Tobach and Rosoff 1994: 70).

Popular discourse about the supposed childlike, undisciplined and indolent state of natives abounded and was published in books like Moore's *Savage Survivals*, a text that purported to be a serious scientific treatise whilst making sexist and ethnocentric statements based on crude Darwinist conjectures about indigenous peoples being at an immature stage of development and ruled by capricious id-like tendencies, while clearly suggesting that women share these traits:

> The savage is in many ways a child. He has the same untrained will as the child, the same unsteadiness, the same tendency to be ruled by the impulses that rise within him from moment to moment [. . .] Women are much more inclined to imitate each other than men are, because they have, on the whole, more of the characteristics of the child psychology.
>
> (Moore 1933: 116)

It seems clear that racialisation of social relations, despite the flimsiest of evidence and, under the cloak of social Darwinism, has also had a marked impact on the representation of gender and sexuality.

BLACK FEMINISM

Black feminism developed from traditions of courage, independence and resistance by black women to the brutal conditions of slavery and institutionalised racism. The challenge of black feminist approaches in Britain, America and elsewhere is their focus upon the simultaneity of oppressions that affect women of non-western origins, especially racism, sexism, class oppression and homophobia. The term 'black feminism' has been criticised for generating essentialist readings of blackness (just as arguably second-wave feminisms have tended to universalise concepts of woman and 'sisterhood'). There have been strands of feminism that specifically focus upon female biological differences. Patricia Hill Collins comments that the

> term *black* and the accompanying assumptions that being of African descent somehow produces a certain consciousness or perspective are inherent in these definitions. By presenting race as fixed and immutable – something rooted in nature – these approaches mask the historical construction of racial categories. The shifting meaning of race and the crucial role of politics and ideology in shaping conceptions of race.
>
> (Hill Collins 1990)

Early feminist Sojourner Truth is a cornerstone of black feminist thought. Her vivid evocation of the 'double burden': sexism and racism (not to mention class oppression) has become well known through her famous 'ain't I a woman?' speech that so directly addresses the fact that she is not treated as a white woman, as a fragile and delicate woman in need of protection. Her speech still rings out with undiminished power because it underlines the distinction made about women on the basis of their race, class and gender. Yet, as Aziz comments, it is also a 'powerful admonishment to her audience (a white Ohio congregation) defying them to see her as nothing more than 'a product of racism-sexism-slavery' (Aziz 1992: 2).

The contribution made by black feminists has been to question feminism and draw attention to the divisions between women that make the essentialist viewpoint of a united 'sisterhood' difficult to maintain. Black women faced multiple oppressions and their identity as an oppressed racial group meant that unity with black men was often more important to them as a bulwark against racism than separation from them as a stand against patriarchy. Black women in the USA were concerned that 'feminism' did not concern itself with their struggle and was a vehicle for white and often middle-class women. Alice Walker proposed the term 'womanist' as one that embodied black women's more serious and mature identity in the face of oppression. Walker's much cited phrase, 'womanist is to feminist as purple to lavender' (1983: xii) clearly seems designed to set up this type of comparison – black women are 'womanist' while white women remain merely 'feminist.'

Concerns that afflicted black women in the 1960s and 1970s were of a different order to those that characterised white feminist struggles. White women were traditionally portrayed as delicate, in need of protection and unsuited for hard labour, whereas black women were presented as quite different beings. At the time that white women were making a strong stand about reproductive rights, the pill and limited access to abortion, black women were facing a willingness to prescribe DepoProvera, a contraceptive drug that was known to cause a high incidence of sterility, in addition to more overt eugenic-inspired programmes (as discussed earlier), as well as different treatment from policy-makers who either saw their families as dysfunctional, culturally deprived and in need of state management or were, at least, critical of black women's abilities as mothers (see Knowles and Mercer 1992: 107).

In effect, black feminism must come to terms with a white feminist agenda blind to racism as well as black or ethnic nationalist movements that fail to confront their own sexism. In each case the tendency towards a form of 'strategic essentialism' is a distorting effect of striving for political recognition, yet clearly the most damaging oppression at one time can shift and expose others who are equally central to the culture and the combination of class, race and gender can be arranged differently depending on the context. There has often been a danger of equating black identity as class identity (typically assuming working-class identity). These and many other internal divisions that require identification have rendered older, more universalist politics unconvincing to many.

There is a clear parallel here to the fragmentation of left-wing politics generally. Although inequalities have actually widened, there seems to be a tendency to disidentify with class (see Bufton 2004), giving way to more subjective notions of *identity*, cutting across class boundaries and involving other divisions that may be seen as more significant. A similar fragmentation is observable within feminism.

However, whether or not some see these disputes as undermining a traditional socialist or feminist agenda, they mark an important critique that recognises the problems of ignoring local differences in the interest of political strength. Black feminists have raised important issues about power relations and inequality. Can women be genuinely said to share a common experience of oppression? What is the relative importance of racism and sexism? Have 'feminists over-concentrated on patriarchy and neglected race and ethnicity as sources of women's oppression?' (Solomos 1996: 13). Do black men share the same positions of patriarchal power as white men?

These questions were posed by black feminists in Europe and America as major challenges to the women's movement.

Just as gender politics can deny ethnic differences, there is a danger that politically a type of 'ethnic absolutism', a conceptual and political view of ethnic groups that sees them as possessing distinct and separate traditions, fixed and absolute, is supported in a struggle for ascendancy and resistance. Black feminism highlights the complex construction of the subject and serves as a reality check to those who eschew difference for the sake of political strength.

The interview in the box below, conducted by Mark Quah (a British-Born Chinese research student), examines one site of the intersection of these discourses in the identity of British-Born Chinese. It becomes clear that personal identity develops at the conjunction of several divisive discourses: ethnicity, gender and class, as well as occupational status and generational differences. The negotiated space that Eve and her mother have carved out is cited between traditional patriarchal Chinese views and the incipient xenophobia and racist stereotypes prevalent in Britain.

BRITISH-BORN CHINESE

EVE: That's the thing you also feel like you don't properly belong[,] like you belong to either set British or Chinese but they don't see you as part of them so [. . .] Being Female[,] well the thing is I don't know if it's just the people in my community back in Wales but they tend to be fairly traditional and quite sexist[,] I don't know possibly more so than your average English family[.] I don't know 'cos being an eldest son is more important than being the eldest daughter and the thing is [. . .] in terms of my education my results have always have been better than my younger brothers so my dad was 'why can't you be a son I wish you were a boy' and [. . .] my dad actually has a nickname for me which is a boy's name but he only calls me that when I've been doing really well and he pats me on the head and says 'my boy!' It's quite weird but I know that's only my dad [. . .] my mum does work with my dad as well but it's just that he expects her to be the little housewife for him but my mum's been trying to break free from that [. . .] I mean she goes to college and she does loads of study [. . .] she's quite an inspiration[.] I'm very proud of her[,] she's doing all of this and she's doing chairperson of the Chinese society and so she is helping a lot of other Chinese women sort of like[,] could say empower themselves to be able to make them feel like they can actually not so much break free but feel like they can be more than just the wife[.]

MARK: Do you think it's a bit confined the roles that they can play?

EVE: The thing is[,] because of my mum's involvement in this Chinese women's society my dad got very very angry and all of the men in the area got very angry with my mum[dot] And it was like [. . .] she's spending far too much of her time away from the family and she's neglecting us[.] The thing is we're all grown up[,] my brother's at university[,] my younger brother is at secondary school and we're all fairly [–] well the eldest two [–] we're fairly independent and the youngest can look after himself and we don't have to have my mum there all the time to look after us and my dad's just [. . .] thing is we're all very supportive of my mum and she's doing her best[.] The thing is she's got accountancy thing something or other[,] she's an accountant anyway and she wants to get a job but my dad won't let her and that was fairly disappointing even though she was feeling like she's doing all of this by herself but she's still listening to my father and kind of like doing what she can to please him [.] It's understandable but yeah 'cos she loves him or whatever (lots of different pressures on) and I don't know [–] there is a fair amount of pressure on her. And my dad I wouldn't say he was a tyrant but I don't know [. . .] oh what has she done[,] she's also be arranging English lessons for the other Chinese women because that's the thing[,] the fact that they don't know any English 'cos a lot of them first generation don't know a lot and they're just trapped in the home working looking after the children [.] A lot of the time it's because they don't know any English and they don't have the confidence to go out[,] because they may know a little bit or whatever but they don't have the [. . .] and they can't read[,] they don't have the confidence to kind of go out.

MARK: Seems pretty essential then that they get these other services[.]

EVE: Mm that's the thing [–] and my mum has been helping, teaching them English I mean she's been teaching them very basic English but also mm helping the women enrol on courses in the local college[.] I'm very proud of her [. . .]

MARK: Maybe they should do something with the Sunday schools[,] teach English as well as Cantonese?

EVE: Yeah well that's what I think[,] a lot of what she also does is you know the Chinese women's society[.] They meet every once a week in the daytime when the men are asleep so you know they don't know the women have gone you know snuck out (that's really good I like that but maybe it shouldn't be like that)[.] That's the thing it's like you know the women have to wake up early in the morning to take the kids to school anyway and they [. . .] I don't know about other women I know my mum does a lot with her day[,] she zooms around doing stuff you know going to college and I know she's done psychology and biology and accountancy and that's the thing[,] that's also why I feel like I should excel 'cos my mum's such a good example can't let her down[.]

MARK: That's really great[.]

EVE: Also gives them a chance to [. . .] as well as learn things [. . .] but to actually congregate and just talk and relax and have someone to talk to as well as umm just as being cooped up at home working their fingers to the bone and whatever[,] I think it's just as important to have friends and have people to talk to[.] I think that was the main point of her society just to have somewhere for the women to go just once a week[.] To relax and not have to be a mother and a wife[,] to kind of be themselves and also teach them various skills[.] I mean I went home the other day and my mum was doing all this stuff on the computer and I was like 'mum how do you know all this' I was so shocked but my mum[,] I can't pull the wool over my mum's eyes over anything[.]

EVE: I just said yeah my parents are but I'm trying to work my way up[dot]

[This point brings up issues of how far to respond to these attempts at being marginalised and how far this marginalisation is itself internalised. The latter point refers to the apologetic nature of the comment by Eve, her reply speaks volumes in terms of the ability of those at the centre to influence the shape of the internal worlds of those at the margins.]

EVE: Actually I remember [. . .] when you're at school and you do work experience I really wanted to be a doctor! That's another thing Chinese parents[.] They want you to be a doctor or a lawyer [*haha*] and I told them I want to be an engineer and they were horribly disappointed and I said I want to be a psychologist and they said no! you'll be surrounded by mad people and then you'll turn mad yourself [*hahaha*] And they wanted me to be a doctor and I quite liked the idea as well and I went and did some work experience at the hospital and I did the rounds with the doctor and I had my white lab coat and everything[,] and then we came round to the bed of this really old woman and she said[,] she sounded very surprised and she said 'I expected you lot to be working in takeaways. And at that minute I thought yeah[.] I can't remember[,] this was so long ago and it wasn't the most offensive thing anyone's said to me but it was like 'cos I'm Chinese you actually just expect me to work in a takeaway[.]

MARK: Did you say anything back?

EVE: I don't remember what I said back I'm pretty sure I said something back but erm [. . .] no I can't remember[,] it was so long ago[,] I [*softly*] just said yeah my parents are but I'm trying to work my way up[.] And I guess part of the problem a lot of Chinese people do kind of [. . .]

MARK: [. . .] mix in[,] keep themselves to themselves?

EVE: Yeah they do keep themselves to themselves and I mean I heard someone say the Chinese people[,] the Chinese community[,] are pretty much the invisible people of the UK – 'cos the thing is we have this huge community of Chinese but you never hear anything about them about what they do and [. . .]

MARK: You hear stuff like oh Chinese food they cook dogs and stuff like that [. . .]

EVE: Yeah yeah, that's the thing[,] we do have a huge Chinese community and there are loads of people that don't work in the Chinese takeaways and restaurants or whatever but the few that are out there and doing their jobs they don't speak up for themselves[.] That's the thing[,] Chinese people don't speak up for themselves and I guess that's why we're the invisible race.

MARK: You're in our country but we don't want you in the mainstream[.]

EVE: Yes I'm sorry about that but I am working very hard[.]

This interview highlights the struggle of British-Born Chinese women. Eve, the young person being interviewed, negotiates the different interpellations of traditional Chinese discourses of femininity and masculinity, stereotypes and expectations about work and cultural dimensions to identity in twenty-first-century Wales. The area is notably monocultural and Eve's mother is a leading light of the Chinese women's association helping Chinese women to adapt to their surroundings and break away from the traditional housewifely roles. Gender relations then are another modality in which ethnicity and class are articulated. Individuals need to negotiate between traditional cultural expectations of gender roles and performances and those that make up the majority culture.

CHAPTER SUMMARY

This chapter has attempted to give an overview of some influential theoretical approaches that have been applied to an understanding of ethnicity. In the main there have been attempts to explain ethnic mobilisation in terms of biological imperatives, class, honour, status, functionality, rational action, pursuit of political or financial power, primordial symbols and concepts of self developed through interaction and the intersection of gender and ethnicity. With reservations about the socio-biologist stance on ethnicity (as by its nature hard to either prove or disprove), ethnicity it seems can illustrate aspects of each of these attributes but seems to be too complex a concept to be reduced to any one theory. Further, the idea of accepting some synthetic form of combinations of each is ultimately untenable as this is at best a mere mosaic of quite contradictory approaches. However, the insights developed by post-structuralists and feminists seem to offer some ways forward by recognising the dimensions of societal structures and their shaping influence on individual subjectivity.

EXERCISE 4.1

1   Consider the phenomenon of racist attacks that are constantly in the media. What is the most convincing cause of such apparent hatred in our multicultural society? Which of the above theories offers the most useful perspectives?
2   John Rex argues "'liberal ideologies" in western metropolitan contexts disallow mention of colour as means of discrimination *yet this is the real criterion'*. Discuss this claim.
3   How adequate is the traditional Marxist model of base/superstructure when explaining racism?
4   Consider a specific act of racism and analyse its causes and consequences and meanings using the following theories: Marxism, Weberian, symbolic inter-actionism, black feminism, Bourdieu, Foucauldian, neo-Marxism. Which of the theories is most relevant in the case you chose and why?
5   After considering the case of Sara Baartman, discuss the function of ethno-graphic displays in museums. Are they a means of educating about other nations and their people or a reaffirmation of European imperialism?
6   Are there other examples of 'human exhibition' that you know of? What function do such displays appear to fulfil? (You might begin to research this

issue by reading a short article available on <http://www.english.emory.edu/Bahri/Exhibition,html>.)

7   Read the interview with the British-Born Chinese woman Eve in Box 4.1. What aspects of identity does Eve discuss? How does Chinese identity appear to be a source of both strength and resistance, while at the same time imposing certain constraints on Chinese women?

CHAPTER 5

Identity

Marginal Voices and the Politics of Difference

In Chapter 4 some of the theoretical landscape was charted, and it becomes apparent that there is more going on within race and ethnicity than can be adequately accounted for by materialist and economic explanations. The movement towards more individualistic and fragmentary views of identity has emerged with increasing emphasis on difference. There has been a 'cultural turn' in theoretical formations of race and ethnicity, and notions of identity take centre ground. This more individualistic and context-specific approach is clearly already visible in the work of Rex and others and affirmed and developed by culturalists like Hall and Gilroy who have selectively applied ideas from postmodern and post-colonial theorising, producing finely tuned studies of the cultural terrain in which ethnic identity and unique forms of sexism and racism are generated and circulate as cultural signs to be consumed. Certainly there is a fragmentation and atomism of left politics. Resistance needs to be re-tooled to account for the hybrid and local voices that had remained marginal for so long. With this variously called 'postmodern frame' (Donald and Rattansi 1992), 'differentialist' approach (Mac an Ghaill 1999) and 'contradictory plurality' of the subject (Laclau and Mouffe 1985), the increasing privilege of identity politics as a unified centre for resistance becomes impossible.

POSTMODERNITY: MAPS AND TERRAIN

It is argued that the conventional theoretical frameworks that informed much of the academic study of race and racism in the course of the 1970s and 1980s are now outdated and inadequate to the task of providing an analysis of the complex nature of the operation of racialised discourse in contemporary society: 'postmodernity means coming to terms with ambivalence, with the ambiguity of meanings, and with indeterminacy of the future; yet acceptance of ambivalence can be life-enhancing, especially when contrasted to the driven world of certitudes that modernity used to foster' (Giddens 1994: 349). Postmodern, post-structural, post-Marxist, the notion that at some juncture in the twentieth century (although the timing is widely contested) the driving force of modernity – the positivist and rationalist project kick-started in the Enlightenment – has collapsed, folding in upon itself. The map has become the terrain (an image popularised by a Borges story (1975) in which map-makers strive for such accuracy, such verisimilitude to the land they are charting that they make a map that exactly covers the country's every contour and feature). The representational has become the real and behind the sign there is nothing (see Baudrillard 1983). In marketing terms, the brand identity has taken over from the utility value of the product and indeed we can see today that products are often bought because they are a specific 'aspirational' brand rather than merely because they are useful. The signifier dominates and the practice of relating to deeper meanings, connotations is passé. The world of images that flow over us in endless pastiche, superficial and meaningless, corporatised and global, the Gulf Wars as video games or Hollywood epics (see Baudrillard 1991), tens of thousands of lives lost are 'collateral damage'. Media imagery has an immediacy and omnipresence today that, like the fable of the map, appears to cover every inch of the world. Similarly, this view of global coverage is an illusion, the media is very narrowly cast to fulfil the needs of its marketplace – the ownership structure and advertising.

HOLOCAUST AND RELATIVITY

Another feature of the 'postmodern condition' is loss of faith in the validity of science and rationalism. Zygmunt Bauman (2002) among others has envisioned the Holocaust, the systematic annihilation of 6 million Jews and other marginalised groups as the epitome of the use of rational positivism. The argument is that the cold calculation needed to effect murder on such a vast scale is something quite different from the barbarism and brutality of the 'wild justice' (see Gilroy 2004) of colonialism (although the same infrahuman vision of beings as human waste surely underlies these atrocities). Instead, the obsession with order and the use of the most rational systems (IBM punch cards in the case of Auschwitz enabled the allocation of the infamous five-figure number tattoos) was necessary to effect this destruction. As Malesevic (2004: 147) notes: 'It was the product of modern "dull bureaucratic routine" governed by the principle of instrumental rationality and a hierarchical delegation of tasks.' Like the infernal punishment machine in Kafka's 'In the Penal Colony' (2000), the state inscribes its will onto the prone bodies of its victims; violence is merely a technical example of the State's omnipotence.

If certainty and monocultural dominance can produce such terminally bleak results then the Nietzchean view of humanity as fatally flawed (as 'all too human') begins to look more plausible. The impact of all this on social theory along with the parallel collapse of theories of representation and the successive fragmentation of social movements through the process of **identity politics** has led to a tendency towards relativism in the face of what appears to be modernity's attempts 'to transgress hybridity and the fragmented nature of ethno-national narratives' (ibid).

Kenan Malik has produced a reasoned scholarly argument against what he sees as a misguided dismissal of the most progressive features of Enlightenment thought: the striving for universal human rights. Rather than pursuing the argument that universalising rationality leads to the death camps, Malik sees the critical juncture in the Enlightenment to be the movement towards making distinctions between human beings rather than recognising their essential humanity. These are differences that are not based on science or rationality but on ethnocentric and romantic notions of the other. Race science which is (as we have seen) unsupported by genuine empirical evidence, provided the spurious rational for racial superiority and the fiction of primordial destiny of the Aryan races.

Malik (1996) has highlighted the manner in which universalist viewpoints have been condemned as implicitly fascistic and ethnocentric. Postmodernists, cynical about the Enlightenment ideals of reason and universal conception of humanity, have favoured a supposedly more open and tolerant approach that promotes diversity. Malik suggests, to the contrary, that an over-emphasis on cultural difference has the possible effect of encouraging conflict and separation and denying the most important realisation of the Enlightenment, which was an affirmation of the equality of mankind. This obsession with difference evolved later with pseudo-scientific topologies used to legitimatise colonialist exploitation abroad and class exploitation at home. The achievements of scientific reasoning that came about in the Renaissance and the Enlightenment have lead to genuinely superior and innovative technologies and political forms and should not be conflated with notions of monocultural dominance, European superiority and racism. Malik shows that the very opponents of western colonialism did not make the same mistake as western liberals. This is remarkable given the fact that colonialists treated the colonised with such disdain and arrogance.

Frantz Fanon, one of the great voices of postwar third world nationalism, similarly argued that the problem was not Enlightenment philosophy but the failure of Europeans to follow through its emancipatory logic. 'All the elements of a solution to the great problems of humanity have, at different times, existed in European thought,' he argued. 'But Europeans have not carried out in practice the mission that fell to them.'

(Malik 2002: 4)

It is difficult not to see the parallels between colonial oppressions and extermination of a whole generation of European Jews. In the 1970s BBC programme *The Ascent of Man*, Jacob Bronowski squatted in the pond at Auschwitz and, taking a handful of mud, he made a powerful gesture in which he said:

It is said that science will dehumanise people and turn them into numbers. That is false – tragically false. Look for yourself. This is the concentration camp and crematorium at Auschwitz. This is where people were turned into numbers. Into this pond were flushed the ashes of four million people. And that was not done by gas. It was done by arrogance. It was done by dogma. It was done by ignorance. When people believe that they have absolute knowledge, with no test in reality – this is how they behave. This is what men do when they aspire to the knowledge of gods [. . .] We have to cure ourselves of the itch for absolute knowledge and power. We have to close the distance between the push-button order and the human act. We have to touch people.

(1976: 186)

Bronowski's is a heartfelt and strikingly potent defence of science – a plea not to abandon rationality but to embrace it and recognise that true adherence to science would never allow callous certainty to triumph but would lead to a more open society. Echoing the words of Oliver Cromwell, Bronowski pleads, 'I beseech you in the bowels of Christ, think it possible you may be mistaken'.

However, it is dangerous to locate the fatal flaw of narcissism and arrogance, of which the Holocaust is an example, as solely a consequence of European modernity. Recent and ongoing blood-soaked rationalisations have taken place in many other parts of the world. Gilroy (2000: 237) conjectures that: 'Though it's neither the flipside of a Europe-centred modernity nor something eternal and evil, outside of history and secular morality altogether, it does have something to do with the pathologies of modern development that Rousseau called "the fatal ingenuities of civilized man".'

While, as Bronowski and others protest that science should not be pilloried for the dehumanisation of which Auschwitz is an especially bleak example, 'scientism', which came to dominate the early twentieth century changed forever the scale and tone of human potential for persecution. 'We have to deal, not only with the old dangers of occultism and irrationality, but with the new evils represented by the rational application of irrationality' (1974: 186).

IDENTITY POLITICS AND TRADITIONAL
LEFT THOUGHT

Postmodernism is a loose amalgamation of theories that attempt to explain the apparent tendency towards fragmentation. While globalisation may increase cultural homogeneity, this may occurr at a fairly superficial level, and beneath this veneer of global brand names, other contradictory forces are arguably eroding ethnic solidarity and monolithic national identity. The traditional Left notion of a unified front against racism or capitalism seems to be abandoned as more specific identity projects are being realised. Homi Bhabha captures the unease of our times, the ominous sense that the driving force towards social democratic commonality has been replaced by

> an anxious age of identity, in which the attempt to memorialise lost time, and to reclaim lost territories, creates a culture of disparate 'interest groups' or social movements. Here affiliation may be antagonistic and ambivalent; solidarity may be *only* situational and strategic; commonality is often negotiated through the 'contingency' of social interests and political claims.
>
> (Bhabha 1996: 59)

McGuigan (1999) shows the importance of considering the commitment of identity politics to equality and, indeed, solidarity across different marginal and subordinate social positions – questions that are much too easily dismissed as illegitimately 'universalistic'.

While McGuigan (1999: 88) stresses the vital role of difference as a 'subversive principle', he highlights some of the concerns that more traditional Left intellectuals harbour about this shift towards identity politics. Hobsbawm is cited in defence of the older tradition (1996: 40): 'The political project of the Left is universalist: it is for all human beings.' Whereas 'Identity groups are about themselves and nobody else' (Hobsbawm 1996: 44).

So clearly if we accept these aspects of identity as realistic, identity politics and the postmodern views about the fluidity and highly constructed nature of identity are very hard to accept by traditional leftist thought. An end to essentialist categories makes power relations difficult to understand and, as Foucault has shown, undermines traditional Marxist thought: how can there be a class enemy or a ruling class of oppressors? 'The political project of the Left is universalist: it is for *all* human beings' (Hobsbawm 1996: 43) whilst on the other hand, 'Identity groups are about themselves and nobody else' (Hobsbawm 1996: 44).

Despite the apparent contrast between modern and postmodern, others argue that postmodernism is merely the latest chapter in the cultural history of western modernity, not a major shift. Sardar has been a powerful critic of those who portray postmodernity as heralding a new radical liberation movement to oppressed peoples around the world. According to Sardar:

> far from being a new theory of liberation, postmodernism, particularly from the perspective of the Other, the non-western cultures, is simply a new wave of domination riding on the crest of colonialism and modernity. [...] Colonialism was about the physical occupation of non-western cultures. Modernity was about displacing the present and occupying the minds of non-western cultures. Postmodernism is about appropriating the history and identity of non-western cultures as an integral facet of itself, colonising their future and occupying their being.
>
> (Sardar 1998: 13)

Sardar is suggesting that postmodernity is another form of colonialism in the guise of liberal values, the postmodern 'we' is never inclusive in Sardar's view; it never refers to the non-western other.

CONSEQUENCES OF POSTMODERN THOUGHT

Postmodernity seems to signal a crisis of uncertainty, complexity and chaos for the project of modernity clad in its armour of assurance of an ultimate understanding of the world. In *The Meaning of Race*, Kenan Malik goes on to critique the post-structuralist and postmodern theories of difference that have become the backbone of contemporary anti-racist discourse and to examine the possibility of transcending the discourse of race.

> The postmodern condition is one in which the 'grand narratives' have become discredited. Grand narratives are attempts to grasp society in its totality, to give coherence to our observations of the objective world. Nationalism is one such grand narrative because it attempts to impose a collective sense of belonging on disparate individuals. Postmodernists reject all the great collective social identities of class, of race, of nation, of gender, and of the West. They reject Marxism too, and in fact any form of emancipatory theory the aim of which is the total liberation of humankind.
>
> (Malik 1996: 218)

Malik goes on to explain that universalism is considered by postmodernists as being inherently racist: a dangerous Eurocentric fantasy that serves to impose European and American culture and values of rationality and objectivity on the rest of the world. Indeed universalism denies the very possibility of non-European viewpoints. In this view, the endeavours of the natural sciences and social sciences such as anthropology are dangerously ethnocentric in their outlook and attempt to construct the 'Other', that is the non-European individual, through their dominant discourses.

However, as we have seen from the analysis of Foucauldian approaches, post-modern views have political consequences. For the very reason that they disallow and decry mass, collective movements, they are pessimistic about social change other than through micro-revolutions. Every case of racism is unique based on different social, political, cultural and economic subject locations.

> belief in the arbitrary nature of both power and truth leads to an extreme relativism [. . .] If power is simply the constituting element in all social systems, how can we choose between one society and another? And if discourse makes its own truth, whose validity is given by the strength of an arbitrary power, how are we to distinguish between different representations or discourses?
>
> (Malik 1996: 234)

So the dilemma of the postmodern (and also the post-colonial) becomes clear: based on a Foucauldian notion of power (the collapse of the concept of ideology), relative values are celebrated and the result could be the impossibility of making value judgements about any cultural practices or recognising any universal human values. Malik directs his criticism towards the current trends in valuing diversity – enshrined in the ethos of multiculturalism – he sees this as leading away from ideas of equality and encouraging separatism and – far from discouraging racism – providing a fertile ground for racists to gain respectability and legitimatise their views.

Hence Malik maintains 'The philosophy of difference is the politics of defeat, born out of defeat' (1996: 265). On the other hand, isn't the celebration of diversity is preferable to enforced integration and aggressive ethnocentrism. Yet when 'valuing diversity' becomes an ethos and the basis for policy, the logical conclusion seems to be divisive policies of education, ghettoisation, hardening of boundaries and a divisive strand of competitive ethnic rivalry and political correctness and identity confusion which the extreme right is able to exploit to their advantage.

POST-COLONIAL IDENTITIES

Examining the contentious territory of the post-colonial entails the study of political, social, cultural, literary and formations of identity. This section is intended to convey an understanding of what Hall (1994) has called the dias-porisation of ethnicity. This indicates that society is moving away from simplistic essentialism in its understanding of ethnic identity. Bhabha, Spivak and others talk about the mythical conception of an essential Other, which in reality is always divided. Many of our conceptions of race and ethnicity assume an original pure form of being; this is a claim that has been strongly refuted by the growing voices of post-colonial thinkers whose key theme could be characterised by the idea that 'The language of the oppressed has yet to be invented' (Petkovic 1983).

Post-colonialism is a complex field of discourse, constituted by responses to colonialism, slavery and the master discourses of empire, those authoritative and learned discourses that purport to speak for the muted colonial subject: history, literature, philology, anthropology, ethnography, philosophy and linguistics. It is the voice of the oppressed emerging and talking back with well-chosen words – a critical assault on the western conceit that it can constitute the colonial Other in its own form. These post-colonial currents in thought have become an increasingly important and challenging canon in the theoretical landscape:

> Post-colonial theory involves discussion about experience of various kinds: migration, slavery, suppression, resistance, representation, difference, race, gender, place, and responses to the influential master discourses of imperial Europe such as history, philosophy and linguistics, and the fundamental experiences of speaking and writing by which all these come into being. None of these is 'essentially' post-colonial, but together they form the complex fabric of the field.
>
> (Ashcroft et al. 1998: 2)

> Post-colonialism is regarded as the need, in nation or groups which have been victims of imperialism, to achieve an identity uncontaminated by universalist or Eurocentric concepts or images.
>
> (During 1995)

Such a field allows new explanatory paradigms for the radical changes that are occurring and the new cultural forms that are emerging.

> Theories of 'cultural imperialism' and 'neo-colonialism', which reproduce the oppositions of 'centre' and 'periphery', 'dominance' and 'submission' that shaped colonialist thinking itself, have seemed insufficient to account for the fragmentations and redefinitions of national boundaries and the shifting, contingent and hybrid forms of cultural and political identification characteristic of the late twentieth century.
>
> (Bennett and Stephens 1991: 5)

Up until the Second World War, most of the Third World, with the exception of some Latin American countries, was ruled directly by western colonial powers (see Chapter 3). These powers controlled monopolies of trade in the 'Third World'. Each European country had a set of 'Third World' countries that were, effectively, captive markets for its manufactured products. As already discussed, this colonial situation was aided by popular stereotypes and romantic myths about, for example, 'their' inherent spirituality as opposed to western materialism. The break-up of colonial states occurred from the end of the Second World War on. Most of the countries that had been in the hands of European colonists were swept with a wave of revolutionary thought. India gained independence in 1950; many African countries were not far behind. The war had drained Europe of money and labour and hence the capacity to maintain colonial rule and infrastructure was seriously threatened. At the same time, the growing nationalist movements were becoming an increasing nuisance to the colonial authorities.

This fracture of western dominance and the regaining of pluralist voices across the globe has meant the further destabilisation of our assumptions of how the subject is constructed; meaning is further displaced from ethnocentric construction. This is another example of the fragmentation associated with postmodernism. The great modernist trends in thought, which centred on the western rationalist, positivist view of the world, have been shaken by the voices of those previously oppressed emerging from lands liberated from colonial rule. The resulting challenges to the colonial powers lead to an unravelling of the global bindings, decentring the previously central place of European thought.

Post-colonialism is a complex set of global cultural formations that bring into question any unifying perspective that foreground dominant Eurocentric values. At another level, it can be narrowly defined as a literary movement, which emerged mostly from within English departments in western universities, that attempts to describe and understand the experience of colonised peoples – before and after colonisation – by an examination of texts: images, movies, advertising and especially literary genres that reflect the colonial condition and imperatives, for example in works by Rudyard Kipling, Joseph Conrad and George Eliot. These texts are examined in the light of the discursive structures prevalent in society, for example in physiology, anthropology and politics.

THEORIES OF POST-COLONIALISM

The publication of Frantz Fanon's revolutionary book *The Wretched of the Earth* (1961) could be argued to mark the birth of post-colonialism. Written at the height of the Algerian war, it has proved an inspiration for worldwide liberation movements. Fanon focuses on the struggle for identity of the colonial subject and the psychological scarring caused by colonialism. It is a rallying cry to the voices of Third World peoples to articulate their own destiny:

> When the nation stirs as a whole, the new man is not an a posteriori product of that nation; rather, he coexists with it and triumphs with it. This dialectic

requirement explains the reticence with which adaptations to colonization and reforms of the facade are met. Independence is not a word which can be used as an exorcism, but an indispensable condition for the existence of men and women who are truly liberated, in other words who are truly masters of all the material means which make possible the radical transformation of society.

(Fanon 1961: 250)

Fanon's work achieved high status as a guiding light for anti-colonial resistance. Fanon believed that there was a redemptive quality in the violent banishing of oppressors from the homeland, which more diplomatic and negotiated solutions did not allow: 'colonialism is not a thinking machine, nor a body endowed with reasoning faculties. It is violence in its natural state, and it will only yield when confronted with greater violence' (Fanon 1961: 61). Fanon practised psychiatry in Algeria and saw at first hand the 'internalization of oppression' that scarred not only the colonial subject but also the oppressors. Oppression was manifest in the body as well as the mind. Fanon has been influential theoretically because he was able to see the relevance of Lacanian ideas of the **mirror stage** to the racialised subject.

Perhaps the most influential scholar and literary theorist to have an impact and to define the post-colonial terrain is Edward Said who was a Palestinian/ American professor of literature, best known for writing *Orientalism* (1985), the seminal work that examines the western construction and conceptions of the 'Orient'. Said defines 'Orientalism' as a sub-genre of post-colonial obsession with 'others'. It is the construction created by the west to manage relations with the east. Said presents his work not only as an examination of European attitudes to Islam and the Arabs but also as a model for analysis of all western 'discourses on the Other'. He claims that the discourse of Orientalism preceded and paved the way for colonial possession and exploitation of the East. Said believes that a society builds up its identity more efficiently by imagining an 'Other', in the same way that Pieterese illustrated the imagined others of Europe in Table 1.1. Hence western identity is defined in relation to the essentialist myth of Orientalism. In this way the cultural and intellectual superiority imagined by the West was foreshadowed by an imagined East that remained forever culturally static and inferior. A similar process has been applied to the western constructions of all 'Others'.

The Orient was viewed, Said claims, as a region outside of the influence of western rationalism and science. It was characterised by 'its sensuality, its tendency to despotism, its aberrant mentality, its habit of inaccuracy, its backwardness' (Said 1978: 205). Orientalism was constituted by an amalgamation of complex interwoven discourses of philology, history, sociology and economics amongst others through which Orientalism not only creates but it also maintains; it is, rather than expresses, a certain will or intention to understand, in some cases to control, manipulate, even to incorporate, what is a manifestly different (or alternative and novel) world; it is, above all, a discourse that is by no means in direct, corresponding relationship with political power in the raw, but rather is produced and exists in an uneven exchange with various kinds of power.

(Said 1978: 12)

Despite this apparently sophisticated discursive argument (Said relies heavily on a Foucauldian notion of discourse in his work), Said's conception has come under heavy attack more recently as being too simplistic and helping to reify the existence of two monolithic entities: the Occident and the Orient. The colonial reality, it is argued, is much more complex and multifaceted than Said suggested. Nevertheless, Said's work has radically redefined the cultural landscape, his further texts have developed and refined his initial contentious and ground-breaking thesis. Feminist critics have both criticised and built on Said's work, which initially seemed to give little recognition of the important role women play in colonial discourses.

FEMINISM AND POST-COLONIALISM

In many different societies, women, like colonised subjects, have been relegated to the position of 'Other', 'colonised' by various forms of patriarchal domination. They thus share with colonised races and cultures an intimate experience of the politics of oppression and repression, albeit from a very different perspective. This is clearly a reason why post-colonial theories have shared concerns with developments in feminist theory. Both discourses endeavour to examine and reassert marginalised voices. Indeed Gayatri Chakravorty Spivak's teasingly rhetorical and ironic question 'Can the Subaltern Speak?' (1985) captures perfectly the dual burdens of post-colonial female subjects. The dual colonisation, both patriarchal and imperial, has rendered women mute.

Feminist critiques of Said's *Orientalism* target the fact that he appears to conceive of Orientalism as a unified discourse. As Reina Lewis points out, the only use of gender 'occurs as a metaphor for the negative characterization of the Orientalized Other as "feminine" [. . .] Said never questions women's apparent absence as producers of Orientalist discourse or as agents within colonial power' (Lewis 1996: 18). It could be contended that Said did not address one of the key elements in the discursive subordination of the East: the portrayal of women as powerless. It is important to see that the power of colonial discourse may be derived from how it positions women. The veil, the *hijab*, has come to be seen as a symbol of this oppression as well as the signifier of romantic mystique of the Orient contrasted to the supposed freedoms of western sexuality. These claims can be contested on the basis that the freedoms of western sexuality are freedoms that still favour hegemonic male sexuality and also that they are used to uphold the spurious notion that Muslim women are the passive victims of an archaic patriarchal culture.

Into the twenty-first century, the veiled Muslim woman has come to represent the ultimate symbol of backwardness and oppression and acts as a visual cue to bolster claims of the 'alarming' rise in Islamic militancy. The groundwork for Muslim women around the world to occupy such a degraded image was laid in the preceding nineteenth and twentieth centuries when European colonialists became obsessed with freeing the 'Other' woman in order to subvert and destroy the indigenous cultures over which they ruled and was further exacerbated by the mistaken belief in feminist discourse that the only true model of emancipation was the western model of feminism (Woodlock 2002).

Meyda Yegenoglu (1998) shows the inability of both Orientalism and feminism not to accept these divisive myths of the other leading in turn to a self-fulfilling prophecy about the state of impoverished developing nations and effectively strengthening the divide. This discourse regarded women of the less democratic, less learned, unstable and poverty-stricken societies as deprived of the possibilities and channels of power that are elsewhere accessible to western women. This 'backwardness', which became a recurrent theme, is of course sustained by a silently conducted comparison between underdeveloped or developing countries and industrialised ones. Such a comparison betrays a difference that remains central to the discourse disseminated by mainstream feminist practices: it reintroduces the 'West and the rest' opposition, thus constructing the sovereign western female subject endowed with all the privileges and powers reserved solely for her. This opposition also brings us back to the problems posed by post-colonial theory in its analysis of how 'Orientalism orientalizes the Orient' (Nezih Erdogan 2000).

Figures 5.1–5.4 indicate some of the ways in which discourses of gender, race and sexuality have been historically combined. In the nineteenth century, the preoccupation with race and 'breeding' led to an inordinate focus on sex and reproducing the race. In the latter half of the nineteenth century an outpouring of concerns about race purity and sexual orthodoxy combined concerns of eugenics and psychiatrics of sexual perversion. Women were delicate vessels for the raising of healthy babies needed to keep the stock pure; non-reproductive sex and homosexuality were treated as grievous waste of the 'germ plasm', the potential for furthering the race was squandered through immoral and hedonistic practices. As Foucault (1981) claims, this inordinate focus on sex and race can be seen as 'An entire social practice, which took the exasperated but coherent form of a state-directed racism, furnished this technology of sex with a formidable power and far-reaching consequences' (Foucault 1981: 119).

Other developing practices reflected this peculiar linking between racism and sexism. Craniology and brain measurement purported to show that blacks and

Figure 5.1 Kabyle. 'Bejewelled Beauty of the Kabyle'

Figure 5.2 Sudanese. 'Circe of the Sudanese Dancing World'

whites had different-sized brains – and the size of the brain was thought to correlate directly to intelligence. Similar findings suggested that women's brains were slightly smaller than men's. As a result, non-western native peoples were often portrayed as feminine, indolent and passive, or fitting other well-worn stereotypes such as being natural mimics, emulating their superiors or as simple-minded and treacherous, having no sense of honour.

Figures 5.1–4 shown above, and thousands of others like them, are indicative of these dominant western discourses. The first three images show the exoticism

ARABIA

Unveiled
Charms of
Beduin Women

This sun-kissed young Beduin mother
carries her baby, according to the custom
of the East, on her back. The child as it
grows older will acquire the dusky hue of
its mother. The Beduin woman, right,
like most of her fellows wears elaborate
ornaments and her silver ear-rings,
brooches, and necklace may represent a
good part of her husband's capital.

Figure 5.3 Arabia. 'Unveiled Charms of Beduin Women'

Figure 5.4 Veils, Egypt. 'Glimpses of Feminine Charms'

and sensuality with which western views of the female Other are imbued. The 'Bejewelled Beauty' echoes codes from classical paintings such as those of Ingres' *The Turkish Bath* and Sophie Anderson's *In the Harem, Tunis*. Lewis's (1996) discussion of the gendered Orientalism provides numerous examples of the portrayals of Oriental women by upper-class female artists and the adornment and posture depicted in these paintings is very similar. The codes by which women are displayed as erotic objects for the male gaze have been discussed at length by feminists and cultural-studies theorists. For example, the screen theorist Laura Mulvey, drawing on Lacanian ideas of **scopophilia** and the Oedipal male look, notes how Woman displayed as sexual object is the leitmotif of erotic spectacle: from pin-ups to striptease, from Ziegfeld to Busby Berkeley, she holds the look, plays to and signifies male desire' (Mulvey 1975: 6–18).

Portrayals of veiled women as in Figure 5.4, 'Glimpses of Feminine Charms', illustrate the voyeurism implicit in presentations of 'exotic' otherness. The male gaze and the desire for the Other – to see beyond and into the other – is reflected in these images. The women in these images are displayed in postures that seem to suggest sensuality and availability. The accompanying text emphasises their colouring: the Bedouin wife (Figure 5.3) is 'sun-kissed', the Kabyle woman has a 'tinge of hue' that 'is but permanent sun burn', the Bedouin's child will acquire the 'dusky hue of its mother'. These markers are, it seems, important when assessing the feminine charms of 'exotic' women. The language used by Hammerton (1933) is both coy and provocative, like the postures and poses that are selected and designed by the photographers. The other theme that emerges is the women's description as being part of the husband's wealth, displaying elaborate adornment which, in the Bedouin's case, 'may represent a good part of her husband's capital.'

In Figure 5.1 the arrangement is voyeuristic and stylised, very obviously posed – almost choreographed (like a Cecil B. DeMille biblical waterbearer or exotic harem dancer). When I showed this image to students, one or two mentioned the old Fry's Turkish Delight adverts – 'full of eastern promise'[1] – featuring the 'exotic' eastern female of countless adverts, television shows and films. The image employs codes from film, dance, costume, romantic painting and literary traditions. Indeed, she could easily come from the pages of that great Orientalist Sir Richard Burton (translator of *The Rubaiyat of Omar Khayam*, *1001 Nights* and the *Kama Sutra*) or from a silent epic, dancing the Seven Veils, a 'bejewelled beauty' from the Bedouin sheik's harem. The use of the ornate jug and the colour of the fabrics, richly woven rug and blanket that frame her are very well recognised signs of 'Orientalism'. The highly produced character of this image, its deep colours and sumptuous textures renders it as more than a photograph (or photogravure) and separates the real woman away from biographical detail rendering the image an icon of the Orient.

This mythologising tendency in these books has been hinted at in Chapter 1. While this treatment undermines the putative use of ethnographic task of recording the detail of life worlds of the other with a degree of objectivity, the fact that these images at the denotative level are photographic, with all the presumptions of unmediated reality, renders them innocent and allows the reader to willingly suspend disbelief and affirm the Orientalist myth of exotic beauty. The discourses that are readily available to replace the anthropological accuracy of these images are compelling ones from popular culture.

The harem has served for the Orientalist as a fantasy stage and the Muslim woman as the anchor that structured this space, enabling colonial discourse to operate on a number of levels. In the past three centuries, the 'enslaved woman' was perceived as a sign of the backwardness of Muslim society, in contrast with the situation of the western woman, who were then heading for emancipation (Erdogan 2000).

In Figure 5.5, 'A Pleasing Contrast', interesting transformations are made. The image is at once chaste and innocent, yet the 'pleasing contrast' being drawn is

---

1 An advert of the 1960s and 1970s for a popular Turkish Delight chocolate bar.

Figure 5.5 'A Pleasing Contrast'

purely one of colour aesthetics, 'the glossy blackness' against 'the whiteness of snow', such is the language of a paternalistic and imperial gaze, which reminds the reader of colour and the Manichean divisions that accompany these oppositions. A contrast would never be drawn in this way of a white person in a black gown, because this girl is closer to the realm of objects than that of human beings, and her colour is her most relevant and distinctive feature.

Racism relies on the invisibility of whiteness and the focus on blackness as particular and deviant. This obscures the fact that whiteness is just as integral to the mechanisms of racism (in the same way that homophobia relies on homosexuality as the defining identity of gays and lesbians and obscures the particularism of hetero-sexuality). Therefore, as Aziz (1992) cogently states,

> white women experience the state (to take one example) as patriarchal, whereas black women experience the state as racist *and* patriarchal: if the state is racist, it is racist to everyone; it is merely more difficult for white people to see this, because part of the racism of the state is to treat and promote white-ness as the norm.

(1992: 298)

Gayatri Chakravorty Spivak is another central theorist to post-colonial studies. She is best known for her essay 'Can the Subaltern[2] Speak?' in which she addresses one of the central issues affecting the field – how to represent the subjugated groups in academic discourse. Spivak 'questions whether or not the possibility exists for

2 'Subaltern' is defined here as one subordinated discursively.

any recovery of a subaltern voice that is not a kind of essentialist fiction' (Ashcroft et al. 1995: 8). In relating the experience of marginalised groups and the disastrous impact on them by western colonialist discourses, she asks can these groups speak for themselves or do they require someone to speak for them? Her frustrating conclusion is that neither option is satisfactory.

Drawing on the post-structural work of Jacques Derrida, Spivak focuses on the impossibility of anyone, even members of the ethnic group themselves, finding a true, unproblematic voice that would adequately express the views of the whole group. To attempt this would be implicitly subjective and, as Derrida contends, all subjectivity is fragmented and therefore tainted. Furthermore, subaltern groups are simply too heterogeneous to allow that any one member could realistically represent the entire group. (For example, Australians frequently refer to 'the Aborigines' as a single group when in fact there are hundreds of distinct cultural segments with unique languages, customs and belief systems that make up the indigenous peoples of Australia.)

Why can't academics speak for them? Partly for the same reason as mentioned above but also, as Spivak argues, those academics (usually from privileged and comfortable western universities) who attempt to speak for the subaltern are unlikely to do more than perpetuate the familiar discourses of domination, to rely on 'fictional' voices to represent the whole – just as Said suggested westerners did with their inventions of the 'Orient'. Therefore we are trapped in a Catch-22; a Babel of voices limited by the subjective nature of the subaltern speaker who cannot speak for all subalterns, or alternatively reduced to academic constructions of the developing world that are seeking the inherent 'otherness' of the subaltern and will frequently fall back on theoretical simulacra (the critical apparatus that has already been developed).

There is also debate around how post-colonial discourse should articulate colonialism and neo-colonialism. Should a stark 'master–slave' dichotomy be reinvented to define the characteristics of colonial dynamics, to help 'recover (a) the socio-economic and historical referents of the colonial encounter, and (b) the agency and oppositional impulses of the individual colonised subject and nationalist discourses and movements in general?' (Loomba 1993: 308). Or is 'hybridity', the ambivalence and duality of the colonial subject, more useful and instructive? Bhabha and others suggest that the coloniser–colonised relationship is not a Manichean divide, but deeply fissured from the start (see Williams and Chrisman 1993).

The term 'post-colonial' itself is fraught with problems:

To reveal 'the continuing persistence of colonial discourse', to question the 'post' in 'post-colonial', as Mani wishes to do, is important; at the same time, if we are contesting the stasis attributed to colonised societies by Orientalist discourse, the 'pre' and the 'post' of colonialism deserve equal attention.

(Loomba 1993: 320)

To conclude: post-colonialism is not an easy term to define. It represents a new socio-political and cultural space, in the aftermath of colonisation. It is an area often chartered through complex, hybrid ethnic forms and literatures. Drawing on diverse traditions of criticism, Marxian, psychoanalytical (especially Lacanian) literary and film theory, post-structuralist practices, it is indeed an important aspect of postmodern theory and practice. It is the caesura left after the brutality of colonial rule and decolonisation wars, and it is within this space that the post-colonial subject, hybrid and diasporic, seeks to find an identity and voice. 'Today the task of social science is to deconstruct the fixation of this essentially racist epistemology. By listening to the plurality of local and subaltern voices the stereotypes of fixed categories, dominant structures become less fixed. Local voices retool the semantics of ethnicity by being specific. Their specificity defeats the manipulation of ethnicity, itself a nexus of power. failing to hear the subaltern voices, still newer forms of oppression may masquerade as "ethnic" and be promulgated as such by intellectuals' (Shoebrun 1993: 48).

However, the privileging of 'subaltern' and specific identities involves a theoretical conundrum: are the claims for self-determination and human rights made by post-colonial individuals from, say, Sri Lanka or Vietnam to be assessed as valid because they are from Sri Lankans or Vietnamese or on the basis of their common membership of humanity? As Tabish Khair comments in a recent article 'Our claim to rights is a universal claim, while our oppression is always specific to our particular, relational identities' (Khair 1999: 2). This is not to deny the validity of claims or the very real oppression that colonial regimes have practised. The problem, as Khair astutely notices, is that again the discourses of post-colonialism, as with postmodernity, are founded on a negative view of ideas that attempt to essentialise or universalise and instead embrace the relative and fragmented view that no one world view is capable of speaking for all 'others'. However as Khair notes (a view echoed by Malik and others) 'exploitation and control work by way of particularities just as much as by way of abstract and false universalisms' (Khair 1999).

Despite the controversy generated and the theoretical complexity of some of these critiques, culture is always 'in the making', never static, and those academics who seek to reduce post-colonial voices to essentialist or determinist categories or outcomes are bypassing the importance of the specific and local.

CHAPTER SUMMARY

There has been a shift towards theoretical approaches to race and ethnicity that deconstruct social meanings and consider the individual subject location rather than more macro-sociological and materially based theories. Postmodernity has allowed a great many synthetic and experimental approaches to defining identity.

This focus on identity politics has been shown to have some positive value for a closer culturalist understanding of the construction of race and racism(s) as well as gender and sexuality. Stuart Hall and others have developed the work of Foucault, Derrida, and neo-Marxists, developing an understanding of ethnicity that is fluid and diasporic. The 'postmodern turn' has been opposed by some who feel fragmentation of identity politics and relativism represent a politics of defeat and undermine anti-racist struggles for equality by over-emphasising difference.

EXERCISE 5.1

1 Consider the images used in this chapter. What are the initial meanings and values you would associate with them?
2 Can you find similar images of the 'Orient'? Have today's images of the Other changed substantially? Why?/Why not?
3 What modern literature are you aware of that develops the narrative of the contemporary multicultural cosmopolitan city?
4 Consider Spivak's question 'Can the Subaltern Speak?' How relevant is it to minority ethnic groups, women, gays and other discriminated groups?
5 Assess Khair's (1999) robust criticism of post-colonialism that 'exploitation and control work by way of particularities just as much as by way of abstract and false universalisms'. Is this view born out in practice? What does this mean for postmodern/post-colonial criticism?
6 Is 'the philosophy of difference the politics of defeat' (Malik 1996: 265)? Why?/Why not?
7 There seem to be many arguments against postmodern theorising on race and ethnicity, but what are the benefits of such approaches to this area of study?

CHAPTER 6

Case Study
Indigenous Australians

There is no greater sorrow on earth than the loss of one's native land.
(Euripides 431 BC)

[handwritten margin note: Social Construct Created problem]

[I]ntellectual faculties have been maintained and gradually perfected through natural selection . . . leading to the gradual extinction of inferior races and their cultures, including the Australian Aborigines.
(Darwin 1952: 352)

Australia's indigenous people have faced more than two centuries of dispossession. Enduring wave after wave of colonialism, firstly external colonialism from Britain, then 'internal colonialism', which meant policies of 'protection' with the overt intention to protect them from the damage done by European culture, but never to restore Aboriginal culture, which was seen as doomed due to an inherent inferiority (see Hughes 1995), post-war policies of assimilation and integration gave way to self-determination and reconciliation. Yet despite these shifts in policy the conditions and treatment of Aboriginal peoples in Australia is uniformly shameful. This chapter includes a recent piece of research and some imagery from a short documentary film, *Framing the Fringe Dwellers*, that the author has produced. First, to make this study more accessible there are some contextual notes.

LAND RIGHTS

The Land Rights Movement claims that Aborigines have the right to own large tracts of land on the principle of being the first inhabitants, and yet before Britain colonised this land, Australia was a wilderness, a land going to waste. Although rich in natural resources and pastoral land, the Aboriginal had not, in thousands of years, constructed permanent dwellings or developed the land in any form. Very little real culture was recognisable today with the technology of the European, all Australians have a nation of which they can be very proud. One which has the potential of being the richest and most self sufficient in the world.

> (Tract 'Threat to the Nation', Union of Caucasian Christian People, Perth 1985)

Perceptions such as those expressed above reflect a popular misapprehension about land rights and would be laughable if they weren't part of an inherently racist view that is shared by Australians from varied backgrounds. These views recall the first settlers' refusal to recognise Aboriginal people as having any prior rights over their land and using the term *terra nullius* (empty land) to describe large areas of Australia on early maps. In an ironic reversal, anti-immigration activists in the early 1990s employed graffiti of an outline map with the word 'FULL' printed inside. The ground-breaking Mabo High Court Ruling in 1992 (referred to in Chapter 2) has further fuelled public anxiety, inflamed by media panics, about claims potentially threatening suburban gardens and vast areas of public land. These inflated concerns backed by powerful industrialists and pastoralists were finally endorsed by what many would see as regressive government legislation. Howard's amendments, known as the Ten Point Plan were implemented in response to a rightist campaign to nullify a December 1996 High Court ruling in the Wik case, which legitimised native title claims on pastoral leases – public land leased to farmers and pastoralists (ranchers). But the polarisation over the issue has been a thorn in the side of John Howard's Liberal government.

At the time this legislation was passed, a series of television ads were infamous for representing this issue as a direct attack on Australian 'battlers', farmers and other white Australians, who were presented as 'sons of the soil' – every bit as entitled to the land as Aborigines. The effect of this has been to inflate an issue from which there was never any threat, and to scapegoat Aboriginal people who compose only 2 per cent of the population.

Over the course of this year [1997], the National Farmers Federation (NFF), [. . .] has spearheaded a campaign asserting that small farmers' right to work the land is in jeopardy from the newly recognized native title rights. This scare campaign is backed by the National Party and sections of the Liberal Party,

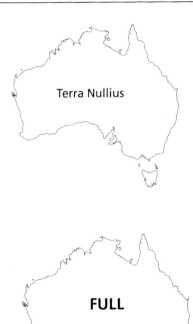

Figure 6.1 Australia, from *terra nullius*, 'empty', in 1788 to 'full' in 1988

including the state governments in Queensland and Western Australia. Howard's measures were drawn up under the pressure of these forces.

(Aiken and Poulsen 1997: 2)

LIVING CONDITIONS

Table 6.1 shows just how inequitable life in Australia is for Aboriginal peoples. The figures present a picture of stark contrast. Aboriginal people make up only around 2 per cent of the population but are around 12 times more likely to be incarcerated, nearly five times more likely to be unemployed and have a chronically shortened life span compared to white Australians. It is important to recognise these details because there is much disinformation about the conditions in which Aboriginal people find themselves.

Figure 6.2 is from the pressure group PARIAH's (People Against Racism In Australian Hotels) web site. Aboriginal people in Darwin and other cities in Australia are frequently victims of racist abuse and are marginalised, moved on,

Table 6.1 Patterns of indigenous disadvantage

NATIONAL INDICATORS	INDIGENOUS	ALL AUSTRALIANS
Life expectancy at birth (male)	56.9 years	75.2 years
Life expectancy at birth (female)	61.7 years	81.1 years
Imprisonment rate per 100,000	1,625	135
Home-ownership rate	31%	71%
Year 12 retention rate	30%	74%
Post-school qualifications	14%	34%
Average unemployment rate	34%	7.5%

(Source: Council for Aboriginal Reconciliation 1998)

Prior to their being 'moved on' by NT Police, these people were peaceably assembled in Darwin's city centre, instead of their isolated and (according to ex-NT Chief Minister Shane Stone) "dysfunctional" communities. Don't you love the Aboriginal Art (for the tourists) in the background.

Figure 6.2 'Breathing while Black'. 'Prior to their being 'moved on' by NT Police, these people were peaceably assembled in Darwin's city centre, instead of their isolated and (according to ex-NT Chief Minister Shane Stone) 'dysfunctional' communities. Don't you love the Aboriginal Art (for the tourists) in the background. (Mick Lambe, PARIAH web site)

and barred from hotels and other public places. On the same site there is a protest against the extraordinary rates of incarceration suffered by Aboriginal people in the Northern Territory. The image shows the group's sense of irony about a legislature that convicts Aboriginal people for the flimsiest of reasons. Because Aboriginal drinkers are refused entry to many pubs, they may be seen drinking in public places such as parks or city squares, their behaviour is considered unacceptable and taboo. As Fiske et al. suggest, there is a cultural boundary for white Australians who would see public drinking as threatening.

> So their drunkenness is more visible and breaks the tacit rule of white drinking; and they get arrested on charges of drunkenness in a vast disproportion to their numbers or even degree of drunkenness and the danger to public order they represent. But the punitive treatment of Aboriginal drinkers in public places serves a double ideological function: it separates them off from full participation and membership of white Australian society (they are 'dirty drunks' whereas whites are 'good boozers'), and it vindicates the magic wall around the pub, which protects white drinkers in their alcoholic anti-society and keeps the subversion and criticism within its safe bounds.
>
> (Fiske et al. 1987: 11)

Stephen Muecke investigates how concepts of aboriginality are constructed through discourse. Muecke argues that 'whatever "Aboriginality" is, it has never always been the same thing from one tribal group to another, from ancient times to the present, or even according to some legal definitions, from one state of Australia to another' (1992: 19). Although arguing that aboriginality has never had a singular definition or meaning, Muecke rightly notes that according to humanist thought, 'the essence of what "they" are, is known intuitively by the people themselves, and no-one else can have access to this knowledge' (1992: 19). This view has underpinned the movement towards self-determination and makes a nonsense of the idea that aboriginality can be quantified in terms of blood, which has been seriously discussed in Australia in the 1990s considering how Tasmanian and other Aboriginal claimants could be tested as bona-fide Aboriginal.

Muecke's work on aboriginality is an important starting point in a discussion about the historical construction of aboriginality in Australian society. Muecke offers a lucid critique of the ways in which aboriginality is represented as a truthful and authentic object by whoever appropriates it. Aboriginality is socially constructed through various representations, for example, in print media, on television, in film, through politics and through music. Muecke's critical and historical approach argues 'that European ways of talking about Aborigines limit their ways of knowing what Aborigines might be' (1992: 20).

> A good example of critical discourse leading to practical change is the legal status of 'public drunkenness'. This offence was constructed during a period of high moral conservatism in Australia, and its existence now appears to be anachronistic. More insidious though is the fact that public drunkenness is the offence which sees many young black men being placed in police custody – a situation which leads to young black men taking their own lives at a

disproportionately high rate compared with the national average for suicides in gaol. It would take a small act of legislative courage to remove the offence of public drunkenness from the statutes thus reducing the possibility of young black men being arrested and possibly taking their own lives.

(Finnigan 2001: 43)

Aboriginal people, as discussed earlier in Chapter 1 with reference to Hartley's (1998) assessment of how the media divides reality, are marginalised – part of a permanent metaphysical otherness (theydom). Media coverage of Aboriginal issues typically constructs them as a problem, depicting them as:

agitators, politicos, welfare-funded drunks or as frequent cause of social unrest in 'stable' white communities. In media discourse, an 'educated' and 'articulate' Aboriginal person is quickly labelled a political stirrer, radical activist, or black sympathiser. News crews are quick to cover community brawls, or scuffles at Aboriginal landright marches or protest gatherings outside courtrooms. Wherever and whenever Aborigines (or other ethnic groups) can be captured on film as unruly, disruptive, and (preferably) violent, the media are present.

(Luke 1996: 6)

[handwritten margin note: result of campaign process]

The following case study focuses on Darwin in the Northern Territory and the Indigenous Australians who live there. Australia has a complex indigenous heritage, several hundred 'Aboriginal' groups with unique languages and traditions. However, the consequences of invasion, rates of incarceration and the legacy of the 'stolen generation' (forcible removal of Aboriginal children) and continuous pressure from developers on already small parcels of land have had a catastrophic impact on many communities, dislocating them from their traditional areas and leading to many indigenous people being trapped in an impoverished and pressured state. There is often a struggle to obtain even the most basic amenities in the midst of monocultural Australian affluence.

This chapter focuses on one specific site of this colonial legacy – Darwin in the Northern Territory; an area with a larger proportion of diverse indigenous peoples than other states of Australia. These disparate groups enjoy an uneasy existence on the edges of the city in a few poorly resourced and crowded housing estates or in informal camps. It is an existence that at times brings them into conflict with the white community and local government's concerns for the image of the city and the burgeoning tourist trade. The strategies employed by Darwin City Council to manage what they call the 'itinerant problem' are a reminder of the divisive tactics employed by colonial overseers. Certain disparate groups of indigenous peoples have been formed into the Larrakia Nation in pursuit of long-standing land-rights claims in the Darwin area. This group has been encouraged to act as 'cultural ambassadors' to persuade groups of so called 'itinerant' Aborigines to return to their own homelands. This chapter looks at the contested notion of 'home', citizenship and nation and focuses on what occurs when lifestyles, cultures and financial aims collide.

CONTESTED HOMELANDS: DARWIN'S 'ITINERANT PROBLEM'[1]

Framing the fringe dwellers

The dry season in Darwin: dragonflies fill the air, back-packers fill the streets, Mindil Beach Markets are in full swing presenting tourists with a multicultural mosaic, and the ongoing campaign to remove homeless Aboriginal people from public view moves up a notch.

Darwin has the biggest Aboriginal population of any Australian city at nearly 9 per cent, and the Northern Territory has nearly 28 per cent of the indigenous population. While the greater majority of the indigenous population in Darwin live in circumstances not unlike their non-indigenous neighbours, a number are, out of necessity, more transient, moving between remote communities and the city, visiting friends and relatives who may be in hospital or prison, seeking work or escaping unenviable conditions in the interior.

It is important to preface the present study with a word on social and historical context, as the representation of indigenous issues in 'the Territory' is founded upon historical and cultural constructions of aboriginality. What underpins this long-running moral panic about homeless indigenous people?

First, the history of Aboriginal people in Australia has been one of dispossession, cultural genocide and displacement.

> During the period of conquest, indigenous people were deprived of their most basic rights, their society and culture were destroyed, and their populations were decimated. Survivors were forced onto reservations and controlled by missionaries and special welfare bureaucracies. They were seen as racially inferior and expected to 'die out'.
>
> (Castles and Davidson 2000: 73)

Second, there is a long-standing and well-recognised cultural defensiveness – the 'cultural cringe' – a deference to European and British culture ('the old country')

---

1 This section is adapted from Spencer, S. (2005b) 'Contested Homelands: Darwin's "Itinerant Problem"' and is published with the permission of the *Pacific Journalism Review*, University of Auckland (Vol. 11(1), April 2005, pp. 174–97).

that has been recently reinvoked with reference to the 'stolen generation' and the current liberal government's refusal to make an official apology to indigenous Australians. Howard has used the term 'black armband view of history' to characterise what he regards as a negative and morose reading of history that reflects 'a belief that most Australian history since 1788 has been little more than a disgraceful story of imperialism, exploitation, racism, sexism and other forms of discrimination' (Howard's 1996 Robert Menzies Lecture, see also McKenna 1997 and Mayne 1997).

stolen generation

Third, in the context of the repositioning of social theory since the 1980s, the exhaustion of the narratives of modernity and the deconstruction of previously unchallenged foundations of national identity have all thrown historical events into sharper focus that had been buried in commonsense ethnocentric credo of Australia as the 'lucky country' (although Donald Horne who popularised the epithet made it with pointed irony: 'Australia is a lucky country, run by second-rate people who share its luck' (Horne 1964)).

The recent scrutiny and documenting of Australian history has challenged a more ingenuous image of Australia as a land of sunshine and opportunity and has led to debates about the intentions behind (as well as the actual extent of) acts that fit international definitions of genocide (see, for example, Windschuttle 2004). These new readings have also produced works of literature such as Robert Drewe's *The Savage Crows* (1976), which draws on the 1829 journals of George Augustus Robinson about the last days of the Tasmanian Aborigines; Robert Hughes's *The Fatal Shore* (1987), a history of Australia as a penal colony; and more recently films such as *Rabbit-Proof Fence* (2002), which powerfully portrays the forced removal of Aboriginal children as part of a systematic eugenics policy. Through these and many other works, a more realistic and plural identity began to emerge. At the same time, the multi-ethnic composition of Australia was also being recognised, previously coercive assimilationist policies were being criticised and multiculturalism emerged as a progressive discourse, despite warnings from conservative historians such as Geoffrey Blainey who argued it would lead to a weakening of national culture (Blainey 1984).

Fourth, there has been a conservative backlash to these shifts in discourse. It seems that there is a popular view, stridently xenophobic, a deep sense of being disenfranchised by liberal, multicultural rhetoric that seems to negate white Australian popular mores. The surge of popularity that swelled behind Pauline Hanson's One Nation Party tapped into these very sentiments. In this context the need to demonise Aborigines serves a long-standing function of reaffirming the civilisation and culture of white Australians, particularly in rural areas and away from Sydney and Melbourne. Hanson was able to effectively exploit a streak of resentment and xenophobia by pointing to benefits that Asian migrants and Aborigines received.

One Nation was a tragedy. By creating a block of 1 million voters strategically placed between Labor, the Nationals and the Liberals, it tempted the parties to pander to its prejudices. The Liberals adopted much of its refugee policy. More importantly they pursued their own similar agenda against multiculturalism and Aboriginal reconciliation.

(Jupp 2002: 139)

Fifth, at the same time that the national climate concerning indigenous politics has encouraged conservatism, economically Darwin has become a premier tourist spot – the gateway to Kakadu and the much-promoted areas to the south (Uluru, the Olgas, Kings Canyon) and of course the crocodile parks and river cruises. Tourism in 2003–4 saw 'visitor spending increased by 8% (to $1.2B), injecting an additional $81M into the NT' (Northern Territory Tourist Commission 2004).

Culturally oriented tourism is heavily promoted as a vital part of this success. Tourists can

meet members of the local indigenous community for an educational experience in bush land setting. Learn of the Aboriginal culture through the wide range of exhibits. See demonstrations of boomerang and spear throwing and learn about traditional sources for food and medicine. There is opportunity to sample bush foods such as Witchetty Grubs, Bloodwood Apples, Bush Bananas and various seeds. Following a morning tea of damper and billy tea, learn about tribal life, languages, art, dance and music, where you can be taught how to play the didgeridoo.

(Goway.com)

As a tourist to the 'Top End', this is typical of the rhetoric one is exposed to. It appears that the static imagery of traditional life-styles unchanged and timelessly pursued in remote settings is the preferred image, the one that is thought to attract tourism. The imagery used in the card in Figure 6.3 is very appealing and unproblematic, yet for many Aboriginal people these images of traditional life are a far remove from their day-to-day reality, living in urban settings often very similar to their white compatriots. This is not to deny the survival of rich and varied traditions of indigenous culture – only to state that the culture is one which, like all cultures, grows and develops, adapting, synthesising and making sense of a changing world.

However, the visibility of impoverished urban Aborigines runs counter to the images of carefree natives in a bush setting, which is the only available image presented for tourist consumption, and since 2003 the Northern Territory government has stepped up measures to remove so-called 'itinerants' from the city.

Indeed, there is the suggestion that Aboriginal people are imprisoned by a timeless view of culture. This view of culture is romantic and static and highlights

Figure 6.3 'Australian Aborigines' – typical representations of Aboriginal culture

undo us power to stolen children

the lack of real communication between indigenous and white populations in Australia: 'they are constantly called upon to display this essence, or this or that skill, as if culture were an endowment. This is an enormous burden, and it is the Western version of culture which gives them this, not the Aboriginal' (Muecke 1992: 40).

Sonia Smallacombe (Head of Indigenous Studies, Charles Darwin University), in a recent interview, supported this view of indigenous people tied to a primordial ethnic identity:

> Some of the legislation is so draconian. To satisfy a land claim you've got to have lived a lifestyle that occurred before 1788 – of course we've changed a lot since 1788! – But the legislation doesn't recognise it – the Government doesn't recognise that cultures change and also we have to change if we want to survive. They look at indigenous culture as static, they don't look at any other culture, but they certainly see indigenous culture as it has to be static which we're certainly not.

(Smallacombe 2004)

Directly racist constructions of aboriginality have used this form of static essentialism based on blood quantum, genealogical test, or ideas of an Aboriginal 'race' to define Aboriginal identity and membership and eligibility to benefits (see Gardiner-Garden 2003). It is clear then that concerns about developing tourism and prevailing trends of ethnocentric self-interest have developed an

145

approach to indigenous culture that divides the 'timeless cultural values' that seem most marketable from the cultural resistance of 'itinerant' lifestyles that are antagonistic to the aims of profit maximisation. The latter lifestyles and communities are a threat that has attracted an extraordinary amount of concern, such that the NT Government has allocated 5.25 million dollars since June 2003 to try and resolve the issue. However, the money has not gone towards improving the accommodation for Aboriginal communities that is wholly inadequate in area and in gross disrepair.

The 'itinerant problem': community conditions

The ideas of 'home' and of being homeless have powerful cultural and normative power. The less formal aspects of the homes of 'long grass' people (generally referred to in Darwin as 'itinerants', which is another very emotionally loaded term) are a cause for concern to white Territorians and hard to equate with neat suburban blocks that most Australians inhabit. To accept homes as being temporary, makeshift or transient spaces is seen as a rather threatening concept. Yet from the work of writers such as Bill Day and Marcia Langton, it appears that these 'itinerant' camps are highly organised and structured with complex relationships and rules by which the campers live (see Day 2001, Langton 1997 and Sansom 1980).

The largest official Aboriginal community in Darwin, the Bagot community in the Ludmilla area, began as an Aboriginal Reserve in 1938. Like a few other communities, the Bagot is under-resourced and too small for the needs of an expanding indigenous community. Bagot has been reduced in area (some land has been taken to build a fast-food outlet – Hungry Jacks. It is in a prime location for passing traffic to the airport and obviously will receive patronage from local Bagot residents themselves. A recent project to build a fence around the community was promoted by local politicians as an investment in the community:

> Mr Vatskalis said the first stage of the $460,000 project is about to start and will involve the construction of a new fence across the front of Bagot community, a new entrance and associated landscaping. Additional new fencing will also be installed around most of the remaining boundary of Bagot community to improve security and prevent vehicular access.
>
> (NT Government 2003)

However, the project may well be greeted with cynicism by some members of the indigenous community. One wonders whether the fencing is for their security and enhancement of the community or to hide the cramped and rundown conditions within the impoverished community from public scrutiny and further stigmatise the people inside. A recent story illustrates the conditions within Bagot: 'A Darwin indigenous community (Bagot) says it does not have the money to remove a run-down house containing asbestos' (ABC Northern Territory, 20 November 2004). The house could not be quickly and safely removed as the costs for such an operation were prohibitive.

Another smaller community with less formal status, closer to the city centre, is the One Mile Dam community. The lack of services here was very apparent when I visited in July 2004. The camp was set up for indigenous people in the 1970s and has received little help or improvement since then. This camp can swell to accommodate nearly 200 people and has only two toilets. Piles of refuse fester in the heat and recent reports have cited faulty wiring exposing residents to danger of electrocution. In addition, nearby fuel-storage tanks overlook the community, presenting an ever-present threat from volatile fumes and residents worry about the pollution of the billabong, which was considered a place of special significance to the community. The new luxury apartments that overlook the community signify another threat as developers look to expand and use the community land for future developments.

The continual pressure on these small parcels of land become intense as local government refuses to build new community sites to accommodate so-called 'itinerants'. The resultant overcrowding and other social problems associated with poverty and living under difficult conditions have blighted Aboriginal communities for a very long time. Different groups are thrown together in these shrinking communal spaces, and arguments and violence are not uncommon. Consumption of alcohol and high incidence of illnesses, domestic violence and child abuse have all been associated with communities. While these behaviours are undeniably a part of life in the cramped and under-resourced areas apportioned to 'itiner-ants', they receive much more public censure than when they occur in the white community. There are a number of possible reasons for this, including the obvious one that this is a group that is much more exposed to public scrutiny – barred from pubs so forced to drink in public, sleeping in the open when accommodation is not available. More than this, however, it appears that any 'official' approach to Aborigines is always from a point of historically constructed paternalism.

Law and order

In 2003, the city council began to look seriously at a number of initiatives that it saw as potential solutions to what had become characterised as the 'itinerant problem'. The Government concern reached a peak around early to mid-2003 as the following extract suggests, even considering a permit system for Aboriginal people who were considered a threat to the law and order of the city. Draconian policing laws under the previous Liberal Party Government had included mandatory sentencing, which led to some extraordinarily harsh penalties for the most minor offences.

> In 1999, an unemployed homeless man was sentenced to 12 months in jail for the theft of a bath towel valued at $15. The court record states that the man took the towel from the backyard of a Darwin suburban house 'to use for a blanket' because he was cold. This was his third property offence since the introduction of mandatory sentencing and he was therefore given an automatic term of 12 months imprisonment.
>
> The man had a history of 13 other property offences, mostly for the theft of food and similar items for his personal survival. He saw no alternative to entering a plea of guilty as he realised 'there was no choice for him but to do his time'.
>
> His lawyer, Kirsty Gowans, said that the penalty far outweighed the minor nature of the offence. 'We have not come very far from transporting people for stealing a loaf of bread', she said.
>
> (Territorians for Effective Sentencing)

Even with a Labour government in office, the policy of aggressively targeting young male Aborigines who were often unemployed or students has continued. In 2003, over 80 per cent of the prison population in the Northern Territory were Aboriginal people. A popular NT tabloid presented this fact thus: 'of 756 prisoners in jail in Darwin and Alice Springs, 612 are indigenous. [. . .] This equates to 82 per cent of the prison population being black. [. . .] And this means they still show little or no respect for the laws of this country' (Col Newman, NT News, October 2003).

Media manifestations

During 2003, the Northern Territory developed a perennial theme through its daily newspaper the *Northern Territory News*. The theme could fairly be classed as a moral panic in the original use of the term whereby 'a condition, episode, person or group of persons [who] become defined as a threat to societal values and interests' (Cohen 1986: 9). Indigenous people have been a constantly demonised and, as shown, criminalised group. The news headlines (see Box 6.1) also indicate possible resolutions to the problem. The use of the term 'itinerants', clearly treated here as a thinly veiled euphemism for Aborigines, is cast aside and almost parodied in the second sample headline. Looking at these and other headlines, a transparent campaign of moral sanction and censure reached a peak around April 2003 as attested to by the headlines in Box 6.1. Many of the stories show the tabloids tendency to reduce complex stories to rabble-rousing slogans and seem aggressive and antagonistic about Aboriginal issues (see Figure 6.4).

▌ BOX 6.1 ABORIGINAL AUSTRALIANS

PERMITS FOR ABORIGINES (*Northern Territory News*, 4 March 2003)

ITINERANTS TOLD BY THEIR OWN PEOPLE: GO HOME
(*Northern Territory News*, 15 April 2003)

GANG OF 30 BASHES 3 TEENS (*Northern Territory News*, 16 April 2003, featuring a photograph of an Aboriginal male and the inset box '"Why? Because there was nothing to do", Darren Duncan pictured at court yesterday').

BLACK v WHITE: ABORIGINES TRY TO REMOVE WHITE WORKERS (*Northern Territory News*, 26 April 2003)

Figure 6.4 Front page of *Northern Territory News*, 15 April 2003

Cohen (1967) and others (Young 1971, Hall et al. 1978, Critcher 2003) have shown how a desire for moral consensus may underpin moral panics, focusing on a group that comes to embody – for a period – evil or moral corrosion in society. Figures of authority, agents of social control, particularly the police, are seen to 'amplify' the occurrence of deviance. The media is a central agent in this process of amplification (and, at times, sheer fabrication) of deviance and threat to a moral order. The headlines from the *Northern Territory News* present indigenous people as a threat; they are repeatedly portrayed as violent, drunk, homeless beggars who are a civic nuisance.

There is, it could be suggested, an ambivalence about these portrayals because, first, the conditions in which Aborigines are living are in the case of some communities shameful and squalid. Second, the derogatory stereotypes about Aboriginal drinking (which have a long history) also draw attention to the Northern Territory's parallel excesses and alarming rates of alcoholism. Third, many tourists are visiting the Northern Territory to visit Aboriginal sites and enjoy the timeless 'cultural performance' of aboriginality.

Chas Critcher, in a recent interview (June 2004), suggested that moral panics often represent the need for moral unity 'particularly at times when moral consensus is hard to come by'. In Australia it could be argued that the moral consensus about historical treatment of indigenous populations and about attitudes of white dominance have gradually shifted and have been exposed to critical scrutiny, as has Australia's less than glorious colonial past as a penal colony.

A key element in the construction of urban Aborigines in Darwin is the discourse around public drinking. There is evidence that the perceptions of aboriginal Australians, which are prevalent today, have their origins in derogatory historical stereotypes.

The caricatures from 1887 editions of the *Queensland Figaro* (see Figures 6.5 and 6.6) portray drink as a central and morally corrosive feature of Aboriginal urban culture. The effects of drinking on indigenous culture has clearly been used by white Australians to affirm their place on higher moral ground, and as a means of racist ridicule and paternalism, bemoaning a loss of noble 'natural' attributes.

The irony, of course, is that it was these very attributes of naturalness that were so despised by early settlers in the frontiers of America, Canada and Australia. As David Sibley suggests, science and Christianity asserted white dominance over indigenous peoples, arguing that 'peoples closest to nature, in a primitive state needed saving. Salvation often involved not only accepting Christianity but also adopting European style of dress and discipline of a Christian education in the mission school [. . .] The civilizing mission distanced them from nature' (Sibley 1995: 25).

However, there is also the suggestion here that Aboriginal people are at best poor mimics of white society. They are portrayed as so far removed from the civilised mores and refined etiquette of English culture that the very suggestion

Figure 6.5 'Amongst the Queensland Blacks', *Queensland Figaro*, 10 December 1888

Figure 6.6 'Nature – Civilization', *Queensland Figaro*, 6 August 1887

of Aborigines adopting such a lifestyle is presented as ridiculous (as shown in Figure 6.7).

This contrast between the raw 'nature' of Aboriginal existence and 'civilisation' (Figure 6.6) recalls another popular discourse, that of Rousseau's 'noble savage', a romantic discourse stemming from a strand of Enlightenment thought. The suggestion that Aboriginal people should remain true to their 'nature' is, as I have illustrated, very much alive and well and is still the abiding 'safe' image of indigenous Australians that white Australians and tourism affirms.

These visions of Aboriginal people as depraved drunks are obviously the basis of the gross stereotypes available to white Australians who often have little or no contact with indigenous people throughout their lives.

As discussed, Aboriginal drinking is always looked at as a problem. Yet there is a contradiction involved when the Northern Territory (especially) is clearly proud of a frontier tradition of excessive drinking. Sonia Smallacombe drew out this point in a recent interview: 'It's basically a contradiction. It's quite celebrated, the fact that the city has a huge consumption of alcohol, [. . .] while they're

Figure 6.7 'England – Blackfellows at home': 'They are kindly received in fashionable circles – ladies play the piano to them etc.' *Sydney Punch*, 15 August 1868

celebrating, they're also saying that indigenous people are the ones who should really control their drinking' (Smallacombe 2004).

In Darwin, the Beer Can Regatta is a public celebration in which rafts and boats constructed from thousands of beer cans (see Figure 6.8) are raced at Mindil Beach. Aboriginal people (as well as other ethnic groups) are notably absent. Anthropologist Bill Day suggests that the festival serves a crucial function:

> in the Beer Can Regatta the Darwin non-Aboriginal settler society conceals its cultural dislocation and dispossession of Aboriginal people, while constructing settler myths on the urban landscape. In my analysis, I suggest that the festival mediates the disjunction between culture and place typical of immigrant people. In contrast, I suggest that Darwin fringe dwellers believe that they are at home on their own land, while their drinking is associated with Aboriginal resistance to dispossession.
>
> (Day 2001: 1)

Further, Day suggests that the regatta reflects British origins of the 'regatta' (as in the regatta at Henley-on-Thames) and further imbues white drinking behaviour with 'civilised' values in contrast to the image of Aboriginal drinking, which is presented as out of control. The Beer Can Regatta is presented as a purposeful and constructive reason for drinking. Originating in the 1970s' Keep Australia Beautiful campaign as a creative solution to the mountains of tin cans strewn around the city, the regatta then was founded on the idea of a constructive and civic-minded activity that would improve the environment. Day suggests that the act of drinking and hence making more cans available for this family-oriented activity is given a positive value.

Figure 6.8
'Purposeful
drinking'. Beer
can boat at the
annual Beer Can
Regatta, Darwin

Heavy drinking was excused as preparation for the beer-can races. One team said they had drunk 3,000 cans of beer in a week. 'If we win we'll get rid of a few more cans of beer – to use in next year's race, of course' (*NT News*, 6 August 1997, as quoted in Day 2001).

Day makes the point that the festival serves as an unspoken affirmation of white domination, especially as it takes place at Mindil Beach, an area that has significance to local Larrakia people as a burial site.

> In postcolonial Darwin where public expressions of racial superiority are illegal, the festival makes a powerful unspoken statement authorising task-directed white drinking in public places. Aborigines, who are noticeably absent from the Mindil Beach festival, are further displaced by the appropriation of the supposedly empty landscape for the predominantly White festival.
>
> (Day 2001: Chapter 9, 11–12)

Drinking, then, is at the heart of the construction of the 'itinerant problem' and of dominant perceptions of Aboriginal people in Darwin. Aboriginal drinking is seen as an example of the corruption of Aboriginal culture (see Pearson 2000), a view that accords with dominant white constructions of Aboriginal culture as tainted by contact with 'civilised' values. Conversely, a number of analysts have equated heavy-drinking cultures amongst 'itinerant' communities as a form of resistance to white hegemony (see Day 2001: Chapter 9). This is not the place to speculate about this, but suffice to say that the treatment of Aboriginal people for very minor offences (for which a blind eye is turned if the person is white) such as public drunkenness appears to be out of proportion and suggests that urban Aborigines are seen as a threat, perhaps at a symbolic level. This is a feature of the moral panic that has led the white authorities in Darwin to focus on 'itinerants'.

Deconstructing 'the itinerant problem'

In June 2003, the Northern Territory Government announced a 5.25 million-dollar budget allocation to develop a strategy dubbed the 'Community Harmony Strategy'. The overarching aims of the strategy were a significant reduction of the incidence of anti-social behaviour by 'itinerants' in all major territory centres and the delivery of infrastructure, intervention programs and health services responding to identified needs of 'itinerant' groups (Northern Territory Department of Community Development, Sport and Cultural Affairs, <http://www.dcdsca.nt. gov.au/dcdsca/intranet.nsf/pages/Home>).

While the ostensible aims of this strategy seemed laudable, a focus on health and well-being and a sort of assisted passage back home for people stranded and penniless in city areas, the terms of reference and the definition of implicitly inclusive and exclusive categories of citizenship raise several concerns.

First, the term 'itinerant' entails assumptions of degradation and exclusion that are never made explicit. 'Itinerant' appears to be a euphemism for Aboriginal Australians who stray into the city limits and do not choose to live in the ghettoised suburban developments where social housing is provided. Mick Lambe, a vocal opponent of local government schemes and racist attitudes towards indigenous groups in the territory, commented that the term 'itinerant ' signified 'Territory-speak for Aboriginal people who choose to live traditionally' and 'Aboriginal people who have escaped from their remote Communities' (Lambe 2003).

Second, the term 'itinerant' is applied to groups who are relatively settled in areas around Darwin city centre. There are a number of camps that have been established since the 1970s with some basic dwellings – now in a state of disrepair: One Mile Dam (also known as Railway Dam) with between 90 and 150 people and larger communities such as the Bagot near Ludmilla in the outer suburbs of Darwin, with over 300 people. In addition there are a number of 'long grass' camps that are more transitory but nevertheless have been a feature of Darwin's foreshore for many years. As Sonia Smallacombe (Head of Indigenous Studies University of Darwin) told me, 'The Government has labelled these people as itinerants, although a lot of them have been around twenty or thirty years so they're actually not itinerants' (Smallacombe 2004).

Third, the term 'itinerant' clearly reflects judgements about lifestyle as well as origins and length of habitation. Indeed, those people known as itinerant appear to maintain some vestiges of a traditional lifestyle and appear to be resistant to the model of citizenship offered by the representatives of the Larrakia nation. Sonia Smallacombe commented:

> They're a group of people who for various reasons are not keen to live in houses, and a lot of people will say things like 'The reason I don't want to go and live in a state house or a housing commission flat is because I can't – I'm not allowed to have my extended family visit me or stay with me – I'm not allowed to have my animals'. Aboriginal people like to have their dogs, they're not allowed to have their dogs with them.
>
> (Smallacombe 2004)

Anthropologist Bill Day suggests that 'itinerant' is a signifier that removes the threat the privileged white society of Darwin feels towards Aboriginal people.

In Darwin it would seem that homeless Aboriginal people become less threatening as 'transients' or 'itinerants'. These categories are often used as the equivalent the iconic 'drunken "Abo"', as described by Langton (1993a). However, as Cowlishaw (1994: 80) claims, the refusal of Aborigines in towns to be passive and silent 'stimulates the fears and feeds the paranoia' that many town residents feel towards the significant minority.

Fourth, the term 'itinerants' disguises (effectively denies) the agency of dominant white Australians in dispossessing Aboriginal groups from their traditional lands, forcibly removing of groups to missions and removing children from their families. Ironically, the approach stemming from the euphemistic 'itinerant problem' is arguably related to the earlier policies characterised by the title 'Aboriginal problem'. 'The aim of these assimilationist policies was that the Aboriginal "problem" would ultimately disappear – the people would lose their identity within the wider community, albeit through continuing restrictive laws and paternalistic administration' (*Northern Territory News*, Editorial, 11 March 1996).

The Government approach to homeless Aboriginal people today appears to be of the same order, removing Aboriginal people from the city centre and using a variety of coercive methods to return them to their 'homelands'. Local Government has mooted the use of permits for 'itinerants' to control their access to the city area in Darwin. When this approach didn't work and when, as stated in the *Northern Territory News* editorial (11 March 1996): 'Pulling down of makeshift camps and moving people on certainly doesn't work. The itinerants just shift to another spot in town. Disliking them and their lifestyle won't make them go away. Positive ideas are needed'.

The most recent scheme has involved the collaboration of the Government with a newly formed Aboriginal group, the Larrakia nation, to give the job of policing itinerants a more ethical and apparently culturally sensitive approach.

Larrakia Nation

The newly formed Larrakia Nation received 500,000-dollar backing from the State Government. The teams of 'Larrakia Hosts' were formed, their function was to persuade 'long grassers' or itinerants to go home and to attempt to reduce 'anti-social behaviours'. Cultural protocols were foregrounded, asking non-Larrakians to respect traditional values when on Larrakia land. The host scheme was fairly ineffective, but signs were put up around the centre, setting boundaries and times for public drinking. This approach was supplemented by intensive policing of the few Aboriginal people who now set foot in the park.

To an outsider, it seems hard to imagine that Darwin has a significant population of indigenous people, as they are noticeably absent from the city centre. A few groups of Aboriginal people were seen in the Bicentennial Park on the Esplanade, small clusters sat conversing and sharing beers. It was hardly the riotous assembly the tabloids had portrayed. There was a very significant police presence in the park, one evening fifteen officers with motor bikes and patrol wagons gathered informally near the Esplanade. Police wagons move in and out of the park during the day checking on the small knots of Aborigines, especially where there are white tourists who are sunbathing. Mission Australia also patrols the park, stopping to investigate Aboriginal needs, distributing fresh water and giving contact details in case they want to use any of the services that the Mission provides, including an assisted passage back home (tickets are purchased for them and the money is reclaimed from their social-security allowance). In short, this surveillance and monitoring seemed inordinately focused on a few transient people who were causing very little fuss.

The focus is on public drinking and tourists and retail businesses in the city receiving harassment from 'itinerants' begging or 'humbugging'. These are the issues that city aldermen insist require drastic measures to counter. Figure 6.2 is from the polemical PARIAH web site and captures the sense of oppression experienced by Aboriginal people in the city centre. The new police laws allow for 'itinerants' to be 'moved on'.

When asking about the Larrakia Nation and its origins, I was told that it represents a newly incorporated umbrella group of collectively defined groups who have long-standing land rights claims in the Darwin area and the Cox Peninsula.

> The Larrakia are unique in the sense that we are identified as the traditional owners and custodians of the greater Darwin area, Palmerston area, rural area which is unique in the sense that most large urban areas, particularly city areas, throughout Australia share a joint ownership of two or more aboriginal groups but we're certainly recognised as the only aboriginal group in the greater Darwin

area as custodians/traditional owners: within that there are 8 identifiable family groups that represent the 1700 Larrakia people.

(Calvin Costello, Head of Larrakia Nation, interview July 2004)

These are people who have struggled for many years for recognition of their lands, and as with all Aboriginal groups, are marginalised and impoverished. The Government's Land Commissioner, Justice Grey, in December 2000, recommended with regard to the 'Kenbi Land Claim' that a large area of land on the Cox Peninsula should be handed back to the Larrakia after a twenty-three-year struggle.

There is a general suspicion about the Larrakia's involvement in city-council schemes to send itinerants home. The recent founding of the Larrakia Nation (1997) is viewed by some as a political bargaining tool. And now members act as hosts who inform other Aboriginal people of the sort of behaviour that is respectful on Larrakia land. The same message was disseminated via a video that features Larrakia elders exhorting other Aborigines to return to their homelands. This is perceived by some 'itinerants' as divide-and-rule tactics by a group who have been lured into collusion by the promise of shared bounty.

The scheme was featured on the ABC's *7.30 Report* (6 January 2004) where it was portrayed as an effective panacea to help Aboriginal people who get marooned in Darwin and cannot afford the fare back home. No mention was made of the long-standing long grass and other communities in Darwin. The Larrakia scheme was presented as a brilliant enterprise that avoids the rough handling that was associated with the Liberals' attitude. The story was presented in the usual magazine style by the presenter Murray Mclaughlin's commentary and a few indigenous voices, interestingly, never dialogues or exchanges, but unitary utterances in terse, almost broken, English. The coordinated and orderly work by many service providers renders the story one of success for the voice of reason, civic pride and responsibility. The itinerants are described as befuddled natives who can think no further than their immediate needs. Keeping them actively employed making paintings and carvings might keep them off the streets. It is paternalism dressed up in the discourse of timeless aboriginality. There was no attempt to highlight or even address the issue of 'itinerants': they have no voice here and are contrasted to the Larrakia 'leaders' and white Australians. However, the division between Larrakia and others is certainly not clearly defined in reality. Sonia Smallacombe commented that the Larrakia had

somehow been recruited by the Government – not all of them, I've met a lot of Larrakia people who don't agree with it – being recruited by the Government to tell other indigenous people that your behaviour on our country is not good enough, and you really should respect Larrakia ways of doing things – when you going up here and drinking, and going up and asking tourists for money

. . . Fortunately it's not been a decisive policy; a lot of Larrakia people actually support the itinerants, and there is an itinerant organisation that's been set up – and there's a lot of Larrakia people in that. . . . I think indigenous people are aware that the Government uses those kind of strategies to try and divide indigenous groups.

(Smallacombe 2004)

The attempt to use Larrakia claims and voices strategically is also echoed by Mick Lambe:

An enormous presumption is being made about the impact of Aboriginal people in Darwin, dressed up in terms such as 'cultural protocols' to conceal its innate contradictions. Does the 'impact' of Aboriginal people on the Larrakia compare in any way [for example] to the cultural and physical impact of European invasion? What right has the government to dictate, when and how Larrakian voices will be heard? And, more importantly – which Larrakian voices will be heard. As June Mills stated in court. The Larrakians did not give permission for the NT Parliament building to be constructed on their land.'

(Mick Lambe, PARIAH web site)

Lambe's comments draw out the extraordinary ironies implicit in this scheme. The apparent divide between two relatively underprivileged groups further amplifies the deviance of the more loosely defined 'itinerants', while the Larrakia 'Nation' becomes a viable partner with the State Government and Council to share in financially lucrative schemes. Furthermore, as with any effective colonial administration, it sets subject 'races' in an antagonistic relationship while reaping the benefits and maintaining control yet disguising the true conditions of domination.

Despite the desperate needs of other indigenous groups around the outskirts of Darwin, Costello takes a pragmatic view of their welfare and struggles with officialdom. Calvin is quick to point out a different side to the plight of One Mile Dam, explaining that they haven't paid rent on the site for over four years. (One would perhaps feel that the suggestion of 'rent' was an insult given the appalling conditions they have to contend with.) Calvin gives a wry smile and suggests that they also have choices – moving into public housing is also an option available to them. There are two sets of values informing this divide, two discourses that give competing readings of the role that itinerants play in Northern Territory society.

Realistically, this situation is not a simple polemic; the waters are much muddier. The Larrakia have struggled for over twenty-four years for the recognition they have achieved. The issue of lifestyle is extraordinarily divisive. Even within the ranks of Larrakia people there are a diversity of views; certainly many Larrakia are keen supporters of groups such as the Kumbutjil Association, established by the One Mile Dam Community to run their own programmes and projects for a safer, active and healthier community.

However, Larrakia people, Costello argues, make up a tiny minority of less formal communities such as the Bagot (he claimed only two people lived there). Instead they have been dispersed into public housing. I asked him about the Community Development Employment Programme. Marcia Langton has called this 'labour apartheid'. Costello simply stated the popularity of the scheme and the fact there was a waiting list of several hundred. If skills and experience are needed, does this scheme provide these? Some have argued that the scheme is merely a means of providing labour under the minimum wage and that the majority of the tasks are menial, degrading and hardly constitute growing a skilled community. Sonia Smallacombe emphasised that developing skills and growth in the community is the only way out of the appalling conditions faced by generations of indigenous people in the Northern Territory.

To the Larrakia, who are more cooperative, membership appears to have potential benefits. Calvin Costello, Larrakia Nation Coordinator proudly showed me a model of the proposed cultural facility, which is planned to be built on Larrakia land near the airport. The multi-million-dollar development is designed to attract tourists to share in Aboriginal culture and will offer employment possibilities for large numbers of Larrakians. This development, however, is not for outsiders or 'itinerants', as the promotion for a 'multi-purpose cultural facility' makes clear: 'All Larrakia people are encouraged to attend a viewing of the concept model for the proposed Larrakia Multi Purpose Cultural Facility. All Larrakia Nation Members and Non-member Larrakia Families are invited to provide input into the development of this major Project' (<http://www.larrakia.com/the website/future.html>).

The implications of this are clear when aligned with a policy of policing the boundaries of shared ownership and disseminating information about cultural protocols. There are effectively two competing groups: one defined by homelessness, poverty, dispossession and anti-social behaviours, the other with official approval and recognition, that has bargaining power, a successful land claim and relative affluence, but a less traditional lifestyle.

These projects represent a financially lucrative arrangement between some of the Larrakia, Councillor Ah Kit (himself of Larrakian origin) and the Labor Government. 'Essentially a plan to remove "itinerants" (Territory-speak for Aboriginal people who choose to live traditionally) has been given a politically-correct fillip by the use of some of the less "traditional", but far wealthier Larrakians' (Mick Lambe 2003).

When I asked Mr Costello about the contrast in lifestyles, he reinforced the fact that the negative impacts of alcohol on 'long grass' communities was having impact on young children with, he suggested, increasing incidence of violent abuse to women and sexual abuse of children. He was unequivocal about the need for indigenous people to move into housing to gain employment and hence self-respect. While speaking with him I felt the pragmatism he exuded was probably one positive antidote to a very hard and demoralising existence. However, there are other ways in which a state with genuine concern for cultural values could give Aboriginal people of all origins and lifestyles a sense of belonging rather than casting some of them as pariahs. A suggestion made by several groups is to re-zone areas that include the less formal camps and to allow those who wish to live less formally with extended family and their animals to do so.

CONCLUSION

> I read somewhere during the Bosnian war . . . I think about 'ethnic cleansing'
> – well I'm beginning to think that that's what's happening here.
> (David Timber, Coordinator of the Kumbutjil Association,
> One Mile Dam Community)

Figure 6.9 David Timber, Coordinator of the Kumbutjil Association at One Mile Dam Community near Darwin

To an outsider from the cramped confines of urban England, it seemed extraordinary to me initially that such vast areas of land could not accommodate a few thousand indigenous people who wish to determine their own lifestyle and to resist being squeezed into new and regulated suburban spaces. However, I came to the conclusion that the recalcitrance of the city authorities is more purposeful and is fuelled by the need for a moral consensus, that the affluent white population wishes to reaffirm its hegemony and that the result has been a moral panic which, over the decades, has demonised and pressured this group. Aboriginality is being used as a 'floating' signifier (see Hall 1997), drawn upon expediently, where there is cultural or economic capital to be gained – tourist dollars or a compliant and malleable indigenous community. Aboriginal people are portrayed, when it suits, as noble custodians of the outback, the embodiment of ancient traditions or dirty drunks who are an embarrassment to the civic authorities and a potential threat to business, and who must be banished from the city environs. The signifier of collective guilt and collective denial of that guilt is never far away, because what happened in the past is still happening today. There can be no solution to this situation until the reality of Aboriginal identity is realised and the history of what has really taken place in the Northern Territory, as in the rest of Australia, is confronted.

POSTSCRIPT

Since my visit in July 2004, several events have occurred that clearly show the acquisitive motives which intervene and prevent reasonable compromise. Sonia Smallacombe of Darwin University writes:

> The Aboriginal Development Foundation that holds the lease [to the One Mile Dam site] is willing to hand it over if the Goverment pays them 1 million Australian dollars!! This group has been responsible for providing basic services to the community (which they haven't) and now that there will be a story on the community, they are concerned . . . The One Mile Community voted no confidence in this group last year. In the meantime, Larrakia Nation is negotiating with the NT Government to erase the community and turn the area into parklands. Interesting how there is money to do everything but supply basic services to a group of long term residents!

THEORETICAL FRAMING

In this section, the case study about Aborigines in Darwin is used as a way of exploring several different theoretical readings. Students may find it easier to comprehend the possible uses of these conceptual frameworks when they can see them as parallel and complementary approaches.

Plural society theory

The Aboriginal diaspora is a direct consequence of colonial dispossession of Aboriginal lands and the disruptive removal of Aboriginal children. The complex and clannish groupings of Aboriginal people has followed a pattern that would seem to support Furnivall's (1948) central importance of the marketplace. Aboriginal people were able to mobilise as the potential for uniting under the newly formed banner of 'The Larrakia Nation'. Interestingly, the prohibitions and aggression of the colonial era clearly shaped practices in ways that administrators did not foresee: alcohol as a sign of citizenship, a communal sacrament to be shared and a form of resistance to the white authorities that condemn Aboriginal drinking but promote white drinking.

Marxist approaches

Conflicts between the white community and indigenous Australians have a long and dismal history. The elite white population is predominantly affluent, and it is common knowledge that the remoteness and 'frontier spirit' of the Northern Territory may serve as a filter to collect people who tend to be like-minded and generally conservative. Certainly, attitudes expressed in the State Government would be less likely to be heard in the larger urban centres. These are attitudes akin to the aggressive colonial history of the region. Marxist approaches could show the colonial strategy of divide and rule is still very much in place; the coopting of the Larrakia people into a favoured position as a bulwark against 'itinerants' (shorthand for Aboriginal people who do not fit into the correct image required for tourism in the city). The conceptual framework employed by each strand of Marxist reasoning could produce articulate readings of the Darwin issue. In terms of hegemony, media resources aggressively demonise Aboriginal people (using the term 'itinerant' to highlight undesirable civic values). Tourism plays a role both in the further exclusion of urban Aborigines and the construction of mythical views about Aborigines. Tourism is a major form of capital for the territory and Aboriginal culture is one of the aspects that draws tourism to the state. The visible presence of Aboriginal people in Darwin city centre is almost entirely associated with the production of Aboriginal art and artefacts.

Althusser's conception of the failure of 'repressive state apparatus' giving way to 'ideological state apparatus' clearly seems to be applicable here. Under the Liberals, the policy for dealing with 'itinerants' was to destroy their temporary dwellings and to confiscate their possessions. Shane Stone, Former Chief Minister, recommended that the police should monster and stomp on them: 'People who are out there causing havoc on our streets, who are defecating in our car parks and our shopping centres, deserve to be monstered and stomped on' (ABC *7.30*

Report). In addition, the mandatory sentencing scheme saw a prison population of nearly 80 per cent Aborigines. None of these schemes worked: no sooner had shelters been pulled down in one area than they were erected again elsewhere. Furthermore, the 'itinerant' problem and the harsh treatment of Aborigines had the possibility of bringing unwanted attention to the Government of the day. Hence, the Northern Territory's Labor Government has pursued an apparently more culturally sensitive approach.

Weberian notes

The Weberian traditions, as articulated by Rex and Tomlinson, amongst others, are very much germane in this case study. The more complex social structures that are autonomous of class are clearly in operation here. Ideas of 'imagined community' and citizenship are an important part of the subjective identity of the groups involved. Bill Day (an anthropologist) recognised the importance of drinking alcohol to Aboriginal people who, he claims, associate it with citizenship because for many years there was a specific prohibition for Aboriginal people to drink in the city environs: 'Remembering the era of prohibition and the campaigns for change, Aboriginal people in the Northern Territory and elsewhere equate achieving the right to drink with "citizenship rights"' (Day 2001: 4).

This presents a very different function behind drinking and the status attributed to it by whites and indigenous people. Some observers have assessed the Beer Can Regatta event in terms of class and masculinity, but Day suggests this is a misreading because it is really a ritual affirmation of dominance over and separation from Aboriginal inhabitants and a way of stressing the legitimacy of drinking for white Australians. Certainly the fact that alcohol is a key social problem for non-Aboriginal Australians could be damaging to the identity of rugged individualism on which the Northern Territory prides itself. 'With Aboriginal citizenship, non-Aboriginal Northern Territory drinkers were faced with the contradiction of deploring uncontrolled Aboriginal drinking while praising the frontier tradition of drinking to excess' (Day 2001: 4).

Taking issues such as this into account highlights the importance of status and social honour as well as monopolistic social closure. A Weberian approach maps social groups and their value systems without the necessary reduction to relationships of production. However, in most cases, neo-Weberian analyses such as those of John Rex and David Mason (1986) could be said to allow that social contexts are underpinned by economic relations.

Nevertheless, there are clearly times where social honour, citizenship rights and other aspects of identity and resistance in the face of dispossession exert more influence than class. Again, Day and others have commented that ultimately

Aboriginal drinking, wherever it takes place, is returning a profit for white Australians. Alcohol is aggressively promoted in areas where Aboriginal people have access to it. Furthermore, the revenue on alcohol could be seen as one means of recouping welfare benefits to Aborigines:

> One submission to the Royal Commission into Deaths in Custody (Langton et al. 1991: 319) stated: 'everyone is just trying to make more and more money from these outlets, and take money from the people'. For some Aboriginal people 'alcohol is seen as a deliberate component of the invasion of traditional lands and the destruction of traditional culture and law' (p. 308).
>
> (Day 2001: 18)

This less deterministic view of class opens up the possibility of more subtle overlapping analyses in which 'ethnicity overlaps with status in one situation, and with class, caste or estate in other cases' (Malesevic 2004: 129).

The competition between groups of Aborigines indicates competition for scarce resources and is reflected in differential market positions (in Weberian terms). In this case, one group has achieved a different market position by forging allegiances with the state government and by providing assistance in projects which encourage Aboriginal endeavour as part of the lucrative tourist market. Conversely other groups (the 'out groups' who have been dubbed 'itinerants') have a relationship to the state which is characterised by purposeful resistance: heavy drinking and living a so-called itinerant lifestyle rather than living in public housing. Cultural identity therefore can be a divisive force. On the one hand, the retention of attachments to the land, to practices of food preparation, communal patterns of behaviour, being surrounded by extended family and dogs (incompatible with state housing in Australia) or, on the other hand, having aspirations to some of the material rewards of white Australian culture and hence having to relinquish or modify practices.

So it becomes apparent that in some instances an analysis that refuses to give any credence to cultural values and status issues that exert influence on ethnicity could be one that misses the complex variables that are contributing to the situation. Interpretations of conflict and cooperation in terms of race and ethnicity (cultural difference) are frequently used by the state to disguise the powerlessness of groups and their disadvantage in the marketplace – a disadvantage that is frequently extremely marked and of long duration.

Elite theory

Classical elite theory re-affirms the Marxist emphasis upon sectional interest (in other words, elites) in determining the distribution of power in the state and civil society. There are clear examples that give credence to the role of elites in constructing political structures of the state, and in guiding policy in many democratic states (not least the US and UK administrations). The theory would encourage us to look at the motives of the power holders in the Northern Territory Government and in other organisations that have a stake in the issues. John Ah Kit (the Minister for Community Development, Sport and Cultural Affairs, himself a Larrakian) has certainly been instrumental in the policies. There are indications that the 'Larrakia Nation' and its social-harmony plans, which are directly funded by the government, have the potential to be very lucrative to Larrakians higher in the hierarchy. Furthermore, stakeholders in other hierarchies are clearly not above sacrificing the 'itinerant' communities who they feel have persisted in negative and self-destructive resistance. For example, the Aboriginal Development Foundation that holds the lease (to One Mile Dam site) is willing to hand it over if the Government pays them 1 million Australian dollars, while at the same time the Larrakia Nation is negotiating with the Government to turn the camp into parklands.

Postmodernity

Postmodern approaches would typically stress the discursive construction of the relationship between Aboriginal and white Australians. The nature of the dominant white discourse on Aboriginal people is one which locates them in the past as part of a static timeless, culture (in fact their sign is 'nature' rather than 'culture'). This discourse has a function in the urban capitals as a romantic marker of white superiority, the so-called 'bush myth', which glorifies the frontier traditions of Australia and white dominance over adversity. Although the fierce wars and conflicts with the original inhabitants are not part of this history, the rugged individualism epitomised by Banjo Patterson's poetry and recent films based on these (e.g. *The Man from Snowy River*) definitely is. Furthermore, the discourse of Aborigines as romantically attuned to the bush and to ancient mystic traditions is a source (especially in the Northern Territory) for the burgeoning tourist trade worth nearly 1 billion Australian dollars a year. Hence there are clear motives to disguise the poor conditions in which displaced Aborigines are forced into near the city. Makeshift camps and beggars are not compatible with the image of Australia being broadcast. Postmodernist perspectives might also consider the situation in terms of identity politics. Competing factions assert their subjectivities, and the fragmentation of indigenous groups into their regional identities is an example of this process of an awakening sense of giving voice to identities too long subsumed under the imposed under the 'subaltern' term 'Aborigines'. Identities are malleable in this view and constantly in the process of being formed. Discursive practices, as Muecke (1982) has shown, constitute the available discourses by which whites can talk about 'them'. Taking this analysis further, Marcia Langton (1993: 33) writes:

> 'Aboriginality' [. . .] is a field of intersubjectivity in that it is remade over and over again in a process of dialogue, of imagination, of representation and interpretation. Both Aboriginal and non-Aboriginal people create 'Aboriginalities' [. . .] This opens up further possibilities for the development of understanding and communication between cultures traditionally located in such isolation. This process appears to be one to strive for but how realistic is this when the average white Australian is highly unlikely to even exchange the time of day with an Aboriginal person?

Symbolic interactionism

In this perspective, the way in which the divisions between and within ethnic groupings are affected is a result of outside categorising and an intersubjective relationship between the in-group and out-group. The formation of self through interactive encounters with other groups and individuals, and particularly as this is transmitted through the use of generalised labels transmitted and given authority through media and other significant institutions. Interactionists say that the world we experience is socially constructed. In this view, ethnic groups are seen as products of social interaction. Ethnicity arises when communication channels between groups are limited and the different groups develop different systems of meanings. In this case, there are certainly different conceptions of what it means to be an Aborigine, each concept derived from different social histories and relations to dominant white society, economic and political meanings that have led to quite different and contradictory strategies for survival.

As Fenton (1999: 63) argues:

> the 'cultural stuff' of ethnicity is grounded in social relationships. In a more or less conscious way, it is a feature of daily practice. This cultural content – the shared ancestry, the claims to a shared inheritance, the common customs and language – are also 'drawn upon' by ethnic group members, to give substance to. It may be drawn upon, too, by those who do not belong and do not share the cultural inheritance – that is, to mark them off from us.

Hence, in the case of Darwin there are clearly quite different perceptions of each group vis-à-vis the other. The white Australians recognise some Aboriginal groups, for example the Larrakia Nation, as sharing aspirations for the lifestyles that they already enjoy. They allow this group a small share in the enormous bounty from white tourism in exchange for some of their lands and for their complicity in being the reasonable face of the Government in dealings with 'itinerants'. Conversely, the tangible dissatisfaction of itinerants is aimed at the lifestyle of some Larrakians, which they see as falsely claimed indigenous credentials when in reality they illustrate a sort of cultural amnesia.

Rational-choice theory

The actions of all protagonists could be partly explained from a rational-choice perspective. The premise is that all action is determined by assessment of gains and losses, and rational calculation indicates the best strategy. Larrakians, whose land claims are at least in principle recognised, have formed into a united group despite considerable differences amongst their members. This could be seen as a rationalist approach to mobilise and claim ethnic unity. Similarly, the Government viewpoint is clear in this perspective. The State (Northern Territory) requires increased funding, and tourism is providing great potential for an area that is often forgotten due to its relatively small population base and the aridity of much of its land mass. Tourism provides the Northern Territory with high profits and increased global status. In order to capitalise on this niche, all efforts are prioritised to promote the tourist benefits of the Northern Territory. The great resources are the unspoilt wilderness areas, the proud frontier image of the area and, of course, the increasing interest in Aboriginal culture and art. However, negative images and bad press about racism and the appalling conditions in which urban Aboriginal people are forced to live are not conducive to the image of green and cultural tourist agendas, hence the remarkable efforts to remove or disguise the problem.

CHAPTER SUMMARY

Australia has a complex indigenous heritage, several hundred 'Aboriginal' groups with unique languages and traditions. However, the consequences of invasion – rates of incarceration, the legacy of the 'stolen generation' (forcible removal of Aboriginal children) and continuous pressure from developers on already small parcels of land – has had a catastrophic impact on many communities, dislocating them from their traditional areas and leading to many indigenous people being trapped in an impoverished and pressured state. There is often a struggle to obtain even the most basic amenities in the midst of monocultural Australian affluence. This chapter highlights one specific site of this colonial legacy, Darwin in the Northern Territory, an area with a larger proportion of diverse indigenous peoples than other states of Australia. Yet these disparate groups enjoy an uneasy existence on the edges of the city in a few poorly resourced and crowded housing estates or in informal camps. It is an existence that at times brings them into conflict with the white community's and local government's concerns for the image of the city and the burgeoning tourist trade. The strategies employed by Darwin City Council to manage what they call the 'itinerant problem' are a reminder of the divisive tactics employed by colonial overseers.

EXERCISE 6.1

1   How does the situation of indigenous peoples differ from those of other groups within plural societies such as Australia?
2   Why might Aboriginal people be disinclined to take part in (or wish to be recognised as part of) Australian multiculturalism?
3   How do lifestyles become a key issue in this case and separate people who otherwise have much in common?
4   Consider Steven Muecke's 'Available discourses on Aborigines'. How do the discourses of the romantic and anthropological operate in this case?
5   What are the signs that there is a moral panic taking place?
6   What paternalistic views are disseminated about Aboriginal people? Why are these views so prevalent and long-lasting?
7   What strategies could be put into place to improve the situation in the Northern Territory and elsewhere?

CHAPTER 7

Conflict

Violence breeds violence [. . .] Pure goals can never justify impure or violent action [. . .] They say the means are after all just means. I would say means are after all everything. As the means, so the end [. . .] If we take care of the means we are bound to reach the end sooner or later.

(Mahatma Gandhi 1964)

Interview with Martin Carter: Georgetown, Guyana 29 April 1991. Martin Carter was one of Guyana's most famous poets and also a political activist in his day who was imprisoned by the British colonial government as part of the independence movement. Martin died in 1999.

Mr Carter beckoned me in to a spacious front room adorned with Amerindian artefacts. Martin Carter projects a largesse, an immediate compassion and seriousness within a frame of gentleness, civility and modesty edged with a certain shambling grittiness. He seemed quite amenable to take part in an unstructured talk, part of which is recorded here.

MC: When a crisis comes [,] belonging to a different race becomes a resource. So I am making the two terms 'crisis' and 'resource'. That is to say that when something happens that an individual of one racial group cannot cope with[,] he regresses towards his racial stock [. . .] as a resource, as a vision to help him [. . .]

SS: So the crudest stereotypes emerge [. . .]

MC: and dreadful things will be said [. . .]

SS: I'm hearing this everyday when people start talking in taxis[,] terrible tirade of abuse [. . .]

MC: You make a very sharp observation about the taxi. For instance in a taxi you may not see it too easily[,] but it happens. Let us assume that the taxi driver is a man of Indian descent[.] There is a tendency for him to ignore the person who is of African descent and vice versa[.] So that would therefore mean that the people in a taxi would more likely be of one group [. . .] and so again you will get what you just described [–] like-minded people you see, who are really reinforcing their perceptions[.] And it is worse now[,] it never used to be like that until ten years ago [. . .] but in the debasement it has now become a sort of protest against [. . .] and it can get ugly [–] at least verbally[.]

As I said[,] when it becomes a critical imbalance [–] and I've seen this in 62 and the dimensions of it are horrendous[.] I'll give you an example and one which sticks in the mind[.] In 1962 this very street [–] not here but further up[,] in which a man[,] a young man[,] riding his bicycle[,] he's wearing a hat, so his head is covered (and in those days people attacked one another, especially if they were in a disadvantaged situation). So this young man came along, and some young dark boys came out of a shop or something and attacked him, started belabouring him with sticks. Now the young man who is riding the bicycle realises what is going on very clearly, because he lives here – and the problem was that he was normal dark brown, but his features were more aquiline than average. So he instinctively realised that these chaps had attacked him because of his apparent resemblance to an East Indian. Realising this he tore the hat off his head – and said to them 'What you beating me for? Look at my hair' (for he had negro-type hair). And then when they paused – only momentarily – he said in explanation, 'My mother was an Indian and my father was a blackman.' And the reply was as follows, which is the real horror, they said: 'Oh so your mother was an Indian and your father was a blackman – well we beat the East Indian within you.'

When you reach that state of irrationality you understand that is why I say it is a resource. That has gone beyond politics, its no longer a disagreement with a party, it's now become existential – in the worse sense of the word.'

The people in this and similar stories in Guyana have probably lived in close proximity, been to the same schools and shared many aspects of culture in their everyday lives. In many ways much Guyanese culture is 'creolised', a synthesis of both African and Indian traditions and their unique adaptation to an alien culture. However, ethnic rivalry since colonialism has reached an intensity which threatens at times to again blow up into inter-ethnic violence. Premdas has noted that in Guyana:

> Inter-racial suspicion runs silently deep, each side engaged in a contrived drama of studied hypocrisy about inter-communal amity. In the deepest recess of the soul runs a torrent of hate that makes everyday a veritable civil war, a struggle for ethnic ascendancy, a neurotic fear of ethnic domination, all enacted as an elaborate ritual of seeming routine and peace.
>
> (Premdas 1992: 3)

Here and in other divided post-colonial nations, the Other has been shaped by political, economic and historical processes. For example, in the run up to independence, parties began to unite along ethnic lines. *Apanjat*, Hindi for 'race vote', was employed by leaders of both ethnic enclaves. Another factor in these situations has been the Cold War fears and military intervention by the USA and Britain to secure countries like Guyana under the rubric of liberal democracy, especially where natural resources and useful markets exist within the country. In the case of Guyana this meant deposing the elected candidate and installing a more favoured statesman.

Figure 7.1 is a photograph taken in a thriving market in Georgetown, the capital of Guyana. Although Georgetown is predominantly an African town, social spaces like this market are areas where all groups come together to buy and sell. Publicly, different groups may be observed making transactions and mixing without any outward signs of conflict, but the boundaries are there and expressed fervently when the groups are 'offstage'; within the private bounds of their ethnic enclave they will drop the stage-managed calm of the public arena and often express deep resentment about the other group.

The nature of boundary-making and the consequences of difference reach extremes in nations that are split into dependent and interlocking ethnic enclaves. These examples of bipolar ethnicity are largely the legacy of colonial divisions fostered by administrators to maintain a competitive workforce and to prevent a unified front being forged between subject 'races'. Donald Horowitz (1985: 36–40) usefully defined ethnic systems as belonging to two major categories: 'centralised' or 'dispersed' forms of multi-ethnic state. A 'dispersed ethnic system' includes states in which the population comprises many small ethnic groups, too small to be able to take control of the centre. Horowitz argues this fragmentation of dispersed

Figure 7.1 'Only believe all things are possible': scene in the Stabroek Market, Georgetown, Guyana

groups encourages inter-ethnic harmony and consensus. States such as India and the former Yugoslavia, he suggests, showed a 'benign complexity'. However, as the bonds that have held the nation together begin to unravel, this complexity is lost and the result is fragmentation into separate national boundaries, each with a single dominant ethnic group.

The situation in Guyana fits with Donald Horowitz's definition of a 'centralised' state. This form of state occurs when the ethnic blocs are so large and strong that the problem of their interactions is ever present and central to the political and economic life of the nation. In Guyana (and countries such as Trinidad, Fiji and Latvia) the situation is one of bipolar ethnicity, which is always likely to be the most problematic. In Guyana, the swing between ethnically partisan political parties has led to catastrophic shifts. Each change is accompanied by allegations of electoral fraud (which was certainly true in the past) and street violence. The state is locked into internal conflict with no end in sight due to the sectoral divisions that are embedded since the end of the colonial regime. Indians (who now have ascended to power with their People's Progressive Party) are the backbone of the country's rural-based economy as well as being the most successful entrepreneurs. The Africans on the other hand are heavily represented in the Civil Service, police and army.

Guyana has been blighted by bitter and protracted ethnic conflict. This conflict may be viewed as a manifestation of a long historical process of ethnic-boundary construction rather than a recent post-colonial eruption of primordial ethnic difference. Indeed, 'ethnic boundaries are constructed from the interaction between groups with shared historical experiences and cultural values and their social environment' (Turpin 1990: 73). Ethnicity is socially constructed and subject to constant re-evaluation. It may well be that the conflict helps to shape and affirm identity on both sides. In Guyana there exists considerable institutionalised inequity in the distribution of power between the two ethnic communities.

Early in the history of indentureship (the transportation of indentured labourers to replace the vacuum left by the abolition of slavery), planters recognised the value of having a working population segmented racially and rarely missed the opportunity of 'playing off the two principal races – by using one to put down any overt resistance by the other' (Rodney 1981: 188). Rodney also quotes evidence given at the West Indian Royal Commission, clearly showing that this manipulative attitude was commonplace in the colony.

> The two peoples do not mix. That is, of course, one of our great safeties in the colony when there has been any rioting. If the negroes were troublesome every coolie on the estate would stand by one. If the coolies attacked me, I could with confidence trust my negro friends for keeping me from injury.
>
> (Rodney 1981: 188)

This active separation of ethnic groups can have long-term consequences. Malaysia, Guyana, Trinidad, Fiji and Rwanda, amongst others, have experienced intense and bitter post-colonial conflicts in which inter-ethnic enmity erupts in the competition for political or financial power. Often the people who are most reviled are the people who straddle the divide, those of dual heritage who are treated as pariahs because they embody a transgression against the imperative of the divide.

'RACE RIOTS' OR SOCIAL AND ECONOMIC EXCLUSION

The phenomenon of ethnic conflict is often the primarily negative context in which the dominant culture reflects on the vicissitudes of ethnicity. The designation of conflicts as racial or as 'race riots' is frequently contentious. Simply because a group of people in an inner-city area clashes with the police or right-wing demonstrators does not necessarily have anything to do with the mobilisation of ethnicity, although it is often all too quickly portrayed as that, which has the effect of locating it within the dominant discourse of law and order, marginalising the participants. Such is the case with the so-called 'race riots' in Lancashire in the UK, in which predominantly Asian youths clashed with police in Oldham and Bradford, and again in Australia in Sydney's Redfern district where Aborigines clashed briefly with police. In each instance, the feature that was emphasised was race. However, neither the long-standing tensions in these areas nor their extremes of poverty were stressed. The area of Lancashire affected by these disturbances is among the lowest economically active areas in the country, and the Block area of Redfern is a rundown ghettoised area with, again, some of the most intractable poverty at the edge of affluent city of Sydney.

It is not new to suggest that there is a tendency to 'blame the victims'. The point is the victims *are* these groups in class terms – under-class communities away from the amenities and services of the more affluent whiter community in which unemployment has become entrenched. These are, also due to their often stigmatised character, more heavily patrolled by police (although not always areas of higher than average crime). The anger of the Redfern community was sparked by the death of an Aboriginal boy, T. J. Hickey, who died in suspicious circumstances that involved being chased by a police vehicle. He was found impaled on railings. A police spokesperson who was interviewed on British television described instead the role Aboriginal drinking might have had on the riot. (This discourse has a long history, as discussed in Chapter 6.)

However, while the riots are perhaps not racial in the way they are glibly asserted to be in sensationalist reporting, these conflicts are certainly a consequence of constructions of race. Both Oldham in Lancashire and Redfern in New South Wales are highly segregated and are among the most impoverished areas in each country. This is not coincidental; both groups involved in confrontations with the police are the most disadvantaged minority groups. Pakistani and Bangladeshi population groups are self-segregated from the white population in Oldham as are indigenous people in the Sydney suburb of Redfern.

> The level of residential self-segregation is great in Oldham, with Asian and white communities concentrated in specific housing areas which all suffer from poverty and lack of opportunity. This has restricted day-to-day social contact between people from different ethnic groups. Some primary schools in central Oldham feature pupils from only one ethnic group, when the area as a whole has a very diverse community.
>
> (Oldham Together, online document, 2005)

Segregation of Aboriginal people in Sydney and other cities (as discussed in Chapter 6) is the result of entrenched inequalities that amount to being excluded from the relative affluence of mainstream Australia. In 2000, the UN made unprecedented criticisms of the Australian Government's out-dated policies, which have not improved the circumstances faced by the 2 per cent Aboriginal population who are seventeen times more likely to be arrested, fourteen times more likely to be imprisoned and sixteen times likely to die in custody than non-Aborigines. Economic disadvantage in each case is underpinned by historical patterns of exclusion. These outbreaks of violence reflect general trends of disadvantage across the country.

THE STRUGGLE FOR SYMBOLIC DOMINANCE

The manner in which ethnic groups face off over historical divisions and stalemates frequently entails the symbolic use of ethnicity or of cultural associations central to the group. Symbolic domination or violence can take many forms, parading significant achievements in sport, cultural capital, the arts, economics, a dominant linguistic tradition, and so on. Many forms of cultural capital can affirm one group as a superior rival. Examples include Greek Cypriots with the emphasis on 3,000 years of Greek culture and the connotations of Greek superiority implicit in classical traditions. The former Yugoslavia is claimed to be a conflict in which 'all the symbolic power that ethnicity can provide was manipulated in such a way that fanned the flames for an aggressive ethnonationalism to emerge as a force that finally led to chaos' (Sotiropoulou 2002: 9). In Guyana and Trinidad, cricket (once a sport that gave heart to colonial subjects as the West Indian team showed their mastery over the British one) has also become an arena for the divided ethnic politics of the region. The West Indies team regarded Guyana as an away match, as the support during World Cup events was directed to the visitors. Many

Indian-Guyanese spectators were jubilant in cheering the Australians when they played in 1991 and projectiles and abuse was thrown at the all-Afro-Caribbean team (see Spencer 2005b).

In Guyana, as in many plural societies, one form of establishing or attempting to establish such hegemony is to deny the reality of ethnic inequality and division and to attempt to instil Guyanese identity among *all* Guyanese (Spencer forthcoming).

The following interviews illustrate one dimension of the divide. Ethnic stereotypes that were produced a century ago are reactivated in these two vignettes and the basic elements are seemingly unchanged. The maintenance of boundaries through the use of stereotyped images is not a peripheral activity governed by caprice, but rather an activity central to one's own identity and security in a recognisable social world. Classifying the Other by reference to their body, size, shape, diet, economic behaviours, and so on is essential in defining one's own social space: 'Nothing classifies somebody more than the way he or she classifies' (Bourdieu 1984: 132). Such images are the boundary markers of identity for the individual member of an ethnic group. They are ways of envisaging the Other and, hence, oneself.

BOX 7.1 CONVERSATION WITH TWO AFRICAN-GUYANESE PROFESSIONALS

During a conversation with two African-Guyanese professionals, Lenny and Griff, in the emotionally charged atmosphere of the Demico House bar in central Georgetown, the following exchange took place after a discussion about a high-profile Indian business man, Yesu Persaud. Neither of my companions rated this figure highly. Griff said, 'You see, in the land of the blind, the one-eyed man is king'.

Lenny called him a 'lackney'. Then they took turns in attacking his credibility. He was given his house by President Burnham as part of an immoral deal. Without any prompting the invective started to flow, both men seemed suddenly excited, needled by my off-hand question about this much lauded Indian entrepreneur. There was much thumping of the table. Griff reached for my empty bottle and said:

'Say the Indian wants your bottle – or wot not. He will be so nice – so very good to you, you would never know. He will offer you money, and if that doesn't work – he will send his daughter to you, and if you don't want her he will send his wife! And as soon as he achieve this end – he take it away, then you know he never speak to you again – never! He only interested in the money. That's how they are.'

I ventured that this was perhaps a generalisation and that surely some Indians had other motives. Lenny could barely contain his impatience; 'It *is* general mon! They all the same – *ALL!*'

(Georgetown, 5 March 1991)

THE PERSISTENCE OF ETHNIC STEREOTYPES

Such vehement expressions of resentment are commonplace and reflect the Indians' apparent ease, relative to many Africans, at managing financial matters and property, causing jealousy and condemnation. The single-mindedness of the Indians to save money and forego present comforts and the good life for future improvement and security was condemned as avarice and caused irritation to the whites and the Africans alike (Vasil 1984: 243).

African-Guyanese stereotypes

The fears of many East Indians seemed to focus on the common perception of the African as overly physical and their dominance also perhaps 'physically' manifest in the state itself (especially through the use of coercive force to maintain their power base). This stereotype was notably strong around Georgetown, the seat of government, where African-Guyanese are in the majority. There was a widespread feeling amongst the Indians that they were vulnerable to attack by Africans. The blame for all muggings, known as 'choke and rob', and break-ins, known as 'kick down door', was always assigned to 'blackmen' by Indians.

BOX 7.2 CONVERSATION WITH INDIAN-GUYANESE MAN

The following is an extract from an encounter with a Georgetown East Indian man in his early twenties who worked as a mini-bus 'conductor'. The exchange took place on an empty bus, the only other person present was the East Indian driver.

SS: Do you feel that there is any racist attitude? . . .

EAST INDIAN MAN (EI): Racist. Yes! Racialism – there is! Yeah very strong. You see the Negro people – them don't – them ain't got this kina way – like you know, building a future. Them only brek it – them ain't got dis ting so. They people avent got the stronghold over this country – is East Indian people and Portuguese – people like Peter D'Aguair . . .

SS: Right I see . . .

EI: . . . like Cayman Sankur and Jose Persuad. Majority is Indian or Portuguese – but no you don't find no black people getting capital investment in this country. Any investment they got – they responsible for is drug pusher . . .

SS: . . . drug pusher – yeah?

EI: Yeah, they jus getting the money – look you'd ah seen em on the streets, riding the most fanciest bike, the most fanciest car to drive in. They dress their self in gold right?

SS: Uh huh. Yes.

EI: They dress their self in gold – Indian can't wear gold and the Negro would wear them in town on the skin. Why? They bully – cause if you wear it they come an choke you. They don't do this no more (here he demonstrated a choke and rob hold on my neck). Years ago they used to choke you . . .

SS: Choke and rob – yeah?

EI: . . . and rob you. Now. Now. They cutting you off! They cutting your finger off and they walking alongside you on the pave and they just take out the knife of the pocket . . . and dis 'don't move' – one on one side – now you can feel something sharp sticking in your side – 'now don't move' – a sudden movement [he became increasingly agitated here] Very bully – black people very very very bully! Black people travelling in this veekle – they arlways shart of money and they need music – they need spacious seat – and they arlways short of money. Yes.

(Georgetown, 13 April 1991)

This sense of vulnerability appears to have, if anything, increased. Since the People's Progressive Party achieved government in 1992 there have been allegations that a great number of aggravated assaults and murders in Guyana are racially motivated and largely perpetrated by African-Guyanese against Indians. Apart from the overt sense of physical threat here, which illustrates the common stereotype of the African as a physical aggressor, there is also reference to another popularly voiced view, that of the African as profligate, flashy and lacking in sound financial judgement. For Indians, the 'economic irresponsibility' stereotype is not peculiar to a segment of the African population, but is true of all Africans generally (Premdas 1972: 290–1).

THE OTHER'S THEFT OF LEGITIMATE PLEASURES

Slavoj Žižek (1990) uses the phrase 'theft of enjoyment' to explain the complex psycho-social perception of the Other. In his article 'Eastern Europe's Republics of Gilead' (1990) he related this notion to the growing tensions in Yugoslavia. Žižek equates national movements and 'causes' with the manner in which ethnic groups 'organise their enjoyment through national myths' (Žižek 1990: 53). Further, he presents the notion of the Other constantly impinging on our senses because of their perceived lack of restraint in the practice of their pleasures.

> In short what really bothers us about the 'other' is the peculiar way in which it organises its enjoyment: precisely the surplus, the 'excess' that pertains to it – the smell of their food, their 'noisy' songs and dances, their strange manners, their attitude to work (in the racist perspective, the 'other' is either a workaholic stealing our jobs or an idler living on our labour, and it is quite amusing to note the ease with which one passes from reproaching the 'other' with a refusal to work to reproaching him for the theft of work).
>
> (Žižek 1990: 54)

The two views of the other, as related by Žižek above, can equally be seen in the African- and Indian-Guyanese stereotypes of each other. Indian-Guyanese often fear the African population, believing that they are responsible for robbery and street crimes, which are especially grievous when related to the loss of their pleasure in adorning themselves with gold and jewellery in public, which was once an important aspect of the culture. Conversely, African-Guyanese feel the Indians' success and facility with money and property is a direct trespass on the pleasure and privilege to which their traditional status as public-service workers entitled them. Indians are seen as workaholics. Their ambitions are often viewed as avaricious and their willingness to save money single-mindedly and to sacrifice the comforts of the good life of the present as meanness (Vasil 1984: 243).

Žižek states that: 'What sets in motion this logic of the 'theft of enjoyment' is of course not immediate social reality – the reality of different ethnic communities living closely together – but the inner antagonism inherent in these communities (Žižek 1990: 56).

This is very much the case in Guyana where tension and suspicion between the groups is deeply ingrained, but rarely voiced openly (see Chapter 4). Žižek compares the threat to enjoyment to Lacan's notion of 'imaginary castration'.

179

Certain aspects of cultural identity, the unique symbols, for example, a long association with the land or a type of traditional work practice, are felt to be inaccessible to the 'Other'. Yet when the 'Other' is seen as a rival for these scarce resources, then the result is a constant state of distrust. This is perhaps the central contradiction of Guyana and other ethnically divided states. Žižek's identification of the psychological threat seen to be embodied in the culture of the 'Other' can be recognised in many nations with a marked ethnic divide.

The next example is drawn from another ethnically fractured state, Malaysia, which again experienced a catastrophic eruption of ethnic rivalries in 1969 that provided justification for some overt political manoeuvring.

CHINESE-MALAYS, INTERVIEWS RECORDED JUNE 2004, SHEFFIELD HALLAM UNIVERSITY

Constituting 27 per cent of the population, proportionately Malaysia has the largest Chinese community in the region. When the British departed, they left a socio-economic and political system divided along ethnic lines. Since racial riots in 1969, the Government has vigorously promoted the advancement of ethnic Malays. This has involved a quota system and other restrictions on ethnic Chinese in religion, business, education and employment. Chinese Malaysians nevertheless control about half the private-sector economy and, in spite of such restrictions, have actively preserved their culture. The Government still occasionally questions their loyalty (Chin 1998).

Fenton gives examples of Malaysia where differences of custom and practice between Indians, Chinese and Malays are reproduced in everyday life: language, religion and cuisine. Malay Islamic practice – halal meat restricts the practice of commensality – sharing a table – which is the basis of much social exchange). These routine patterns of behaviour and preference are reproduced in everyday social interaction, just as in the Guyanese example. Similarly to Guyana too there are marked economic and political divisions between the three main groups. Everyday examples of difference are exacerbated and collect a negative charge as any marker of difference becomes operationalised as a marker of domination or a reminder of political or economic struggles between the ethnic enclaves.

In Malaysia the political dominance of the native Malays has been formally ascribed into constitutional law. The Bumiputera Movement creates quotas and systems of positive discrimination for these 'sons of the soil' who have maintained political ascendancy. Meanwhile the Chinese have maintained their dominance of the economy and Indians make up the workforce of the nation.

However, to ensure that Malays are not left out of the mainstream economic system, laws were passed that allowed Malays to take a slice of all businesses in the country (even though their role in these businesses could be said to be negligible). Also Malays make up the main student body of public universities, 60–70 per cent of places are reserved for them, whereas Chinese and Indians have to compete for the remaining places, take up positions in expensive private institutions or, of course, study overseas.

Speaking to three Chinese-Malay students, I discussed their feelings about the current social and political relations within the republic.

SS: Could you talk a little about the dynamics and perhaps the boundaries of ethnicity in Malaysia. How does that work for you?

PUENG: We have to come back to during our colonial times under the British. The differences are that the Malays more to the political side, Chinese more on the economic side and Indian is more on the labour side. But after the so-called 1969 May 13th incident[1] – because of the economic gap between these three – the riot arise. So government has come up with our new policy – Desai Economic Baru – a new economic development plan to try and get the three races closer within the main economic trend . . .

SS: Do you feel this harmonising programme is working out?

KAREN: I don't think it's working – it's still improving.

SS: So it's got a way to go yet to achieve its goals?

JAS: But you can still see that some Malays have more politicians and the Chinese, they are still a lot of business and, as for the Indians, they are still maintained as labour.

SS: Could you please explain to us about the Bumiputeras?

PUENG: Er . . . Bumiputeras . . . you can refer to two groups, OK? We can divide it into two categories: one the Malay Malay – the native *orang asli*, someone who has been in the motherland before the Malay immigrants from Indonesia or Philippine Islands came to the peninsula of Malaysia.

SS: Like an indigenous people?

PUENG: Yeah, like the natives in Australia before the English moved there.

SS: How do non-Malays feel about this possibly privileged group? How do you feel about the Bumiputera movement?

PUENG: I must say that they enjoy some sort of privilege . . .

KAREN: A lot!

PUENG: . . . A lot that we don't enjoy – like when purchasing a house they enjoy a 5 per cent discount on any house off the total value – and they enjoy the quota – the education quota in the local public university. Maybe 60–70 per cent of the places are left for them and the rest we have to share among.

KAREN: Well basically Malays are the majority and for Chinese and Indians is a minority – but of course among the three races we feel sometimes it's quite unfair – but that's how it is . . .

PUENG: They can get into the local university easy even though their results may be not as good as the Chinese . . .

JAS: And they can easily just get a loan.

SS: . . . So it's not based on merit?

JAS: No it's much more to quotas.

PEUNG: No it's based on quotas.

KAREN: No . . .

JAS: . . . which most of us find unfair and dissatisfaction.

PUENG: And those companies – if you like to do your business you have to take in at least 30 per cent of bumiputera to work in your company – directors also, 30 per cent – if you want to get involved in a company government project you must have at least one or two Malay directors in your company.

SS: Has the system arisen because there was seen to be some disadvantage for Malay people – in other words that they were poorer at one stage? And this was to reset the balance—was there some of that motive or . . .?

PUENG: I must say that this kind of system exists because of the new economic development, because as I mentioned, most of the Malay they focus on the political side and lose their power in economic side – So that's why the Government, after the riot, they want to get balance, so they must move the company, move the Malay into the main economic stream – so that they set such rules to encourage the Malay to get involved in the economy.

SS: So because the Government itself was heavily represented by Malay Malays.

PUENG: For us you can say it has both advantage and disadvantage as well – because its advantage is to promote the unity among the races. Because our country without those policies might be the next Indonesia where . . .

KAREN: . . . there's no democratic . . .

PUENG: There's no democratic . . . and they treat Chinese very bad like what happened in 19 . . .

KAREN: Yes, very racist.

PUENG: Yeah, very racist, not like today we can share the unity – peaceful life in Malaysia.

---

1 The 13 May 1969 incident referred to here was a major riot in Kuala Lumpur at the time of the federal elections. Long-standing tensions erupted and, in the aftermath the Government imposed emergency powers, suspended the press and the parliament and established a National Operations Council which ultimately functioned as a de-facto government for nearly two years. When the parliament finally reconvened in February 1971, it announced that certain racially sensitive issues, now known as *isu-isu sensitif,* were henceforth not to be openly discussed under any circumstances. This amounted to a decree which forbade any further questioning of the special privileges of the Malays. A contemporary European analyst commented that 'perhaps the most serious consequence of May 13 [. . .] is the apparent decision of the Malaysian rulers to render Malay status inviolable by thought, word, or deed' (Short 1970: 1089).

The alignment of class relations with ethnicity is very marked in the case of Malaysia, as Fenton (1999) convincingly shows. The post-May 13th New Economic Policy (NEP) was designed to reduce poverty (especially to redress the balance in favour of the rural peasantry who were mostly Malays), to break the ethnicity/class structure and to avoid the threat of future violence. In terms of economic success, the NEP was undoubtedly successful although it has not managed to significantly change the predominant ethnic class sections. The problem of rural peasantry in poverty is deeply entrenched and Malays are still highly represented in this sector. The other problem articulated by these young Chinese Malay students, and a source of hurt and resentment, is the draconian policies the Government has in place to disallow any criticism of the inequalities enshrined in state policies. There has been a good deal of criticism both within Malaysia and around the world about the effective gagging of any sort of a free press in the federation and of the Internal Security Act.

Clearly, the Chinese Malays interviewed here, while they recognise the injustices of the Malay-dominated state bureaucracy, find this preferable to the open and violent confrontations that occurred in the past and especially the extreme anti-Chinese ethnic cleansing under Suharto in 1960s Indonesia in which many thousands were killed. Some have equated ethnic conflict with ethnic loyalties based on kinship and extended kinship. This produces a hardening of boundaries and leads to antagonism, violence and conflict. The frustration with the present regime was apparent in these students' concerns and also evident in their comments about the Internal Security Act, suggesting that taking part in political debate in a public place in Malaysia could have severe consequences:

SS: OK, I understood from what you said before that these issues are very sensitive and really not spoken of publicly. And that there is some problem if people speak too publicly about this. Is this the case? What would be the situation in everyday life? Are people concerned? They wouldn't talk publicly?

KAREN: They'd be thrown into prison . . .

JAS: [*laughs*]

KAREN: [*nudges Pueng*] Tell them about the . . . ISA.

PUENG: Oh yeah ISA is still not the worser if you don't talk openly. OK if you want to talk in the café with your friends – have a normal conversation – chit-chat – that is OK but you don't try and influence the public on a certain policy, . . .

KAREN: . . . go on a demonstration . . .

PUENG: . . . go on a protest – all those things OK. If you want to openly influence the public you will be retained under the ISA, with which they will detain you . . .

KAREN: . . . without any reason for two years – and after two years you will only be put to court.

PUENG: . . . not without *any* reason – they suspect you. If you get involved in certain activities that may bring harm to the public . . .

KAREN: Ahh, still they don't have to prove it to put you in the prison . . .

PUENG: Yeah, they put you into prison – no visitor – no judgement.

SS: So obviously people are reluctant to demonstrate . . .

PUENG: Yeah, especially those opposition party leaders, they're always being detained under ISA . . .

SS: So it's not really tolerated – too much criticism about the Government?

KAREN: they won't tolerate at all . . .

It would appear that in Malaysia dominant cultural interests are protected by racial quotas and overtly partisan legislation, the ISA

provides for preventive detention for up to two years with the possibility of renewal every two years. Any police officer may, without a warrant, arrest and detain anyone he has 'reason to believe' has acted or likely to act in 'any manner prejudicial to the security of Malaysia.' The act also allows for restrictions on freedom of assembly, association, and expression, freedom of movement, residence and employment. It allows for the closing of schools and educational institutions if they are used as a meeting place for an unlawful organization or for any other reason are deemed detrimental to the interests of Malaysia or the public.

(Human Rights Watch, 21 September, 1998)

In situations like this the state often imposes constraints on democratic freedoms: the press becomes a mere mouthpiece for government viewpoints and opposition parties as well as individual expression and association are heavily restricted.

RELIGION

In 2001, the former prime minister Dr Mahathir Mohammed declared Malaysia an Islamic state. The reaction to 9/11 in Malaysia may lead to a watershed of opinion between moderate and more radical Islamic elements:

> on the one hand, some Malay Muslims may see it fit to de-emphasise their Muslim public image and, on the other, some may now be motivated to profile their Muslim image more strongly, either openly or silently. It is the latter that may worry the Malaysian government which is doing its best to fight against Islamic fundamentalism and extremism. It is not improbable that the opposition Parti Islam would take up this issue and turn it into political capital to attack the ruling party, especially UMNO [United Malays National Organisation], and demonstrate that its strategy to please the West by declaring Malaysia a 'moderate Islamic state' has backfired and could be seen a dismal failure in international diplomacy.
>
> (Shamsul 2002)

The increasing power of the Islamic lobby and its impacts on non-Malays had also been noted by my respondents:

ss: And I heard that in some states holding hands in public would be frowned upon . . .

KAREN: Right it was a year ago . . .

PUENG: Yeah, it's true – it's already happened to some Chinese students.

KAREN: Yeah, I heard the rumours that one of the victims, *tashens*, they were just holding hands in the park, in a public park, when they were confronted by Islamic officers that you are charged with public holding hands. That is not right. Some people are very unsatisfied – because I'm not a Malay – first of all and I'm not under Islamic ruling, so practically this rule does not apply to me – but still they get a fine for it. They got a fine for it – they were lucky they weren't thrown into prison.

The form of internal colonialism, through a policy of containment and control, which is going on in Malaysia, is perhaps viewed as preferable as one of the students suggests, to out and out violence, but the unrest and frustration of those subsumed under the dominant political culture is tangible in these interviews. Malaysia has developed affirmative-action and quota system that, as the interviewees recounted, require businesses over a certain size to have Malay partners and that 'ring fences' 45 per cent of the spots in the public university for Malays. Clearly, a governing class of Malay technocrats has been created. The bitter memories of the violence of 1969 live on, and there is a tense stand-off, which may be more fragile in the face of increasing Islamic militancy.

CONFLICT RESOLUTION

Conflict can take many forms from the tense stagemanaged inter-ethnic harmony of Guyana and Malaysia, where there are struggles for symbolic domination in a game of cricket, places at the local university and political and economic rivalry, through to full-scale inter-ethnic violence. The causes are many and complex and often (as in the cases reviewed) have a long and inglorious history that has been marked either by colonial rule (Malaysia, Guyana, Rwanda, Egypt, Algeria) or super-power intervention (Guyana, Afghanistan, Iraq, Iran and scores of others). The possible solutions of conflicts where there is a desire for self-determination are of two kinds: coercive and non-coercive.

Secession is rarely successful. There are a number of movements currently: Chechens in Russia, Basques in Spain, Quebeckers in Canada, Sikhs in India. The majority ethnic group which forms the state fights to retain those territories in question. The coercive means of resolving conflicts are all too familiar, and the consequences of such approaches show that they are unworkable and lead to increased violence and human suffering (international involvement often is necessary): elimination, ethnic cleansing, forced assimilation, containment and control.

Ethnic cleansing, which can involve genocide, is witnessed in the ongoing murder of southerners in Sudan, Rwanda in 1994 where the Tutsi minority were slaughtered by the Hutu majority, Bosnian Muslims in the former Yugoslavia in the early 1990s, Cambodians under the Khmer Rouge in the 1970s,[1] East Timorese by Indonesia about the same time. The list is very long before as well as after the Nazi regime. Another form of ethnic cleansing is the inhumane idea of forced

---

1 Despite the global outcry over the slaughter by Pol Pot's Khmer Rouge, this would not have easily occurred without the carpet-bombing of Cambodia by the USA which killed an esti-mated 2.5 million people (see Herman and Chomsky 1995). There are also claims that the USA covertly supported Pol Pot as the Prince Sihanouk regime did not want to become another US client state.

assimilation or homogenisation. In the 1980s, ethnic Turks in Bulgaria were forced to take on Bulgarian names, while mosques were closed and ethnic ceremonies and practices outlawed. Similarly, the mixed children of Aboriginal parents in Australia were removed (often forcibly) from their parents and given new names with white Australian families. Containment policies can starve minorities of resources, oppress them politically or culturally by refusing to accept their languages (e.g. Basque, Catalan, Welsh). These are the types of policy which may take place within a situation of what Hechter has called internal colonialism. Such oppressions often become the focus of resistance movements.

Clearly these approaches lead to greater violence and suffering and do not attempt to resolve the conflict in a collaborative fashion. Less coercive approaches require active recognition of the group in question and can include: autonomy, forms of power sharing, or the multiculturalist approaches discussed earlier.

CHAPTER SUMMARY

Conflict situations can be of several kinds depending on the form of ethnic system. Where there are multiple 'dispersed' groups too small to individually take control of the centre a tacit harmony may exist, but this may dissolve into ethnic rivalry (as witnessed in the Balkans and in the former Soviet territories). Centralised states like Guyana, Trinidad and Fiji may experience increasing polarisation as ethnically based enclaves become mutually exclusive, and ethnic competition for political and economic power becomes a zero sum game. The solution may be to struggle towards a grand coalition which breaks the division into race-based constituencies and refocuses onto an earlier creolised national character.

The causes of conflict can be complex; there are no magic solutions, and we must find ways to get along rather than partitioning the world into tiny pieces. It seems that political intervention may be part of the solution where it can lead to an acceptance of heterogeneity rather than division. All too often the political system itself is a key cause of ethnic disaffection and resentment. In polarised states like Guyana, electoral competition becomes part of the cycle of ethnic violence as allegations of vote rigging and politicisation of ethnic constituencies further polarise the divide (these are often one of the tragic legacies of divisive colonial systems). A thorough and realistic analysis of the sources of the conflict is essential and must take account of the unique features of the rivals involved and make direct reference to the socio-political structures of the society. Donald Horowitz (2003) suggests that despite the enthusiasm of many politicians for secession and separation, they do little to create long term harmony and may exacerbate conflict. Living together is fraught with difficulties but the alternatives are much worse.

EXERCISE 7.1 GUYANA

1 What are stereotypes? What purpose do they serve?
2 List stereotypes you have about ethnic groups.
3 Consider the Guyanese interviews in this chapter. In what way are the stereotyped views they have functional?
4 How might these images of the Other be considered mutually dependent, even complementary?
5 The process of 'creolisation' is a form of cultural adaptation very visible in Caribbean cultures. Why do you think this has not lead to a more harmonious culture in Guyana?
6 Ethnic conflict such as that in Guyana has many possible causes. Which are the most plausible?

EXERCISE 7.2 MALAYSIA

1 Do you recognise key similarities and differences in the Guyana and Malaysia cases of conflict?
2 What aspects of the situation are most likely to appear as threatening to the Chinese Malays?
3 What aspects of the situation are most likely to appear as threatening to the Malay Malays?
4 What is your opinion of 'affirmative action' policies as adopted in Malaysia?
5 How might colonialism have played a role in sowing the seeds for future conflicts in both countries? (This question may require further research.)

EXERCISE 7.3

1 What policy initiatives might improve the situation in both countries?
2 How far are conflicts such as those in Guyana and Malaysia concerned with class and the relationship to the means of production?
3 How far are the conflicts in Guyana and Malaysia to do with what Žižek has called 'theft of enjoyment'?
4 Look at the definitions of genocide and ethnic cleansing. Are there other acts, crimes against humanity, that should be included?
5 When could the United Nations intervene in a situation of ethnic cleansing or genocide? How much power should the UN be given? Should such intervention be brokered with other regional organisations?

CHAPTER 8

Living the Contradiction

> Identity politics must be based not only on identity, but on an appreciation for politics as the art of living together.
>
> (Phelan 1989: 170)

> Home is where I want to be/But I guess I'm already there . . .
> (David Byrne (Talking Heads), 'This must be the place (naive melody)',
> from *Speaking in Tongues* (1983), Sire Records 23883-1)

DIASPORA AND HYBRIDITY

BOX 8.1 BUXTON, GUYANA 1991

'Dis-en-chant-ment'. Disen-chant-ment'. Louis dreamily segmented the word savouring its nuances; speaking it like a spell into the gathering dusk of Buxton. Goats, chickens, assorted croaking, bleetings, yelps, late kiskadees, laced in the mellow lugubrious musak spilling from the rumshop; an over-drowsy saxophone waltzes from the horn of a drunken b-side busker. Two gangly Indian figures worked by the roadside husking coconuts and collecting for copra, exhausting endless work.

Louis's apparent worldly musings on the word seemed to embody a history of broken dreams, not especially his, but of the country itself – if not the world. Yet enchantment – the bonds of colonialism and empire – a misty nostalgia for the 'mother country' was alive and pulsing in his voice, in the faraway look he cast across cane fields, the polders. The spell still cast its magic deep in the folds and resonances of his voice.

(S. Spencer, field notes, 1991)

The above sketch from rural Guyana attempts to capture the poignant feeling of the colonial (post-colonial subject) for whom there may be many layers of memory for the lost but dreamed-of communities, never seen but imagined and ingrained in family history, in tales of the brutality of slavery and constantly remembered in the broken and dissolute condition of the towns and in the origins of the sugar cane. A sad and distant memory indelibly stamped with the trauma of removal and dispossession. Populations who have been removed from their cultural background, divested of traditions, prey to a sort of cultural forgetting. African-Guyanese people, like Louis in the above example, are the descendants of slaves, part of a *victim* **diaspora**.[1] The Indian-Guyanese in the example on pp. 177–8 make up what has been named *labour* diasporas; their fathers arrived as part of the waves of indentured labour that replaced slavery. Both groups could also be considered part of a *hybrid* diaspora as they are the result of creolised influences of colonialism.

Diaspora: the term which has come to be used for this post-colonial sense of dislocation has also come to convey the dream of a homeland, a shrine of the past where the flame of memory is kept alive for the migrant group. Yet the return to some idealised pre-colonial culture is perhaps more a symbol than an attainable reality. A number of religious and messianic cults embody this idealised culture: Rastafarianism and **Kali Mai** sects in the Caribbean have been influential for their promises of deliverance from the increasingly difficult reality of grinding poverty as international debts have bitten hard into the economies of the region. As conditions have deteriorated, the growth of these forms of religion have been seen to increase (see Bassier 1980). 'Thus, colonised peoples cannot simply turn back to the idea of a collective pre-colonial culture, and a past "which is waiting to be found, and which when found, will secure our sense of ourselves into eternity"' (Hall 1994: 182).

Hall maintains this aspect of diaspora is not a romantic naïveté that stubbornly holds fast to an imagined idealised past but rather a symbol of a new becoming:

---

1 Cohen (1997) gives five types of diaspora.

it is no mere phantasm either. It is something – not a mere trick of the imagination. It has its histories – and histories have their real, material and symbolic effects. The past continues to speak to us. But it no longer addresses us as a simple, factual 'past', since our relation to it, like the child's relation to the mother, is always-already 'after the break'.

(Hall 1994: 183)

Grossberg suggests that 'diaspora emphasises the historically spatial fluidity of identity, its articulation to structures of historical movements (whether forced or chosen, necessary or desired)' (Grossberg 1996: 92). The 'diaspora space' is a critical concept created by the tensions of power between old and new identities, in which the parameters of inclusion, exclusion, otherness and belonging are challenged. This may be a useful way of envisaging post-colonial relations as it places both natives and migrants in the same conflicted and negotiated space: 'diaspora space as a conceptual category is "inhabited" not only by those who have migrated and their descendants but equally by those who are constructed and represented as indigenous' (Brah 1996: 181). This is a space that recognises the reciprocal affects for those established 'natives' as well as for migrant groups, hence it is a radical re-configuration of the centre/periphery relationship implicit, as Soysal argues (2000), in the common use of 'diaspora', which reaffirms the centrality of the nation-state with all its ethno-centrism and chauvinism. However, the 'diaspora space' developed by Brah subverts this meaning, for although migrants and established communities are not equal they are each recognised to be in flux, destabilised and hybrid.

In our pluralistic societies there are now several generations of migrant groups. This section looks at issues of belongingness, citizenship, sense of home and the forming of identities across boundaries. Colonialism displaced millions of people forcibly or, for the promise of a better life, under indentureship which in many cases was not far removed from slavery. This 'body snatching' as Sharrad (1993) has described it, has had a profound and continuous impact on the world. How do those children of many diasporas see themselves and their place in society? How easily are they accepted by the mainstream culture?

The concept of hybridity has come to be one of the cornerstones of post-colonial thought. In his essays, Stuart Hall suggests that there is something significant developing within our multicultural diasporic communities. Posed next to the globalising forces that seem to be suturing together world cultures, creating more homogenous 'third cultures' – there are equally powerful social processes that, quite to the contrary, seem to be unravelling these global certainties; unitary definitions of nation and identity are eroded away. Hall, Gilroy and Bhabha have all been proponents of a fluid, hybrid conception of ethnic identity, which insists that the notion of 'rooted' identities is a delusion. Instead, discussion which centres around the celebration of more marginal, creolised, diasporic voices, which recognises 'the transgressive potential of cultural hybridity' (May et al. 2004: 132). In *Signs Taken For Wonders*, Bhabha identifies post-colonial hybridities as a source for new subjectivities and as locations for alternative strategies of resistance to colonial power. He borrows from a number of lexicons expressing the subtle and elusive nature of hybridity which is also the reason for its power (1985: 153–4):

> Hybridity is the sign of the productivity of colonial power, its shifting forces and fixities; it is the name for the strategic reversal of the process of domination through disavowal (that is, the production of discriminatory identities that secure the 'pure' and original identity of authority).

The state of being in between cultures is a reality for migrants as we have seen but, by the same token, the flow of migrants has a reciprocal influence on the indigenous population – in the diaspora space where struggles and adaptations take place. However, there are discursive rela-tions of power operating within this interactive space. In Britain, the notorious 'rivers of blood' speech made by Enoch Powell in 1968 mobilised native fears of a lost (yet always hard to define) 'British way of life' and, as Gilroy (2004) suggests, provided the justification for many a pre-emptive strike like the one that took Stephen Lawrence's life in 1993 (On 22 April 1993 Stephen Lawrence was murdered in a racist attack.) . . . Racist violence provides an easy means to 'purify' and rehomogenize the nation (Gilroy 2004: 111)' There are challenges to the idea of hybridity and not just from the mainstream culture. For example, there have been strands of ethnic separatism operating in the midst of these pluralities. As we have seen, there is resistance to mixing, and 'mixed race' or hybrid identities are often seen as transgressive and at times are treated as a threat (perhaps a threat to the collective power of ethnic essentialism).

Despite much conjecture about a 'multicultural drift' in the UK, the insistence on the preservation of a nation-state is certainly strong in western governments recently. Recent debates about the consequences of 9/11, global politics and the ensuing 'war against terror' in the West, and about identifications of members of the Muslim community in our inner cities has yielded some interesting pictures of these dynamic and fluid identities.

A recent BBC Radio 4 broadcast entitled *Don't Call Me Asian* by Sarfraz Manzoor examined the politics of identity of young British Asians. It seems that there is a resurgence of religious identities, amongst Hindus and Sikhs as well as Muslims. They are eschewing the descriptor of themselves as 'Asian' in favour of more specific religious identifications. There was also the suggestion that a number were making a conscious decision to distance themselves from Muslims, who have been demonised since the attempts to link Islam with terrorism after 9/11. There seems to be a trend for some Asians to emphasise their religious identities in reaction to the stigmatised identity of Islam, which they had experienced as a spoiled identity. Merely looking Asian could inspire racist abuse. This is not a sudden change, however, as many Asians have been critical of this homogenised Balkanised cultural branding for years. It was enough to bring down the ire of one of Britain's consecrated black spokesmen, Darcus Howe, who saw this as another fragmentation of lost essentialist identity and even as undermining to Britain's secular society. The remnants of the old Left – amongst which Darcus is clearly proud to be counted – find identity politics (whether to hyphenate or not) ideologically unpalatable. Howe commented in the *New Statesman*:

> And what of the vast number of young Asians who are Sikhs, Hindus, Muslims only in name and do not wish to be saddled with a religious label? [. . .] Manzoor is going down a rocky road. Those of us who came from former colonies to the UK first defined ourselves as 'black', presenting a united front as we entered the struggle against racism. Margaret Thatcher led the demonisation of our communities; she claimed that we had swamped this country with an alien culture. The pace of the struggle quickened, and successful Indians and Pakistanis demanded to be known as 'brown'. They were saying to our detractors that they were closer to white people than to us darkies and therefore merited better treatment.
>
> (Howe 2005)

Well known for courting controversy, Howe's hyperbole is probably only slightly tongue in cheek. Certainly, the strategic value of the term 'black' was recognised by a spectrum of Asians and others. In the US, even Koreans and Cypriots have been known to align themselves strategically in this way. It seems clear that the reasons why people identify with religion or with more secular descriptors or politically motivated standpoints can be many and various. Certainly some identities become stigmatised and the reality is that to be a Muslim in Britain today is to be treated as an embodiment of a tradition characterised as fundamentalist and anti-western. The suggestion that religion divides more than common ethnicity unites may be regarded as politically unsound by some, but is inevitable in the light of a divisive 'war on terror'.

Hybridity, as a theoretical concept, also receives criticism from many directions. Here are a few examples:

- That hybridity presupposes 'the prior existence of pure, fixed separate antecedents as with the race theorists in the Nineteenth Century'. Young's critique (1995) suggests that the new cultural theory of hybridity implicitly legitimates race thinking.
- Others, such as Stephen May, suggest that advocating hybridity encourages the view 'that all group-based identities are essentialist'. And, further, that while the world is increasingly fragmented into fractured identities – these identities are generally *not* hybrid; just the opposite in fact (May 2004: 133).

- The 'subversive potential once invested in notions of hybridity has been subjected to pre-millennial downsizing. Indeed hybridity has spun through the fashion cycle so rapidly that it has come out the other end looking wet and soggy' (Mercer 2000: 510).
- Modood comments that the reaction against essentialism can lead to excesses in the other direction that are 'inherently destructive' because 'Reconciled to multiplicity as an end in itself, its vision of multiculturalism is confined to personal lifestyles and cosmopolitan consumerism and does not extend to the state, which it confidently expects to wither away' (Modood 2000: 178).
- Valdaverde (1995) commented in a book review that Gilroy and other hybridity writers' discussions of hybridity tend to be weakened by a 'romanticism of the in-between that is perhaps more politically palatable but no more theoretically sound than the romanticism of identity politics'.
- Hybridity fails to address adequately the social and political continuities and transformations that underpin individual and collective action in the real world (May 2000: 134). Indeed, in the real world, May, citing Ahmad (1995: 14), suggests political agency is historically anchored to time place and sense of 'stable commitment to one's class or gender or nation.'

These theorists draw up a reality checklist, warning against self-congratulatory discourses of hybridity which, carried away by a sort of anti-essentialist euphoria seem to float away from the realities of everyday material existence in multicultural societies. However, as Les Back reminds us, at some level hybridity is a fact. By using the term 'the fact of hybridity', he is insisting that hybridity is not a mere intellectual construct but reflects the truth that human lives are inseparably intertwined, there are overlapping histories that make the total separation of the self an impossibility (Back 2000: 450). The following conversations present some of the real-life experiences of living 'between cultures', not as a romanticised concept but as a challenging and at times painful negotiation between attitudes and values that are resistant to merging.

BRITISH-BORN CHINESE (BBC)

The experience of hybridity, as we have explained it, relates to the sense of dislocation. This sense of being in between cultures is a complex one, and as can be seen, relates also to generational, gender and class differences. Mark Quah's interview demonstrates the manner in which individuals attempt to navigate their place in the culture, drawing on some concepts that they feel reflect their developing identity and dis-identification with others who may seem to trap them into stereotypical roles.

British-Born Chinese, border crossings. Interviews by Mark Quah

This case study is based upon interviews with British-Born Chinese people. It brings attention to the tenacity used to negotiate cultural boundaries and the confusion that ensues when boundaries are regarded as closed or impassable. The interviews were conducted with the aim of uncovering shared experiences amongst second-generation BBCs that had, up to this point, often been hidden from view even amongst and between British Chinese people themselves.

Win lives in Sheffield. He is twenty years old, a full-time student and also works part-time in his parents' take-away. He attends Chinese school where he learns how to speak, read and write Cantonese

MARK: Do you think it's a positive thing, having a British perspective and a Chinese perspective? Or do you find it confusing?

WIN: Probably confusing at times[,] because you don't know where you fit in[,] it's difficult[.] You need to find an answer for yourself I think[,] where do you think you belong[?] Which is right for you[,] and if you think that's right you're just gonna go for it [. . .] Like where do you belong[?] where's your identity[?] Is it disappeared[?] It's like disappearing in the western world isn't it[?] The more you think about it [. . .] It's like the next generation and the next generation [. . .] and get worse [. . .] like Americans they've lost it[.] Like whenever I go on holiday it's like[,] or any BBC[,] the first thing they want to do is eat British food[,] isn't it[?] Not Chinese food[,] so where's the first place they look? [. . .] McDonald's[,] and they want to eat it everyday[.] like my brother[,] he just eats McDonald's, McDonald's, McDonald's when he could eat something else[,] but he doesn't want to 'cos he wouldn't know it [. . .] his taste [is] all British.

Will is a student. He grew up in Manchester and works part-time in his parents' restaurant during the weekends and holiday time.

WILL: If you're in a Chinese community[,] you just naturally go into a sort of Chinese community state[,] a Chinese state[,] when you're with English people in English society you just act more English type[.] So it's not really I can do this in a Chinese community and then I can change over to that in an English community[,] it just comes naturally to you.

At the time of this interview Eve was twenty years old and a full-time student. As she described it, there was a sizable Chinese community in the places where she grew up.

EVE: I'm very much part of this British society but also I very strongly identify with being Chinese and more specifically with Hong Kong [. . .] you feel like you don't properly belong[,] like you belong to either set British or Chinese[,] but they don't see you as part of them so [. . .]

MARK: Win[,] what's life at home[?] Did your parents stress to you you're Chinese[?] Act this way [. . .] or you're Chinese you shouldn't act that way [?]

WIN: At home like your parents try to bring you into Chinese but if you don't want to learn they can't make you[,] basically it's for yourself to sort of like judge if you want to learn like[.] When you're like brought up accustomed to all these things isn't it[?] You're brought up to like[,] say dating they prefer you to marry your own race isn't it[?]

MARK: yeah[,] my mum says that [. . .]

WIN: [. . .] whereas if you don't they'll be disappointed but when you have kids like they'll probably forgive you innit[?]

MARK: Yeah

WIN: In Hong Kong you get called banana boy[!] [laughs]

MARK: One thing with me is one girl from Hong Kong she was speaking to me and she's speaking English with a Chinese accent[,] and fair enough it's not her first language[,] I don't take the piss [. . .]

WIN: [. . .] yeah we don't take the piss [. . .]

MARK: [. . .] and I say a few words in Cantonese to her, she laughs, yeah

WIN: That's [. . .] the way it is[.]

MARK: sometimes that makes me feel like giving up why should I make an effort if [. . .?]

WIN: You can laugh at [them], if you want [. . .]

MARK: it's not me though [. . .]

WIN: 'Very good!' [Chinese accent] 'Very good!' [. . .] We don't really do that though[,] we're less likely to take the piss out of them [. . .]

MARK: There's something strange[,] here we get taken the piss by the English guys and Chinese but we don't take the piss out of either, yeah [. . .]

WIN: Both of them think they're better than us [. . .]

MARK: Did your parents say to you be proud to be Chinese[?]

WIN: Yeah they say it's good to be Chinese [–] I think it's good to be Chinese but there's some[,] I know some[,] Chinese people that reject [. . .] they

don't like being Chinese and stuff like that[,] which is weird if you're
brought up that way[.]

MARK: What does being Chinese mean to you[?]

WIN: Everything basically[,] life[,] the way I study[,] the way I talk[,]
characteristics[,] everything – so I'm proud to be Chinese[.]

Mark and his respondents have a strong if conflicted sense of identity and are
conscious of navigating between cultures. The middle ground is hard to find as
it is constantly clawed back by each culture. Terms like 'banana boy' may be used
by some who are grounded in the home culture. In Hong Kong to suggest that
the hybrid individual has a veneer an outward appearance of 'Chineseness' which,
if scrutinised will reveal a white English core. However, the social mores that the
Hong Kong Chinese person aspires to may, it is suggested, be those very white
European attributes and cultural knowledges that the above respondents cannot
disguise.

The next interview further strengthens this assessment of hybrid identity. Stuart
is a British Born Chinese in his twenties. Articulating a strong sense of his Chinese
identity, which endures despite his Englishness, Stuart recognises identity as almost
physically ascribed, similar to the way in which Mauss talks of the habitus as
internalised dispositions or bodily orientations (Mauss 1979). He also notes the
automatic nature of racisms that employ well-worn stereotypes and assumptions
about Chinese people.

BOX 8.2 BETWEEN TWO CULTURES

SS: First could you tell us a little about yourself Stuart?

STUART: OK, I was born in England in Leicester, spent most of my life in
the UK, went over to Hong Kong when I was about seven for a year so
I adapted to the culture then, but most of my life I've been in the UK.
But I feel that – even though I've only lived in Hong Kong for a year, in
my heart I still feel Chinese. Even though my behaviour is very English
– I still feel inside my heart I'm very Chinese. I have friends in Hong Kong
who are totally Chinese, when they come to England they want to
be English – even though their experience of life is Chinese – they want
to be English, whereas me I'm opposite: I'm totally English behaviour
and in my heart it's very Chinese.

SS: That's interesting then that there are these different aspirations that people from Hong Kong have got, the English side of it – they've got the colonial thing – and you've been over here [. . .]

STUART: [. . .] yeah I'm the opposite [. . .]

SS: [. . .] you're looking over that way [. . .]

STUART: [. . .] but I strongly believe that this is me[,] I'm one individual[,] everyone's different [–] OK my experiences have brought me the person I am[,] yeah[,] even though I was born in Hong Kong or China I would be the same[,] but even so my environment would have shaped me to a degree to the person I am [–] my inner self [–] I still believe would have been the same but different like[,] maybe slight differences outside in what I perceive[,] but inside my heart I still believe I'd be a Chinese human being[.]

SS: Have your parents had a big influence on the fact do you think[?] I mean do they keep the cultural traditions going quite strongly[?]

STUART: I personally think that Chinese as a whole whether you're born in the UK[,] America[,] Hong Kong[,] China[,] the values[,] morals are very deep rooted[,] it's passed on from generation to generation[.] That's the bottom line[,] the bottom line[,] the basis for Chinese humanity[,] the bottom values and like[,] the cornerstone to build it on[.] So whether you're born in UK[,] Hong Kong[,] China[,] you still have this deep-rooted tradition[,] culture which is embedded[.] It's hard to like to disassemble[,] it's deep rooted[.] [*Makes building motions with his hands simulating bricks and mortar.*]

SS: Yeah [. . .] so presumably you've learnt some of the languages which embody the culture as well[.] I mean having to learn that [–] I mean that embodies all of the cultural traditions presumably[?]

STUART: It's true what you say because like in psychology[,] I can't remember who it is now [–] they say the language itself will shape the personality[.] We have words like rice that is cooked and uncooked[,] you only have rice (you don't know if it's cooked or uncooked)[.] Your mum's brother or your dad's brother there's different words for it you just say 'uncle' what can it be[?] So we have more different sorts of words that can add to the meanings and that [–] icy[,] rainy cold [–] we have different words and that [–] so obviously that's going to affect your vocabulary and your knowledge of how you say things in life[.] But that's just a part of it [–] I think mostly it's to do with the individual[,] yourself[,] you as a person[.] [. . .] It's like with me my experiences in the UK people say that there's no racism[.] Then in the end I believe I'm Chinese[,] whether I'm black or white[,] I believe that we're human beings and we live in this world and you cannot possibly as a human being put yourself above another human being [–] not everyone is like that some people are more narrow-minded[,] some are like, I don't know[,] disturbed in the head[,] I don't know[,] but some people are like that[.] In this world we are seen as one thing [–] we can't just get on with one another [–] people just resent you jealousy[,] envy[,] I don't know[,] it's just human nature to be like that[,] irrespective of your colour[.] So in my upbringing [–] I went to school in England [–] but lucky for me I had brothers and they all just assume that because your brothers do kung fu that you do kung fu[.] It's like stereotypical thing about Chinese [. . .]

SS: [. . .] What[?] The kung fu[?]

STUART: Yeah[,] it's always the case[,] always the case [. . .]

SS: Do you ever feel that you're stuck in between two cultures?

STUART: Yeah yeah [–] because people always assume black white[,] black white[,] it's not[.] The way I look at it is black[,] green[,] none white and white[,] ethnic minorities and white[.] On the exterior say it's cosmopolitan[,] equal opportunities but in the heart[,] deep rooted[,] there's still that resentment[,] that hatred for colours[,] that's the bottom line[.] OK [. . .] First, I see myself as a human being then I see myself as an Oriental[,] Far East[,] not an Asian[,] Far East – Oriental[,] Middle East is like Arabs and that[.] Then I see myself as an ethnic minority[.] So I see myself as a human being[,] Chinese[,] oriental[,] ethnic minority[,] then coloured[,] non-white[.] So when I see an Oriental with a white European[,] an Asian[,] a black African[,] I don't give a shit[,] if they're happy they're happy[.]

(Recorded 16 February 2005)

Stuart's identification with a primordial sense of Chineseness comes through strongly, a foundation that is structured in the language but arguably, as Stuart says, goes further, suggesting an embodied sense of being Chinese.

Many migrants are only short-term: they travel for work or education and return after a period of months or years to their countries. However, this temporary immersion in a culture so different may, at times, bring about transformations. Inhabiting the 'diaspora space' may enable unique perspectives and comparisons for both the visitors and the people they associate with. This is certainly the case in the next interview in which a Mexican subject, Diego, who was a research student in the UK and, after several years, developed a critical detachment. There are several points of comparison made throughout the exchange and Diego was able to recognise flaws with his country (as well as with the UK) despite an obvious pride and a deep-seated sense of the country as a moulding influence. Diego expresses the sense that ethnic identity is not an issue in his community due to the relatively homogenous composition (at least superficially). However, the issue of the Chiapas uprising has allowed many Mexicans like Diego to consider a side of themselves that Diego suggests is typically denied.

CONTRASTING NORMS BETWEEN THE UK AND MEXICO

SS: You will soon be back in Mexico [–] and I was wondering what contrasts you expect to notice having lived here in the UK for several years[?]

DIEGO: When I arrived here[,] if there is a health problem and you have to go to the doctor[,] here in the UK you have to wait because there is a queue and you have to respect this[,] and you cannot make use of other people [–] we call this 'traffic of influence' when you make use of other people in order to take advantage of this. And for me this represents a big impact [–] because in Mexico it's very common that you should have something like a file and each record in the file represents a contact[,] maybe I should say 'traffic of contacts' I'm not sure[,] a contact for medical problems[,] for example[,] and a contact for education problems[,] a contact for administrative problems[,] a contact for tax problems [. . .] a contact for everything[.]

SS: Right[,] so people in influence who can help you out [. . .]

DIEGO: Right and that doesn't exist here[,] and now when I go back [–] I hate that [–] I prefer to go to the tail of the queue [–] I just want the same treatment or the same deal as everyone else[.] So this was a big impact for me [. . .] [*laughs*] My Mexican friends disagree with me they think this is not the real situation[.] At the end I do not fit in my country [–] in the Mexican culture [–] of course I love my country[,] but I hate corruption[,] I hate all of those things so [. . .]

SS: You suggested there is a language of this corruption[,] you call it *la transa*[?]

DIEGO: Yes[,] of course[,] *la transa* is part of our lifestyle [–] it's part of us[.] I'm sure if you were able to remove this habit of our culture[,] I'm sure that we'd be a very different culture [–] I think we should speak like English[,] German[,] American[.] Gringos, For example you can go to an academic meeting[,] a conference[,] you can ask many many questions and there isn't any problem if you disagree with the guy[.] In Mexico it's a bit difference[.] If you express your disagreement there is a problem [–] my impression is that we are very sensitive persons[.]

SS: So things are taken personally[?]

DIEGO: Yes[,] yes we take things personally[.]

SS: Just talking about identity again[,] Mexico has quite interesting different layers of ethnic identity[.] What's your impression of how that operates in everyday life [–] is it a big factor [–] the ethnic identity of people[?]

DIEGO: In this aspect it's very difficult for me to give an opinion to you[.] I live in the northern part of the country[,] and I think you can perceive this in the capital and the south of the country because in the capital and the south it is very common that you can see these groups[,] but not in the north[.]

SS: Do you think the history of people all over Mexico is really the history of these different mixtures of groups in the country[?] I'm just wondering what impact that has on personal identity and how people look at themselves[?]

DIEGO: At the end we all know that we are a mixture of indigenous and Spanish people[,] but my perception is that we are racist persons[.] There is a racism[,] my perception is that we don't want to recognise that there is indigenous in each Mexican [–] that's my perception. Maybe the origin[,] part of the problem in Chiapas. The conditions in which indigenous people live in Chiapas was very[,] very poor[,] ten years ago with Zapatism[.]

SS: Do you think the Zapatista movement actually had an impact on the average Mexican's feelings about these things[?]

DIEGO: Yes[,] yes[,] I think that the problem's still there[.] The current President claimed in his campaign that he would be able to solve the problem in just five minutes, and in four years he hasn't solved anything[.] But yes I think it's not the same Mexico as before and after Zapatism [–] even when many people don't agree with the movement[.] I think it's not the same[.] At least we are conscious about the problem that indigenous people have[,] but before we ignored all these things[.]

(Recorded June 2004)

The above interview implies that Mexicans tended to deny their own indigenous heritage, and the treatment of the indigenous population has long been harsh and unjust. The indigenous groups in the border region of Chiapas live in appalling conditions with few rights over the land, although some communities exercise considerable local control over economic and social issues. They continue to remain largely outside the country's political and economic mainstream and, in many cases, they have minimal participation in decisions affecting their land, cultural traditions and the allocation of natural resources. These powerless people of Mayan ancestry, with Sub-Commandante Marcos at their head, drew attention to their plight and the movement developed an international following and a strong identification with the two iconic figures Marcos and Zapata. There was a magical moment in which the mythic quality of the uprising held world attention as an unlikely challenge to the hegemony of global marketing. The uprising was timed symbolically to the day the North American Free Trade Agreement (NAFTA) came into effect. The impact of the agreement was perceived as a death sentence to indigenous cultures as it allowed the break-up and privatisation of land used collectively (*ejidos*) upon which the many indigenous farmers in Mexico survive.

Zapata's significance for Mexico and the importance of land rights to the peasantry had become again a powerful symbol for the emancipation of these sons of the soil. Many Mexicans, like Diego, must have been deeply affected by these events. The Zapatistas became a focus for cultural renewal and identification with the origins of Mexican society. This illustrates how aspects of a country's shared traditions can revitalise ethnic identification and can become the focus for a deep re-examination of the hybrid nature of the country, a truth that has been denied and an identity which has been coded as 'primitive'. The image of Zapata is installed deeply in the Mexican psyche, seen around Mexico City in the murals of Diego Rivera (at the Presidential Palace in the Zocalo) and as a station sign for the underground train (see Figure 8.1). It was in this vast central square that the Zapatista's historic march from Chiapas culminated:

> On 13 March 2001 the Zapatista column came to Mexico City. It was the culmination of an extraordinary three-week march through Mexico, accompanied by tens of thousands on its way. The delegation attended the Indigenous People's Conference before moving on to the capital, where it was met by a huge crowd in Mexico City's main square – the Zócalo. The British media contemptuously described the crowd as 'several thousands strong' – but anyone who has ever stood in that vast colonial square knows that 'several thousands' would barely occupy one corner. There were hundreds of thousands there.
>
> (Gonzalez 2001: 1)

Indeed, estimates of 300,000 or more have been given. This was undoubtedly an event of enormous symbolic importance, even if the conditions in Chiapas have changed little apart from a small measure of autonomy and accommodation from the Government including the removal of some of the troops from the region. As Mike Gonzalez (2001) suggests, this was extraordinary in enabling the 'representativity' of indigenous peoples on a global platform, because of the advocacy of Sub-Commandante Marcos.

Figure 8.1 Zapata sign for underground station Zapata in Mexico City

There was no doubt that this was a historic victory for Mexico's indigenous people. But it had other consequences and implications. The Zapatistas, above all through the prolific writing of Subcomandante Marcos, claimed a representativity – a right to speak for a movement of many struggles united against globalisation and its impact. This is the central reason why the Zapatistas have come to symbolise the anti-capitalist movement worldwide. Yet the negotiations behind the accords, and the agreements themselves, narrowed and limited the nature of the Zapatistas' demands. Slowly, imperceptibly, and with the collusion of many of their external supporters, the Zapatistas were redefined as a movement exclusively concerned with indigenous rights.

(Gonzalez 2001: 2)

The plight of indigenous people in Mexico may not have changed in any substantial way as a result, but it could be suggested (as Diego said) that now there is a new popular perception of both the plight of native Indians as well as a way of broaching the question about a facet of most Mexicans' hybrid identity that was always denied before the Zapatistas. This was a movement that captured popular imagination and reinvoked images from Mexico's revolutionary foundations.

More recently, there have been further disruptions to the collective psyche of Mexicans. A new book by Marco Polo Hernández Cuevas (2005) suggests that Mexico may have a strong African heritage, as an estimated 300,000 African slaves were brought to Mexico during the colonial era. The suggestion made by Hernández Cuevas is that this large number were absorbed into the population and that some prominent national leaders during Mexico's revolution were black. However, it seems that there has been a policy to systematically erase African heritage (as well as indigenous antecedents) from national memory. Hernández Cuevas recognises the importance of reclaiming lost histories in forging identity and links this shared heritage to peoples throughout the Americas, 'Mexicans, Hispanics, Latinos and African Americans will recognize one another in our common African heritage and bridge the gap that divides us' (2005: 2). Someone who so effectively portrayed Mexico's rich cultural mixture heritage without recourse to 'whitening' the makers of Mexican history was Diego Rivera who painted the extraordinary series of murals depicting Mexico's turbulent history; these paintings surround the walls of the National Palace in Mexico City.

Figure 8.2 Beginning the struggle – Zapatistas in San Cristobal de Las Casas 1991

The struggle for 'Tierra y Libertad' was reignited by the Zapatistas in 1994. This time the enemy was the global forces of capitalism (see Figure 8.2). The struggle became an exciting rallying point for Left politics worldwide. However, slightly removed from some of the leftist rhetoric, but equally significant, is the emergent identity of a post-colonial society still in the shadow of a European self-image – a self-image that is apparently beginning to unravel.

The way that national identity is forged, as we have seen, often involves attempts to disguise or revise significant historical occurrences, to excise aspects of colonial history that seem to reflect badly on the proud image of nationhood. However, the past thirty years have seen increasing awareness of the multi-ethnic, plural nature of many western cities. There is a new confidence, a more mature expression of diversity than before, but how pluralism should be managed is an issue for considerable discussion and disagreement. Futhermore, much of the debate around multiculturalism in Europe is set against an increasingly open racism based around anti-Muslim sentiments. Le Pen in France was the focal point for this, and his meteoric rise reflected that Muslims were the new demonised group.

MULTICULTURALISM

In the 1980s in several western countries, the discourse of multiculturalism was being consecrated and enshrined in policy. In Australia a new ministry, Immigration and Ethnic Affairs, was instituting educational and other policies at the local level, and significant amounts of research and academic concern with the new ethos made it a very public and highly respected approach. In the UK, in the grip of Thatcher's radical Right, Labour councils were sites for research into pluralism in ethnicity, gender, sexualities, age, disability and combinations of these. The rate-capping of these outposts eventually curtailed some very interesting research.

The discourse of multiculturalism attained respectability, seen as progressive and a positive break from the ugliness of nationalism. In Australia, where a 'White Australia Policy' had been in place into the 1970s, multiculturalism seemed to be an antidote to the essentialist views that tarnished Australia's image. But today it is presented by an increasing number of academics as conservative and even reactionary.

History and the conception of the multicultural state

Britain, France, the USA and Australia are broadly comparable since the 1960s. All three have largely abandoned their policies of 'out-and-out assimilation' (Grillo 1998: 168). They now embrace more pluralistic solutions described variously as 'integration', 'insertion', or 'multiculturalism' (Grillo 1998: 168). This movement in Britain was partly a response to the degree of jingoism and patriotic fervour noted in political discourse during the 1980s, including the Conservative Government's rhetoric over the Falklands War. Jingoism and xenophobia were regularly used by the tabloid press, especially when commenting on the European Union. Also, as Grillo suggests, 'Britain seemed an increasingly ugly, nationalistically minded society. The lager-swilling young men rampaging through the cities of Europe dressed in Union Jack shorts and T-shirts may have been untypical, but they offered a compelling, and repellent, vision of the new Britain' (Grillo 1998: 168).

What is multiculturalism?

Fleras defines 'multiculturalism' as 'a set of principles, policies, and practices for accommodating diversity as a legitimate and integral component of society' (Fleras 1994: 26). The way these policies come about and how they are manifest varies considerably, depending on national context. For Canada, the USA and the UK, the term is implicitly linked with questions of racialised differences. In Canada and Australia official policies have been launched (Australia in 1978–9 and Canada in 1988), while in the UK there has simply been an unofficial 'multicultural drift' (Hall 2000). In Australia and elsewhere, as Gunew (1999) comments,

> While there have always been migrations and disaporas, after two world wars and many other conflicts this century the mix of people within borders increasingly rendered traditional national models anachronistic. Multiculturalism has been developed as a concept by nations and other aspirants to geo-political cohesiveness who are trying to represent themselves as homogeneous in spite of their heterogeneity.
>
> (Gunew 1999)

Further, Gunew correctly notes that the concept, as a result, is considered a revisionist one that implies 'an identity politics based on essentialism and claims for authenticity which automatically reinstate a version of the sovereign subject and a concern with reified notions of origins. Thus it becomes impossible, it seems, to mention multiculturalism and socially progressive critical theory in the same breath' (Gunew 1999).

Hall suggests that multiculturalism functions in a similar way to diaspora – as a means of reifying and fixing cultural distinctions and of drawing hard-edged boundaries to demarcate ethnicity. Hence, an ostensibly well-meaning approach to diversity may create similar divisions to one that is founded on racist principles: 'this is what my friend Farand Maharaj has called sometimes "a spook look-alike apartheid logic": apartheid coming back to meet you from the other side' (Hall 2000).

It is important to recognise that the ideal and intent of multiculturalism may be confused with the practice and reality of multiculturalism. Racism still exists in spite of multiculturalism, and ethnic inequalities in income and political participation have not been removed. There is still very unequal treatment of some minorities in education, employment and the justice system.

While these are legitimate complaints, multiculturalism is not responsible for racism. It could just as well be argued that there is not enough multiculturalism. Malik has argued that discourses of diversity and difference have tended to lead to segregation rather than to more robust anti-racist strategies confronting examples of racism within a mixed community. Racism is able to flourish within the divided communities, cloaked in a politically correct gloss. Separation occurs both spatially (cities such as Bradford have become as segregated as ghettoised areas in the USA) and mentally segregated too – creating not cooperative communal structures but stark internal as well as external divisions (see Malik 2003, BBC2 documentary *Disunited Kingdom*).

Promise and reality: life in a multicultural society

The gradual movement of multiculturalism, which has been fomented by the struggle and strife of nearly fifty years of migration, is not a formally constructed policy like those launched in other nations, but what Stuart Hall calls:

> *multicultural drift*, that is to say the unplanned, increasing involvement of Britain's black and brown populations visibly registering a play of difference right across the face of British society. However, this creeping multiculturalism remains deeply uneven. Large areas of the country, most significant centres of power, substantial areas of racially differentiated disadvantage, are largely untouched by it. Outside its radius racialised exclusion compounded by household poverty, unemployment and educational underachievement persist, indeed multiply.
>
> (Hall 2000)

Multiculturalism has received muted support from politicians. The celebration of multicultural populations was, as Hall relates, part of Blair's Cool Britannia promotion of New Labour. Such pageants, it could be argued, are superficial and not noticeably supported by policy but by occasional rhetoric such as the comments made about Chicken Tikka Masala by former foreign secretary Robin Cook in 2001, which has apparently become the most popular dish in Britain, heralded as an example of Britain's successful melding of cultures. The speech was significantly made before the tide of opinion was turned against Muslims, and recent events have lead to government concerns over British identity and citizenship, and David Blunkett's insistence on some kind of citizenship ceremony to show a commitment to British values.

In America, as well as in Australia and Europe, there are sporadic concerns over the effects of migrant populations on the national identity, security and economy. In the USA, the Hispanic population is among the fastest growing, constituting about 12.5 per cent of the population and projected to increase by 39 per cent from 2000 to 2010 (US Census Bureau). Popular concerns about these changing demographics are often expressed in terms of the groups' separatism and refusal to properly assimilate 'American values'. In addition, there is the ideological freight of concerns about illegal immigrants and the quarrel over amnesties that the Bush regime has promised to grant. In Australia, the very hard-line stance against immigration has threatened the country's reputation as a land of the 'fair go'. The current conservative (Liberal) government has made a point of harsh treatment of 'asylum seekers', as John Pilger reported:

> Those Iraqis and Afghans who have succeeded in reaching Australia receive treatment which, for a society proclaiming humanist values, beggars belief. Many are imprisoned behind razor wire in some of the most hostile terrain on earth, deliberately isolated from population centres in 'detention centres' run by an American company specialising in top-security prisons. In their desperation, the refugees, many of them unaccompanied children, have resorted to suicide, starvation, arson and mass escapes.
>
> (Pilger 2002: 2)

Critics of multiculturalism

In Australia, where a much more formal policy of multiculturalism was launched in the 1980s, there were rumblings of misgiving about multiculturalism. In an interview with Brian Bullivant of Monash University, Bullivant aired his misgivings on what he has called the 'pluralist dilemma' based on ideas about the logical extensions of the policy leading to virtually separate and probably antag-onistic enclaves that would refuse to be subsumed under a common law. To Bullivant and other conservative critics it was an untenable ethos that reflected a liberal neglect for the integrity of the Australian state. See the following quotes from Geoffrey Blainey, a conservative historian: 'Multiculturalism is an appropriate policy for those residents who hold two sets of national loyalties and two passports. For the millions of Australians who have only one loyalty this policy is a national insult' (Blainey 1988: 22); 'The more emphasis that is placed on the rights of minorities and the need for affirmative action to enhance those rights, the more is the concept of democracy – and the rights of the majority – in danger of being weakened' (Blainey 1993: 3).

From a quite different political and theoretical stance, Kenan Malik has presented a case against the consequences of praising difference as something intrinsically good when the struggle for British black and Asian communities has been to be treated the same. His argument derives from the premise that multiculturalism stems from a resistance to the basic principles of Enlightenment rationality. The Enlightenment philosophers' vision for humanity united by common nature and universal principles of reason, tolerance and fairness, initially permitted only descriptive divisions between 'races'. Differences between human beings were not like the differences between *species*. '"It's good to be different" might be the motto of our times. The celebration of difference, respect for pluralism, avowal of identity politics – these are regarded the hallmarks of a progressive, antiracist outlook. At least in part, the antiracist embrace of difference is fuelled by a hostility to universalism' (Malik 2002: 1).

These views are articulated even more strongly by Ayn Rand:

> Multiculturalism is racism in a politically-correct guise. It holds that an individual's identity and personal worth are determined by ethnic/racial membership and that all cultures are of equal worth, regardless of their moral views or how they treat people. Multiculturalism holds that ethnic identity should be a central factor in educational and social policy decisions. Multiculturalism would turn this country into a collection of separatist groups competing with each other for power.
>
> (Rand 1998: 1)

Whether the concerns are articulated from right- or left-wing perspectives, they seem to agree that multiculturalism is an unworkable and fatally flawed ethos. The sentiments expressed by Rand, Bullivant and Blainey envisage a chaotic mosaic, the country riven by warring fiefdoms, each holding fast to fundamentalist tenets that will not allow any rapprochement. However, is it really multiculturalism that can lead to such divided cities? Are we in fact investing these often ineffectual (and in the UK certainly very marginal) policies with more power to transform communities than they warrant? Should we not be looking, on the contrary, to the signs that racism, long-term impoverishment and structural inequalities are the real impetus behind the worrying signs of division in our communities?

Impact of multiculturalism

Chas Critcher, whose work has focused on the operation of 'moral panics' (2003) and the state's uses of race rhetoric (Hall et al. 1978), made the following comment when asked about the impact of discourses of multiculturalism on communities in the UK:

Well first of all you have to say that multiculturalism is not a very significant factor anywhere. It's a set of arguments by a small number of liberal elite that has had a small effect on local authority policies. I'm not aware that any major corporations are committed to multiculturalism or that it's been a driving factor behind much government policy for example. So what we're talking about is a squabble among a small number of liberal intellectuals about how they should think about race. Now, it has been suggested that the problem with multiculturalism is that it stressed too much acceptance of diversity and difference, that there ought to have been limits to multiculturalism, that certain things which were never acceptable should not have been accepted, that we need a different way of thinking about our common values, and that we should put more stress on the core values that we should share rather than the acceptance of diversity. . . .

I think what's happening is that the issue of Islam and our attitude towards it is being used as a pretext to rethink some of the terms of that debate. Now, I think it was always true that there were areas that, if you have a multicultural society and if either or any group in the society has practices to do with (for example) eating which other people find unacceptable, at what point do you say, 'Well they can eat that because that's their religion', or you say, 'Well in our kind of society we don't eat that kind of food and we've got moral scruples about eating that kind of food', I've deliberately chosen a fairly uncontroversial area – right!?

Now to say there is a problem there about what multiculturalism means; does it mean we tolerate everybody's food – whatever they eat, however they eat it – because that's what multiculturalism means – it's an acceptance of diversity – or is there an argument saying that certain practices are beyond what we would accept to be the consensus? About drawing a line. A lot of this conversation seems to be about drawing a line. So, yes, there's always been an argument there about the extent to which accepting diverse cultures means you accept practices you don't find acceptable in your own culture. I think that's true – but say again – (a) This is an intellectual debate among a very small number of actually not very influential people and (b) I'm concerned that it has only arisen in the context of the prejudice against Islamic fundamentalism. Though I'm a bit suspicious about where these people are coming from and what their agenda is, to think that the way we think about (what we ought not really think about as 'race' – but as ethnicity) the way we think about ethnicity is somehow to blame for the current situation – that's balderdash!

People who believe in multiculturalism have never had the power to define the situation or to have a radical effect – I mean what do the kids on the street of Oldham or Burnley care about what white liberal intellectuals think? – come on! Live in the real universe – this is rubbish! Face up to some realities you know: lots of kids from ethnic minorities, for all kinds of reasons, have come out at the bottom of society's pile, and kids at the bottom of society's pile end up doing one of two things: they either take to crime or they riot – by and large that's what happens. So don't then turn around and say 'Ooh you liberals are to blame for this' – I'm not having that put on me, not for one moment!

(Interview, June 2004)

Chas Critcher's exhortation to 'get real' about issues of multiculturalism is a salutary point. Academic debate is no substitute for lived experience. It is interesting that even those with a mandate to promote multiculturalism seem to have turned against it, is it one of the most talked about entities that never was? Trevor Phillips the current Director of the Commission for Racial Equality felt the term had outlived its usefulness:

Trevor Phillips – who chairs the Commission for Racial Equality – meanwhile repeated his assertion that the term 'multiculturalism' suggested separateness and had ceased to be useful in modern Britain. It was necessary to 'assert a core of Britishness' for all citizens which meant stressing shared values such as believing in democracy and the rule of law. One of the founding principles of the commission Mr Phillips oversees is multiculturalism – a policy followed by successive government since the 1960s. It was originally designed to strengthen engagement and relations between Britain's different ethnic communities. [. . .] Mr Phillips said the term suggested 'separateness' and was no longer useful in present-day Britain. 'We are now in a different world from the 60s and 70s,' he said. 'For instance, I hate the way this country has lost Shakespeare. That sort of thing is bad for immigrants.'

(BBC News, 5 April 2004)

There is a sense that the manner in which multiculturalism has been taken up by those advocating identity politics has polarised the debate. Malik's *Disunited Kingdom* (BBC2, 2003) presented a snapshot of the country in which identity crises seemed to have reached surreal dimensions. A situation was reported in which the radical right-wing leader of the British National Party could find sanctuary in the multicultural camp. Because of the focus on cultural difference, Nick Griffin and his ilk could argue for the supremacy of English culture and take an aggressively separatist stance supporting the impoverished and ideologically disenfranchised whites at the expense of ethnic minorities, while cloaked in politically correct rhetoric of multiculturalism. By the same token, radical anti-racists were advocating separate recognition of ethnic enclaves.

However, despite the rhetorical shifts and the bad faith in former notions of equality, which have been distorting aspects of the 'multicultural brand', this is a concept that is evolving and requires a more mature response to the embedded diversity that characterises our cities (see Figure 8.3). As Lord Parekh recently

Figure 8.3 Celebrating diversity: CRE poster

stated, 'Multiculturalism basically means that no culture is perfect or represents the best life and that it can therefore benefit from a critical dialogue with other cultures. In this sense multiculturalism requires that all cultures should be open, self-critical, and interactive in their relations with other each other' (BBC News, 5 April 2004).

Multiculturalism it seems can be a double-edged sword. As a liberal ethos it certainly appeared to mark an enlightened advance over post-war chauvinism with the emphasis on aggressive assimilationist and integrationist approaches. Yet an inordinate emphasis on cultural difference may run counter to the necessity of working towards a genuinely equality within respectful diversity and instead encourage a hardening of boundaries rather than bridging of them.

Guyanese anthropologist Brackette Williams (1992) notes that Guyana's polarised ethnic relations have a dual nature – on the one hand there is an egalitarian and uniting tradition forged under oppression of colonialism, but on the other there is also a deep-seated hierarchical order (another colonial legacy). In the latter perspective different groups are measured in terms of their relative contributions – who gives most and who takes the most. As we have seen, ethnic communalism operates by closing ranks and accepting a general vision of the other group as a potential threat to prosperity or political power.

In this instance, two forces – egalitarianism in recognition of the Indian as desirable and hierarchy in the recital of markers of ethnic status – seem to be the site of an individual struggle to transcend prescribed boundaries. What is extra-ordinary here is, first, that the young African-Guyanese woman should feel it necessary to put the object of her affections through this test when it seems unlikely that, at least on surface appearance, there could have been any mistaking his 'Indianness'. Second, the recital of cultural markers is surprising in that it seems so fluent and detailed an inventory that, had even these been thwarted, one imagines she would have been able to continue the litany of distinctive features until she struck one that would have achieved the desired result. This aspect of boundary-crossing points to the possibility that subjects are not constrained by any simple determinism, and they may be knowledgeable and able to consciously manipulate elements in the social world.

GUYANA: BOUNDARY CROSSING

This section has discussed the recognition of otherness and the possibility of forming contingent identities based on mutually exclusive categories of difference. However, in situations where different cultural enclaves live side by side there is a mutual ownership and recognition of these differences in trait and practice – and there are numerous examples of border-crossing. The following story was taken from an interview with Dr Dennis Bassier: a Guyanese anthropologist. This intense awareness of ethnic hierarchy was highlighted in the following anecdote. In his student days, he told me, an African girl became attracted to him. The manner in which their relationship developed highlights not only the intense awareness of ethnic difference, but also the fact that such differences can be negotiated and overcome.

DENNIS: Umm, I was a student here in the early 70s and there was a black girl who would sit in class with me and so on. And she became attracted to me, but her orientation was so strong that she could not accept that she was falling for an Indian – and she looked at me and said: 'You know you're not Indian.' I said 'Yes I am Indian.' She said, 'Oh no no your hair is kinda curly, wavy when it's long.' And I said, 'No Indians do have wavy hair – look at the Madrasees, for instance, the Dravidians?' She said 'Ah no no – do you eat roti in the morning?' (Now this is Indian food.) I said, 'No most mornings I eat bread, crackers what have you.' She said 'Oh Ok then you're not Indian.' She said 'When you eat, before you eat do you feed your dog or cat?' (And this is true, this is very very marked among Indians – they would take a little of their food and give it to the dog or cat before they eat themselves.) I said, 'No I don't, whatever is left I give.' 'Oh then you're not Indian – all Indians do that . . . [*laughs*] So what I say is, it comes back to the stereotypes we have of these categories . . . and since I don't do those two things among the others then, OK I feel satisfied to myself that this man is not Indian so I can go ahead [*laughs*].

(Interview, 9 April 1991)

CHAPTER SUMMARY

This chapter has suggested some of the dynamics of our multicultural cities. Diasporic communities exist in an uncertain space that is dynamic and reciprocal in its effects on flows of migrant groups as well as on the indigenous 'locals'. This is not a utopian situation in which hybridity offers new post-racial reality, but it is a space where boundaries may be challenged and broken down or shifted. Individuals may increasingly find themselves, due to circumstances of birth or migration, between two or more cultures and facing conflicted and contradictory views of themselves, their life styles, identity. These hybrid patterns of ethnic identity, articulated as 'border lives' by Bhabha and existence within 'diaspora space' by Brah are identities in constant transition which pose a challenge to foundationalist thinking. Much of the writing about hybridity suggests that fluid postmodern ethnicities are the emergent form. Now while this may be, it is as well not to ignore the reality of our increasingly diverse cities, where there is often all too little cultural mixing between the diverse groups. However, as the examples given here have shown, boundary crossings *do* happen, people are able at times to forge relations across the hostile boundaries of traditional divides.

EXERCISE 8.1 BOUNDARY CROSSING

1   What were the boundary markers sighted in the Guyana example? In what instances do you imagine that such attributes of distinctiveness might be used to reaffirm distance rather than to lower boundaries?
2   Can you cite other examples of ethnic boundary markers from your personal experience? From the media? What was the context in which these differences were raised?
3   Have you ever experienced a boundary crossing? If so what form did it take?
4   Conversely, have you ever experienced ethnic differences being brought forward to strengthen boundaries?
5   What about other social divisions: age, gender, class, sexuality? In each case, list up the distinctive features that are at times used as barriers. How can these be overcome? Are they substantially different (or similar) to racial/ethnic boundaries?

EXERCISE 8.2

1   Being between cultures, like the people in the interviews in this chapter, may actually provide a stronger, more realised sense of national identity(s) than the identity of a white English person. Discuss.
2   The Zapatista uprising has implications for the world as well as for Mexico. Discuss.
3   Assess the contribution of two contentious terms in the understanding of post-colonial identities: diaspora and hybridity. What are the benefits and drawbacks?
4   Both diaspora and hybridity appear to promise a world in which racism is a spent force. What is the problem with such celebratory discourses?

EXERCISE 8.3

1   Looking at the quotes and the concerns about multiculturalism in this chapter, what signs can you see that multiculturalism leads towards separatism rather than a more holistic society?
2   Which view of multiculturalism do you see as the most realistic and why?

CHAPTER 9

Futures

> Our challenge should now be to bring even more powerful visions of
> planetary humanity from the future into the present and to reconnect them
> with democratic and cosmopolitan traditions that have been all but
> expunged from today's black political imaginary.
>
> (Gilroy 2000: 356)

The previous chapters have offered some sketchy details of the topology of race
and ethnicity, an ambiguous landscape with many ideological pitfalls. In this
final chapter some snap shots of current trends are presented, and visions of how
future meanings of race and ethnic relations might develop.

It is very important that the issues of race and ethnicity are discussed not as
positivistic boundaries which exist eternally, but as transitory social constructs
liable to change and shift, elusive meanings which float on the surface of our
everyday reality.

The issues which form our values are those everyday incidents and visions
which this book has drawn upon. Race can be thrown into sharp relief by: political
campaigns, media stories, incidents in our workplaces, discussions between
students in a seminar, or an argument about racism in a pub.

The strands of theory which focus on race as flows of social meanings should
not be mutually opposed to a keen recognition of the political and social realities
of racism or the embedded structural inequalities which divide our cities. In Europe
and America and much of the world, difference – whether it's equated with
essentialist myths of 'race' or religious or other cultural practices – is a cause of
impoverishment, ethnic cleansing and genocide.

To challenge these reactionary forces it is necessary to develop an analytical
eye to question and deconstruct ideas of subjectivity – without losing sight of the

necessity of supporting those who are disadvantaged as a result of our society's discourses of exclusion.

What trends are recognisable and likely to shape our conceptions of race and future ethnic identities? At the beginning of this book, we showed the apparently functional necessity of relationships of otherness in determining and affirming identities. Pieterese's work suggests that 'others' of one sort or another have always been with us, but that the basis for 'othering' does not need to be embodied by the concept of race. Indeed, we have seen that 'race' is a fluid and floating signifier which is parasitic on the political and social realities of the day. Such 'out groups' rather result from social and political discourses and vary considerably over time and between cultures. The impact of colonialism and dispossession altered the course of history and set up adversarial relationships with powerful aftershocks today. Not only are these impacts part of ethnic memory but they are also part of the daily reality for most of the non-western world. The expansion of global capitalism and the logic of domination and exploitation of human resources has widened the gap, leaving 'developing nations' in a situation where their debts – brokered in the 1970s and 1980s – have produced auto-colonialist regimes allowing the wealthy western nations to dictate terms at a distance and puppet economies from Washington, London, Rome and Paris.

Further one cannot talk about the likely scenarios for futures without recognising the strategic geopolitical goals of the world's superpowers, and the successive US military interventions, more than fifty since the Second World War (see William Blum 2004), which have had a marked impact on ethnic relations within those countries. While there is little space here to discuss this in detail, it must at least be recognised that the long-term picture of race and ethnicity and global relations is deeply affected by market competition, forces of globalisation and the economic autonomy within countries.

Globalisation is an elusive concept and definitions frequently deal with only economic or easily discernable global processes. Cultural and sociological aspects are far more complex and contradictory. Waters (1996: 157) outlines the principles behind the process of social change in these arenas as governed by the tendency 'that material exchanges localize, political exchanges internationalize, and symbolic exchanges globalize'. The more symbolic and fluid the exchange, the more rapidly it will span the globe. Therefore, it was no wonder that financial exchanges were rapidly globalised but flows of people seeking work were resisted, and in some cases boundaries have been tightened against those seeking work. In many cases this may be based on irrational fears, which are too often politically exploited, that the country could be 'swamped' with migrants.

But are we placing too much faith on the dominant western view of globalisation? Is this in fact such an inexorable process that affects cultures so profoundly and permanently? This is a difficult question but at least to ask it cautions us to not be swept along by what may seem to be the inevitability of homogenising forces and to look critically at other processes that may operate in the opposite direction or despite globalising trends.

In a recent interview, Francis Fukuyama takes a more circumspect line on the effects of globalisation, suggesting that much of globalisation has been relatively superficial and that the claims about global media homogenising the world are without foundation. Indeed, the impact of such media might, on the contrary, present a less favourable image of 'western' culture:

> [Forty] years ago, in the 1950s and '60s, Asia looked up to the United States as a model of modernization. Now, Asians look at American urban decay and the decline of the family and they feel that America is not a very attractive model. Communications technology has allowed both Asians and Americans to see each other more clearly, and it turns out they have very different value systems.
>
> (Fukuyama 1999)

Robertson adapts Tolstoy's aphorism to characterise these social forces as: '*the interpenetration of the universalization of particularization and the particularization of universalism*' (Robertson 1992: 100, emphasis in the original). In order to reconcile these social processes Robertson coined the term **glocalisation**, suggesting the unity as well as the difference between the local and the global. Smart also recognises the duality of global processes, 'the fragile unity ascribed to national societies has begun to dissolve, to fragment, as transnational and global exchanges and communications have gathered momentum, and infranational differences expressed in the form of "local, regional, and ethnic cultures" have been reconstituted or regenerated' (Smart 1993: 135).

Giddens is optimistic with regards to the process of globalisation. He takes the view that globalisation is something of an equalising process, since it gives hitherto disempowered groups and nations the potential to realise their goals. Indeed Giddens (2000) has even spoken of globalisation generating what he calls 'reverse colonialism'. The movement towards supranational entities loosens the bonds that have prevented expression of local ethnic identities.

At one level the current acceleration of globalisation could be seen as destabilising in relation to ethnicity, and seems to suggest that ethnic identity will not easily survive. However, globalisation does not necessarily entail homogenisation or integration – it means greater connectedness and **deterritorialisation**, a term that implies that ethnicity is increasingly removed from its traditional base and becomes a floating signifier divorced from connection to a homeland, which is replaced by diaspora space leading to an increase in ethnic pluralism detached from a specific territory or polity. Waters usefully summarises the impact of globalisation on ethnicity thus:

- Globalization is a differentiating as well as homogenizing process – It pluralizes the world by recognizing the value of cultural niches and local abilities
- Weakens the putative nexus between nation and state – releasing absorbed ethnic communities and allowing the reconstitution of nations across former state boundaries
- Centre moves to periphery – as introduces possibilities for new ethnic identities to cultures on the periphery (via electronic images and affluent tourism)
- Periphery moves to centre – flow of economic migrants – and e.g., black culture taken up by white suburban youth.

(1996: 136–7)

These processes can be seen as having impacts for expressions of ethnicity. Media imagery and consumer products utilise peripheral popular culture more and more rapidly. Meaning also flows back to the outer edges rapidly. Media and mobile communications that link up people mean the dissemination is accelarated. However, media messages are increasingly unified by ever-growing global media monopolies, which suggests that despite the apparent variety of media channels, the message is becoming more politically homogenised and market directed.

Hall (1992) notes two possible adaptive responses by ethnic groups to globalisation. First, translation – syncretistic response: such practices can be seen in many post-colonial societies, in which a process of **creolisation** has occurred that has formed syntheses of cultural values and social practices (hybrid ethnic identities and the possibility of boundary crossing discussed in the previous chapter). Second, tradition – ethnic fundamentalism: this could stem from a sense of cultural values that are under threat from outside 'foreign' influences. Charismatic leaders sometimes emerge who are seen to embody the threatened values. There may be the 'rediscovery' of these defining religious or ethnic core values. For example the rebirth (and possible reinvention) of ethnic identities in the former Yugoslavia or the popular revolution in Iran which coalesced around Ayatollah Khomeini's regeneration of fundamental religious tenets in the face of the decadent elitism of the Shah. Cultural globalisation based on hybrid ethnic identity has been perceived as a challenge to ideas of ethnic essentialism. An understanding of the multicultural state can certainly be informed by recognising the influences of these global processes on ethnicity. On the one hand, localism, the fragmentation into regional parochialisms, and, on the other, globalisation challenging the nation-state boundaries from the outside as supranational ethnicities are created.

There are three recognised approaches to managing cultural or ethnic diversity:

1 A model of the state, which sets core values that must be upheld in the public domain. The French state, for example, will not recognise the existence of

national or linguistic minorities within its borders. French citizens, of whatever ethnic origin, enjoy equal civic, cultural and linguistic rights as individuals, but not collectively as minority groups. This could be called an integrationist approach.

2 In contrast, nations such as Germany, Singapore and Japan use a model founded on the principle of '*jus sanguinis*' (blood based). In other words, citizenship depends upon ancestry. This, for example, prevents third-generation Turks born in Germany and speaking German from obtaining nationality.

3 Nations such as Canada, Australia and the UK (although in a less official fashion), which have adopted policies of multiculturalism, through which they formally recognise the unique cultural status of all minorities who have made their home in the nation.

It seems that global processes will continue to impact on ethnic relations, in some cases drawing groups together and in others pulling them apart: 'Increasing changes associated with globalisation and the dynamic changes involving population movements will inevitably produce newer forms of ethnic contact and dynamic pressures for internal changes. The potential for ethnic conflict to remain a major social phenomenon is unlikely to end' (UNESCO 1995: 14).

So what is the potential for a global culture? Is multiculturalism the way to subsume diversity within a benevolent dominant culture and allow for hybridisation to occur over time? Multiculturalism, which teaches tolerance, acceptance and even celebration of diversity is certainly a step forward, despite the dangers of tokenism and structural inequality (political and economic power is typically a 'next wave' phenomenon). We must be cautious about the supposedly homogenising effects of globalisation. Theories of cultural imperialism and media imperialism assume that 'local cultures are necessarily battered out of existence by the proliferation of consumer goods, advertising and media programmes stemming from the West (largely the US)' (ibid.). Featherstone (1995) makes the point that we must be careful not to over-simplify the complex negotiation, absorption, assimilation and resistance strategies within the culture, plus the mediating influence of the nation-state. Both the shape and identity of existing national societies are being challenged both from within and without, by ethnic and regional expressions of difference and parallel demands for autonomy and independence, as well as by global population movements, transnational communication networks . . . etc.' (Smart 1993: 136).

Three issues are briefly examined to indicate the changing global parameters of race and ethnicity: mixed-race relationships, the Internet and cyberidentity, and terrorism and global risk.

MIXED RACE

'Mixed race' is a misleading term since it implies that a 'pure race' exists. Like its alternatives, 'multi-racial', 'mixed parentage', 'dual heritage', it refers to people who are visibly identified as embodying two or more racial or ethnic groupings. It appears to emphasise physically hybrid features but also broader ethnic and cultural syntheses. The concept highlights the borderlines between the terms 'race' and 'ethnicity' and the inadequacy of existing terms to articulate hybrid identities. It seems there is always this tendency to imagine the world in absolute terms, but 'mixed-race' individuals are a living challenge to this absolutism. Britain currently has one of the highest rates of interracial relationships in the western world, with 50 per cent of all black children born having one white parent.

> The controversial new 'mixed' category in the 2001 census attracted 400,000 ticks. One in ten ethnic minority Britons is the product of 'mixed' parents; one in 20 pre-school children in the UK is thought to be of mixed race. Britain has one of the highest rates of inter-racial relationships in the western world. Whether you view this is as a positive sign of a new multi-ethnic melting pot, or a negative watering down of the UK's minorities, it is a fact.
>
> (*Observer*, 25 November 2001)

Children born with dual ethnic heritage may face identity issues. They may feel ambivalent in terms of their identification. From an early age, incipient racism by peers and teachers might lead to a fluctuating identification. Tizzard and Phoenix cite experiments that have explored young children's racial identifications. When asked to choose between a black and a white doll – and asked to choose the doll that looked 'bad' – half of the black children chose the black doll. Even more worryingly a third of the same children misidentified themselves – selecting the white doll when asked to 'Give me the doll that looks like you' (Tizzard and Phoenix 1993: 29). These studies were used in arguments that black children suffered from low self-esteem and identity confusion because they internalised negative views of black people from the white community, leading to calls to desegregate American schools. However, more recent studies show contradictory results.

The following observations (Box 9.1) come from Yvonne Howard-Bunt, an academic and mother who asks some pertinent questions about the meaning of 'mixed race' for herself, her family and wider society. Her examples indicate that we are at the cusp of change; in the uneasy borderlands between the reliance on clear 'colour-coded' boundaries and realisation of a new hybridised social reality.

BOX 9.1 INTERVIEW WITH YVONNE HOWARD-BUNT

I am careful about how I define/label myself and to whom. It changes according to the overall context and purpose, and whether it is for data collection, subject discussion or simply responding to an individual querying my 'racial, ethnic' background. I have difficulty with defining myself within these narrow parameters because I find them misleading and inappropriate. What does 'mixed race' mean when 'pure races' do not exist as a discreet biological entity? 'Black' is a conceptual term of historical social, economic and political significance. Aside from this factor, does the term 'mixed race' have any lesser or greater definitive validity than 'black' and 'white' classifications? At what point and in what way do generational time frame and genetic-distribution factors impinge upon definitions of 'mixed race'? Does the possession of the gene for colour automatically preclude 'mixed-race' people from certain categories? If it does, then the construction of 'race' in terms of 'whiteness' and genetic 'purity' must be unravelled. What would be the implications of a heritage link to 'black' Africa measured in declining genetic kinship percentages? For example, parent, grandparent, great grandparent, great great grandparent, and so on.

And where on the continuum of 'race' and ethnic classification would I place my 'white' complexioned, straight-haired, blue-eyed babe of dual 'mixed-race' and 'white' heritage? Three of his grandparents are 'white' UK citizens and one is a 'black' African UK citizen. Is my child 'black', 'white' or 'mixed race'? What are the parameters of defining my child within these subjective constructs? Should I consider his identities in terms of colour, citizenship or inaccurate and outmoded concepts of 'race' and ethnicity?

The issue of colour symbolism as a conceptual determinant of classification blurs boundaries and influences understanding at a 'grass roots' level. For example: my brown-pigmented 'mixed-race' brother was out with his 'white' complexioned child, the baby's 'white' mother and a 'white' male friend of theirs. A stranger walked up to them, peered into the pushchair and established eye contact with the 'white' parties he presumed to be the parents. The man said, 'What a lovely baby, how old is she?', paying no heed to my brother who was not perceived as the father of the child.

In another situation, a mother enrolled her child in school and was cautioned against classifying her 'white' complexioned child within a 'white' category. The mother, of dual 'Indian' and 'white' UK heritage, positively identifies herself as 'mixed race', but did not define her daughter in this respect.

She stated that this would not have been an issue if the child's 'white' father had enrolled the daughter in her absence. Caution is required here in the view expressed by some authors. This position labels the mother as misguided in terms of defining her child's identity and attributes simplistic notions of identity confusion and self-esteem.

These cases are indicative of the borderlines where assumptions and common-sense perceptions are challenged. However, such confusion often accompanies major shifts in social dynamics and this is clearly the fastest-growing ethnic grouping certainly in the UK, but also in the USA where it is also breaking records and meeting certain forms of resistance. There appear to be important and contested issues below the surface of the celebratory discourses. A *US Today* report (1992) suggests that US resistance to the mixed category may be motivated by powerful lobby from other ethnic groups who may consider the creation of a new and rapidly growing group to be a threat and a drain on resources they might expect; a reminder, again, that how boundaries are drawn can have political and economic consequences.

In addition, the struggle for identification as black or Asian has lead some groups to embrace a relatively essentialist viewpoint, partly as a strategic means by which to gain recognition. As Hall comments:

> I have the feeling that, historically, nothing could have been done to intervene in the dominated field of mainstream popular culture, to try to win some space there, without the strategies through which those dimensions were condensed into the signifier "black." Where would we be, as bell hooks once remarked, without a touch of essentialism? Or, is what Gayatri Spivak calls strategic essentialism, a necessary moment? The question is whether we are any longer in that moment, whether that is still a sufficient basis for the strategies of new interventions.
>
> (Hall 1993: 104)

The manner in which hybrid categorising operates and the social meanings that circulate vary in relation to the existing ethnic divisions and the social and political tensions between these groups. In Guyana's ethnically polarised situation, African and Indian offspring are called '*doogla*' – a somewhat demeaning term. This is a negatively charged political identity given the long-standing rivalry between African- and Indian-Guyanese. However, by contrast, as Parker points out, 'in Central and South America those who are "mixed" predominate with often incalculably fine grained pigmentocracies crucial to the operation of social hierarchies in Brazil for example' (Parker 2004: 109).

Terms such as 'black', 'brown' or 'white' are political and social boundary markers rather than iconic signs representing actual categories, and function in an interlocking fashion to raise or lower boundaries, to exclude or to unite. In a TV documentary on Channel 4, *Brown Britain*, Pauline Black (a woman of mixed race) commented on her self-designation as 'black': 'I will still continue to define myself as black, until white people turn around to me and say, "Hey I'm mixed race as well." You know – the Vikings came over one time, the French came over one time – and actually recognise that everybody on this planet is really a mixture' (*Brown Britain*).

This is a clear example of Hall's 'necessary moment' when individuals make a conscious choice, a strategic way of dealing with the obdurate whiteness of the majority culture that defines identity by difference of colour. People of mixed race are in an anomalous situation – pigeon-holed by others, often in racist or disparaging form. Such experiences of incipient or confrontational racism may start very early at school depending on class and gender. Also, racism is less likely to be directed towards middle-class girls, whereas working-class males were more likely to be target for racist taunts. One student described the racist taunts as 'constant dripping'; racist language was used in a joking yet pointed way. Tizzard and Phoenix's (1993) subjects report mixed-race boys as finding name-calling racist and tiresome, but coped with this by laughing it off and, in some cases, by indulging in racist jokes about black people themselves. Their research found that 85 per cent of the mixed-parentage sample had experienced racism in one form or another – most frequently name-calling in primary school. Crime figures note the high frequency of assaults on people of mixed race:

Asian and mixed race people experienced higher levels of victimisation than white people, but for Asian people the difference was no longer apparent after allowing for age. For mixed race people the difference remained even after age, and also area lived in, had been allowed for. [. . .] People of mixed race were at greater risk of crime than all the other groups. Risk had increased significantly between 2001/02 and 2002/03 for this group.

(Research Development and Statistics Directorate 2004)

SIGNIFICANCE FOR THEORISING RACIALISATION

David Parker (2004) points out the unique opportunity that 'mixed race' allows for a perspective on the process of racialisation. Mixed-race people are the fastest growing ethnicity in the UK, and while multi-racial or mixed-heritage populations are clearly increasing rapidly in the USA, the official figures do not allow for a mixed category. 'There are three ways in which "mixed race" has been conceived:

as a stable social identity in its own right; re-expressed as "multiracial"; and a temporary pre-figurement of a post-racial future' (Parker 2004: 115).

In Britain, the term 'mixed race' is now widely recognised as the identity of self-designation by people with mixed ancestry (Tizzard and Phoenix 1993). Older and more derogatory terms such as 'coloured', 'half-caste' and 'half-breed', although still in circulation, have been displaced. For all the difficulties of invoking a concept 'race', which it then places under erasure, the notion of 'mixed race', by drawing attention to the permeability between so-called races, may have a role in weakening the hold of racialised forms of thought and action in the years ahead. However, as Parker also notes, some restraint is required when we look at the worrying level of racism that exists. A more radical shift in perceptions of identity is needed because currently: 'The social constructions of norms of physical appearance still decisively influence identity formation. In the light of the continuing salience of this and other forms of racialisation, the declaration of post-racialism seems premature' (Parker 2004: 118–19).

Also, as discussed in the previous chapter, the underlying values in British society seem to advocate separation based on difference around a core culture of Britishness rather than a future in which mixed race reflects a view of society which:

> is not dominated by any one cultural tradition but rather allows 'a free flow of contributions from all possible sources'. Rather than having to assimilate (a word which means to be absorbed, swallowed up) to one dominant culture there would be individual freedom to experiment and choose whatever cultural style one felt was most meaningful. The cultural practices within such a state would develop organically from the mixture and interaction amongst myriad cultural forms; this holistic vision would mean that new synthetic forms might emerge over time.
>
> (Bramann 1999: 5)

Is Bramann's vision utopian? A view in which humanist ideals supersede nationalism, where society is open enough to gradually adapt to incorporate new cultural forms. Perhaps it is significant that Britain shows a marked tendency towards mixing despite those who perpetuate segregationist ideas of culture and wish to draw rigid boundaries between ethnicities: Britain 'has the highest number of interracial relationships in the world' according to the Institute for Social and Economic Research. This supremely natural and healthy state of affairs is, however, not due to multiculturalism but in spite of it. For multiculturalist ideology, which believes that 'culture makes man' rather than the other way round, sets its face firmly against miscegenation, integration and assimilation – on principle (Reilly 2001). These are clearly trends which open up discussion of the possibility of a world which is not riven by ethnic conflict and racism. The rhetoric if not the reality at least recognises the desire to be part of a post-racial world.

RACE IN CYBERSPACE

The development of Internet-based cultures and communities is certainly a new cultural form that is worthy of research. Virtual environments raise a host of interesting questions and baffling metaphysical issues about the meaning of such encounters, the nature of being and of reality. Inevitably, rather grandiose predictions have been made: cyberspace has been heralded as a post-racial utopia. According to some media advertising, there is no race, gender or disability on-line: 'There is no race. There is no gender. There is no age. There are no infirmities. There are only minds. Utopia? No! . . . The Internet!' (MCI television commercial, 'Anthem').

This promise of value-free cyberspace, a metaphysical space in which diverse subjectivities can reinvent themselves away from the male, straight, ethnocentric gaze all too prevalent in everyday life, is far from being borne out in reality. There are a number of problems with the Internet as a socially transformative force. Cyberspace has the ability to connect people across the globe, but also disseminates dichotomies that exist within our culture. Identities can be invented and individuals cross (virtual) boundaries, but is this a substitute for, or of any relevance to, the real world? There is the chance of being unmasked for those who practise deception – and the sense of betrayal seems to be just as trenchant as in real life. The example cited by Stone (1995) of 'Julie' illustrates this point well. Julie was a neuropsychologist who was disabled after a horrific accident which left her mute, paraplegic and so disfigured that she could not bear to meet people face to face. This vulnerable character soon became a fascinating participant across virtual communities. She set up help groups for depressed women and counselled them – privy to their most intimate feelings and anxieties. Julie began to develop a flamboyant personality and took her virtual associates on a rollercoaster ride of emotions. However, finally the identity of Julie was exposed to be that of a rather staid but able-bodied Jewish psychiatrist called Sanford. 'Many felt betrayed, cheated, assaulted and even raped. They had poured their lives out to her . . . but Julie had only ever existed in text while their text was also written in flesh and blood' (Stone 1995: 83).

Nakamura (2000: 716) discusses the way Internet fantasists often adopt Asian female identities (males tend to be the most prevalent in cyberspace). This is another example of how the Internet, while it arguably allows people to experiment with fantasy personalities, cross-dressing and some vicarious pleasure from masquerading as a desired object, may also reinforce racist stereotypes by 'exploiting and reifying through performance notions of the Asian female as submissive, docile, a sexual plaything' (2000).

These and other encounters suggest claims that the Internet opens up a prejudice-free, colourless realm are very doubtful. An article by Susan Zickmund (2000) shows to the contrary that cyberculture allows another channel to articulate extremist ideas. Members of the US radical right, the Ku Klux Klan and other Nazi-based organisations have found a collective voice using web sites. Zickmund's belief that confronting the radical right on a newsgroup is a 'step towards forcing subversives into open interaction with society' (Zickmund 2000: 252) is not very convincing. Far from becoming 'an ally in the struggle against bigotry and racism' (2000: 252), there is the fear of accelerated membership and of groups becoming less open (hermetic isolation is achieved by use of secret passwords, etc.) and much more organised. A recent development has been the discovery of Islamic fundamentalist web sites which nurture the anti-western jihad (*Guardian*, 12 May 2004). A number of sites apparently featured live footage of hostages being beheaded in Iraq. The Internet is clearly an enormously powerful tool – but it seems very questionable whether the escape into the virtual will provide 'real time' solutions for intractable ethnic and ideological conflicts.

A PAIR OF BROWN EYES

Before reading this section look at the poster (Figure 9.1) and consider how you would interpret its message.

These visions can assail us in the most ordinary and mundane social spaces. This time it was a shopping trip to the city centre. Through an arcade we passed a well-known catalogue shop when my partner stopped me and drew my attention to the poster which was stuck in the window of the store.

A pair of attractive female brown eyes stared out from the cutaway in the poster like a pill box slot or like a Muslim woman's face wearing traditional garb. The dilated hyperreal eyes captured my attention – in just the way those ads are said to have enlarged the pupils to make you feel the woman in the picture is interested in you. The accompanying text also seemed weird and incongruous.

'Terrorists need places to live and make plans . . . they need vehicles and people to help them. If you have any suspicions about terrorist activity DON'T HESITATE . . . call.'

It has been suggested that the purpose of highlighting the eyes was merely to indicate a person who was alert and vigilant to the threat of terrorism, but this is not likely to be the interpretation most people would arrive at.

Less than 100 yards away in the main shopping area of the city was a small group of Muslims with a table set out with books and leaflets asking us to 'Discover Islam'. I asked them what their opinion was of the poster. To my surprise they were not especially concerned about it although they immediately noticed the similarity of the image to a 'sister' wearing a veil, they felt rather than an intentional anti-Muslim campaign it represented an error of judgement

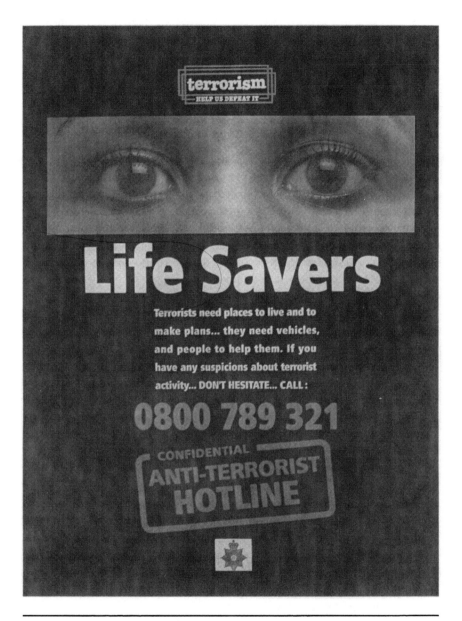

Figure 9.1 'Life Savers'. Police anti-terrorist poster

and perhaps a lack of sensitivity. They also mentioned that there were two other posters, one of a white woman and another of a black man, which suggested that this was not an intentional focus on Muslims. However, the *Guardian* reported that the posters have caused a storm of protest from Asian and Muslim groups around the country. Abdur Rahman Jafar, who represents the Muslim Council of Britain on the safety forum, said: 'We are quite infuriated by it. 'It looks like a woman with a niqab on, which is one version of the veil where women cover up their face and the top of their head.'

(Dodd 2004)

Post 9/11 the climate of fear in the West has – it appears – led to greater victimisation of Muslims. At the time in 2004 when I first saw this poster I felt it was adding needlessly to a climate of fear and a burgeoning moral panic about terrorism and Islam, a view which has been echoed by others in this text.

After the events of 7 July 2005 in London, the implicit assumption in such images is no more useful. Indeed locating repugnant terrorist violence as a feature of Islamic cultural difference only adds fuel to the fire and inflames the sense of alienation which engenders such actions. The impact of such campaigns is especially felt where Asians are a small minority.

> Kauser Ahmed, of Exeter's Mosque and Islamic Centre, refused to put the poster up. She said that in her area 'there are very few people of colour or who are Muslim, so they stand out, and we will be the target of suspicion and hostility. We already feel very marginalised, ignored by the authorities until it suits them. It was very obviously Asian eyes.' 'During the IRA bombings in the 1970s and 80s the posters did not depict someone's eyes; it had a picture of a bag.' Dodd's story goes on to explain that after the September 11 attack the Exeter mosque was desecrated by youths who placed severed pigs' heads outside it.
>
> (ibid.)

The Metropolitan Police have since withdrawn the posters after many complaints from Muslim communities around the country. This poster is clearly open to different interpretations and misinterpretations. One of the features of life in a multi-ethnic society is the need to develop a keener recognition of multiple meanings of such messages, a sensitivity to meanings and interpretations that are less normative and equally valid, exposing the myth or our supposed consensus on a wide range of social and political issues.

The unfolding issue of terrorism is having an unprecedented and distorting affect on perceptions. Some, like Samuel Huntington (1998), draw the battle lines of the future based not on ethnic identifications or desires for empire but on the 'Clash of Civilizations' (as if these are real and separate bases). Further, he suggests that the West is the only civilisation to value individualism, democracy, equality, liberalism, etc., and that the main threats stem from Islamic states and Confusianism (China). These are ultimately inviolable, essentialist categories that are intrinsically opposed. The West must therefore be prepared to use military force to deal with the threat of these dangerous civilisations. This strand of unreasoned cultural pessimism represents real concern when it is apparent that world's only real super-power (US) has advisers who genuinely believe in the righteous dominance of American culture (see, for example, the Project for the New American Century, a neo-conservative think tank that promotes an ideology of total US world domination through the use of force. This is reputedly a strong influence on the current US administration).

CONCLUSIONS

The images, news items, theory and dialogues presented in this book were chosen in an attempt to expose and problematise concepts of race and ethnicity. No single theoretical explanation of racial or ethnic divisions appears to entirely account for the diverse phenomena contained by these contentious terms. Most theoretical frameworks are too crushing in their generality, too reductionist or else too abstruse and fragmentary to recognise the complexity and variety of ethnic relations. Nevertheless, these varied explanations are of interest – not only for the extent they are able to account for race/ism and ethnic identity, but because their emphases are instructive and highlight the dominant ideas which shape our perceptions of difference.

Neither ethnicity nor race can be understood without reference to other social relations. Ethnic identity is recognised by and contingent to divisions of class, gender, and political and economic contexts in which social relations take place. In racism there is fear and a desire for a moral consensus stemming from embedded value systems and a sense of national unity. Some, like Samuel Huntington, draw the battle-lines of the future based not on ethnic identifications or desires for empire but on the *Clash of Civilizations* (as if these are real and separate bases). He suggests that the West is the only civilization to value individualism, democracy, equality, liberalism, etc. and that the main threats stem from Islamic states and Confucianism (China). The West must therefore be prepared to use military force to deal with the threat of these dangerous civilizations. These are ultimately essentialist categories which are intrinsically opposed. This strand of unreasoned cultural pessimism represents real concern when it is apparent that the world's only real superpower (the USA) has advisors who genuinely believe in the righteous dominance of American culture (see, for example, The Project for the New American Century 1997). Paul Gilroy in *After Empire* states that:

The resolute enthusiasm of postmodern ethnic cleansers and absolutists apparently knows no colour lines. Hendrik Verwoed, Samuel Huntington, Ariel Sharon, Slobodan Milosevic, Osama Bin Laden, Condoleezza Rice, and a host of others have contributed something to the belief that absolute culture rather that colour is more likely to supply the organizing principle that underpins contemporary schemes for racial classification and division. These distinctions may be far removed from the warring totalities of blackness and whiteness but are nonetheless likely to be scarred by the Manichean relationship they exemplify.

(Gilroy 2004: 39)

One arena which has fuelled these absolutist sentiments is terrorism. The recognition of global risk (Beck 1992, 2002) through terrorist activity like 9/11 has served to reinforce the autocratic state. Yet, as Beck comments, terrorism diminishes the nation-state leading to greater transnational cooperation as a necessary means of securing internal security (Beck 2002: 14), perhaps the opposite of what the 9/11 terror had intended to achieve.

Beck envisages two types of transnational cooperation emerging. On the one hand, states could become even more fortress like – an all too believable prospect given the heightened surveillance post 9/11. Such states would be rigidly resistant to external cultural influences. Such states would dispense with freedom and democracy and become increasingly authoritarian. Conversely, Beck believes that some states could become what he calls 'Open world states' which emphasize the necessity of self-determination and take a proactive role at not only combating terrorism but also the causes of terrorism. Such an imaginary state would be based on the need for using openness and a belief in the need for unification between its own citizens and foreign nationals, rather than use of rigid and ethnocentric protocols to oppose terror.

Clearly, the initial reactions to 9/11 have followed a course similar to Beck's suggested 'Surveillance state'. The excesses of Guantanamo Bay and Iraq are the brutal mirror held to the 'Other'. The perpetuation of imperial high-handedness finds its reflection in live beheadings broadcast via the Internet and the desperate rage of suicide bombers. The gross disparities of power between those reaping the benefits of the new world order and those who are excluded from a share will not be healed by military might. At present it is hard to imagine the open state approach Beck advocates being adopted. Neo-colonial exploitation has been the road map which seems to lead inexorably towards 'the war on terror', and western nations seem reluctant to relinquish this dominance.

In late 2005 the western reaction to the continued terrorist attacks post September 11 (the Madrid, Bali and London bombs) has been to try and push through increasingly draconian measures. The perpetrators of terror, whether individuals who cynically plan bombings in the name of religion or western governments perpetrating terror through economic or military might, are locked into an ideological impasse. The actions of each side merely reinforce their sense of righteousness and moral outrage.

This book has discussed how placing the emphasis on difference may exacerbate ethnic violence both at the level of individual and subcultural dogma as well as at the national level of structural disadvantage, institutional racism and political violence. The clashes in areas as diverse as Kuala Lumpur, Oldham, Sydney and most recently in the banlieues of Paris, Lyon and Toulouse bear witness to the impact of ghettoisation and exclusion.

One of the rapidly eroding principles of an open society is the ability to criticise practices which are unsound and undermine human dignity and respect for human rights; and this is true whether these stem from small beleaguered and marginalised groups or from super-powers. No belief system or social political practice whether religious or cultural, scientific or divinely inspired should be exempt from critical analysis and examination.

The USA and other western nations may identify certain groups as legitimate targets as terrorists or freedom fighters, they may quietly but implicitly condone the use of extreme measures such as torture to interrogate prisoners in the war against terror. The tacit ideological rightness of their actions is presented as almost beyond question. In reality although the western powers are not beyond scrutiny, their hegemonic power over news values and ownership of media sources allows them to foreground their values; dissent is marginalised and can be ignored. On the other hand, moral criticism of Zionism or the adherence to Sharia law is seen by some as impermissible, as anti-Semitic or Islamophobic, or an example of a neo-colonialist assault on cultural integrity.

So caution is needed; the encompassing ideologies of the state need to be recognised for what they are, their motives and impacts on vulnerable groups exposed and resisted; but the zealous pursuit of relativism as a reaction to the excesses of western imperialism may constitute a defeat of enlightened and universal values of humanism.

If race was an invention of modernity – it had a beginning – then is a time imaginable where race will pass into insignificance, become a difference that doesn't make a difference? Will newer divisions arise and take the place of race? The form and focus may change but it is a delusion to assume that we will stop drawing boundaries, whether they are based on blood quantum, colour, cultural differences, citizenship, employment, or something else, the one thing which seems certain is that identification of 'others' will continue to shift and reflect the political and social trends of the time. Difference is part of social unity. However to deny difference and naturalise traditions of dominance by segregating and staying within defensive cultural boundaries may mean the avoidance of confrontation – but confronting injustice is necessary if we are serious about finding mutual solutions and sharing the future.

1 Is 'mixed race' a sign that we are transcending the boundaries of race and entering a post-racial era?

2 What signs suggest this is an overly optimistic interpretation?

3 Is the Internet a genuinely radical space in which identities can be detached from their material origins?

4 Consider the image used in the anti-terrorist poster (Figure 9.1). What are your impressions of this image?

5 Several other posters showing white blue-eyed faces were also used. Does that then justify the use of the one shown here?

6 Considering the global shifts commented on briefly in this chapter, give examples of these processes in your own town.

7 How does the media of film illustrate both the homogenising and differentiating meanings of ethnicity that are the result of globalisation?

GLOSSARY

aberrant decoding a term coined by Umberto Eco (1965) which highlights the problems of interpreting (decoding) a message by means of a different code from that used to encode it. In effect, whenever there are social or cultural differences between the encoder and the decoder of a message then the reading (decoding) of the message will be 'aberrant'. Fiske (1990: 78) gives the example of an interviewee wearing a pair of jeans at a job interview. The sub-cultural status of jeans, he argues, might have high value to the young man, but to the employer they may seem to be an inappropriate code and represent non-conformity. Many examples of aberrant decoding are apparent when there is an ignorance of cultural codes in a multicultural society. For example, some Aboriginal groups may find direct eye contact with a person in authority to be disrespectful and look away in deference. However, the white European (and Australian) codes for eye contact may read this as a sign of guilt or dishonesty.

affectivity primordial attachments are in essence emotional and based upon strong affective ties (this is akin to the belief that kinship exerts a powerful influence; the 'blood is thicker than water' argument), which again makes such bonds quite impermeable to other social influences.

apriority this is an idea which in contrast to sociological views posits primordial attachments as part of an individual's makeup, given or prior to all social interaction.

biopower/biopolitics a term used by Foucault to designate a form of power that marked the beginning of a historical era (beginning in the eighteenth century) in which 'there was an explosion of numerous and diverse techniques for achieving the subjugation of bodies and the control of populations' (1981: 140). The rapid development of educational, criminal justice, military, medical and labour-management systems of discipline and organisation and their control over the body are mentioned by Foucault. The control of the body rather than level of consciousness or ideology is an important and neglected theme for Foucault. While he recognises the insight of Marx, he views the state-centred model of power as self-defeating because to succeed, the forces of resistance will need to mirror the very state they wish to overthrow. Instead, Foucault's writing traces the biopolitics – the discourses or technologies of power by which bodies and indeed whole populations are controlled. (He particularly focused on punishment, surveillance, medical technologies and sexology.) Many have found Foucault's articulation of power unsatisfactory as it allows for no clearly defined force to oppose.

commodification is a term which indicates the transformation of items, activities, concepts and relationships, which would not previously have been considered as the object of trade or exchange, into commodities, and can, for example, include ideas, aesthetics, spirituality, the family, gender relations, cultural ceremonies and artefacts, and many other things. This process was noted by Marx and Engels in the *Communist Manifesto* in 1848:

> The bourgeoisie, wherever it has got the upper hand, has put an end to all feudal, patriarchal, idyllic relations. It has pitilessly torn asunder the motley feudal ties that bound man to his 'natural superiors', and has left no other nexus between man and man than naked self-interest, than callous 'cash payment'. It has drowned out the most heavenly ecstasies of religious fervour, of chivalrous enthusiasm, of philistine sentimentalism, in the icy water of egotistical calculation. It has resolved personal worth into exchange value, and in place of the numberless indefeasible chartered freedoms, has set up that single, unconscionable freedom - Free Trade. In one word, for exploitation, veiled by religious and political illusions, it has substituted naked, shameless, direct, brutal exploitation.
>
> The bourgeoisie has stripped of its halo every occupation hitherto honoured and looked up to with reverent awe. It has converted the physician, the lawyer, the priest, the poet, the man of science, into its paid wage labourers.
>
> The bourgeoisie has torn away from the family its sentimental veil, and has reduced the family relation into a mere money relation.

In Chapter 6 it is clear that sacred and ceremonial places, art and objects associated with the traditions of Aboriginal people and indeed the people themselves have become commodified.

creolisation the concept of cultural creolisation, introduced in anthropology by Ulf Hannerz (see Hannerz 1992) refers to the intermingling and mixing of two or several formerly discrete traditions or cultures. In an era of global mass communication and capitalism, creolisation can be identified nearly everywhere in the world, but there are important differences as to the degree of mixing. The concept has been criticised for essentialising cultures (as if the merging traditions were 'pure' at the outset).

cultural capital   Bourdieu made the ground-breaking realisation that 'capital' in its broadest sense is the key to understanding the structure and function of the social sphere. He believed that economic theory had served to create a false dichotomy between exchanges which could be counted as purely financial and self-interested and all others which were then considered non-economic and hence disinterested. However, cultural capital is deeply intertwined with economics, although disguised as immaterial and disinterested. It can be embodied in the form of '. . . long-lasting dispositions of the mind and body . . .' or objectified through consumer products of all kinds and especially, perhaps, those which have an aesthetic or status value (books, music, pictures, interior design, electronic gadgetry, etc.) However, Bourdieu also makes particular reference to the acquisition of cultural capital through education (various linguistic and cultural knowledges and competencies) attained by middle-class children specifically and restricted and channelled away from working-class children (or in many cases children from non-white ethnic backgrounds) (see Bourdieu in Halsey 1997: 46).

culture   'the set of human practices that produce meaning and the objects that are the result of those practices. It encompasses all forms of human engagement in those practices, and their effects on humans acting together as a "culture"' (Kress 1988: 182). Further analysis yields other complex distinctions within 'culture'. McGuigan (1993: 6) states:

> Culture is ordinary: that is the first fact. Every human society has its own shape, its own purposes, its own meanings. Every human society expresses these, in institutions, and in arts and learning.
>
> A culture has two aspects: the known meanings and directions, which its members are trained to; the new observations and meanings which are offered and tested. These are the ordinary processes of human societies and human minds, and we see through them the nature of a culture: that is always both traditional and creative; that it is both the most ordinary common meanings and the finest individual meanings.

This definition also gets across the understanding that culture is dynamic and always in the making rather than the more static and elitist possession (which were implicit in traditional notions of High and Low culture).

deconstruction   a term first used by the post-structuralist Jacques Derrida to refer to the way in which the deeper and multiple meanings within a text can be deduced (these meanings may contradict and undermine the ostensible surface interpretation of the text). For example, in the headline 'Five die in riot', the agency is effectively removed and hence we have an incomplete understanding of the context – did the 5 die of sun stroke, heart attacks, old age? Were they killed by other demonstrators, army or police? Similarly, there are assumptions in the word 'riot'. Drawn from a paradigm of similar words 'riot' is different to 'demonstration', 'fracas', 'street battle' (a careful study of the ideological basis of media presentations of reality can be found in G.R. Kress and R. Hodge (1979) *Language as Ideology*. Hence the deconstruction of the surface manifestations of cultural codes can yield insight into the choices and preferred readings of such texts.

deterritorialisation the process by which identity becomes detached from its location and material base. The process of diaspora and hybridisation are elements in the radical displacement of 'rooted' identities, becoming 'routed' in Bhabha's description of the 'border lands' of ethnicity. More generally in postmodernity, the term indicates the compression of time and space suggested by Harvey (1989) and the erosion of meanings from a foundationalist base to becoming free-floating signifiers. The process of globalisation is certainly accelerating the pace at which physical location is decreasing in importance for social relationships.

diaspora a complex term often associated with migration and dispersal of peoples over time. The 1989 edition (second edition) of the OED traces the etymology of the word, 'Diaspora,' back to its Greek root and to its appearance in the Old Testament (Deut. 28:25). As such it references God's intentions for the people of Israel to be 'dispersed' across the world. 'Diaspora' now also refers to 'any body of people living outside their traditional homeland.' Victor Hoboken (2004: 202–3) cites the five types of diaspora. These are:

1 The 'victim' type includes communities which were forced to leave their homeland as a result of political, ethnic or religious conflicts. Among them were Armenians, African captives in Americas and Palestinians.

2 'Labour' diasporas (Italian, Chinese, Japanese, Turkish communities) emerge when the movement of people is caused by unsatisfactory economic conditions in their home countries.

3 'Trade' diasporas do not necessarily mean an escape from home, but are the result of both an individual and a collective (state-sponsored) effort. Chinese trade communities in many countries of south-east Asia illustrate this form.

4 The 'imperial' or 'colonial' type of diaspora – for example Europeans, who found themselves outside their countries of origin after the collapse of colonialism, such as the British in Africa or Russians in the former Soviet republics of the USSR.

5 The 'cultural' or 'hybrid' type of diaspora is best illustrated by the Caribbean peoples abroad. The peoples of the Caribbean are the descendants of the European colonists (imperial diasporas), the Indian migrant workers (labour diaspora) and the African slaves from west Africa (victim diaspora).

differance in this term (from Derrida) 'meaning is always deferred, never quite fixed or complete, so there's always some slippage' (Woodward 1999: 21). Meaning is derived from both identity and difference – it is a continuous dialectic between the two and hence never complete, always open. 'Differance' is Derrida's attempt to combine these aspects of the process of sense making in one word which combines both difference and deferral (see Appignanesi and Garrett 1995: 80). As we have seen in the early chapters meaning and identity are always contingent on 'the other' or the subaltern, this is a necessary and destabilising force within the identity of the dominant term. In other words the marginalised and subordinate term is functionally opposed and a negation of the dominant term, yet actually constitutive of it. This is easy to see in terms like gay/straight, black/white, male/female, sane/insane, etc.

discourse discourses are those broad patterns of institutional thought, or as Foucault suggested 'regimes of truth' which define and limit what can be said about a specific topic. Muecke's (1982) article called 'Available Discourses on Aborigines', suggested that white Australians were limited to only four ways of speaking about Aborigines: via the anthropological, the romantic, the literary and the directly racist (see Chapter 6). Discourse in Foucault's conception is the manner in which power is constituted. This was a radical departure from the notion of power as a possession installed and wielded by (for example) an all-powerful authoritarian state. Foucault instead sees power as the result of the association of various disciplinary practices and knowledges and the resistances to these. His analyses traced the origins of the Asylum (*Madness and Civilization*) the prison and regimes of punishment and surveillance (*Discipline and Punish*) and the different social formations around sexualities (*History of Sexuality I, II, III*).

Discourse is an elusive term which refers to overarching canons of meaning which constitute knowledge and lived experience. Discourse affects and is affected by subjectivity and directs and focuses complex power relations. Discourse is constituted by language but also by apparatus of the state (as shown in Foucault's analyses of prisons, torture, asylums) and the ideas and practices of resistance movements. It can be manifest in linguistic structures: the examples given in this book of 'race' and 'ethnicity' illustrate that these terms are the complex surface of many historical discourses (see Chapters 2 and 3).

essentialism the belief that categories or individuals and groups of human beings have innate, defining features exclusive to their category (for example, the belief that different races have inherent characteristics that differentiate them from other races). Essentialism has been challenged by social constructionist theories which have shown that while there may be some biological predispositions identity and meaning are culturally produced, there is evidence that social-isation, and the discursive practices of a society will shape our sense of self and that this is being constantly modified by a dialectic process. It is quite clear that ethnicity and race, age, gender and sexuality and other aspects of culture are interpreted differently and the practices associated with social divisions vary between cultures.

ethnic cleansing 'the attempt to create ethnically homogeneous geographic areas through the deportation or forcible displacement of persons belonging to particular ethnic groups. Ethnic cleansing sometimes involves the removal of all physical vestiges of the targeted group through the destruction of monuments, cemeteries, and houses of worship' (<http://www.britannica.com/eb/article?tocId=9390062>).

Ethnic cleansing is distinguishable from genocide, because its intent is expulsion, rather than physical destruction of a group. But genocidal massacres are a common tactic in ethnic cleansing. Genocide and ethnic cleansing are not mutually exclusive. A common misconception about genocide is that it requires the intent to destroy an *entire* group. But the Genocide Convention clearly states that it only requires that a *part* of an ethnic or racial group be destroyed for the term genocide to apply. If the victims of mass murder are selected solely because they are members of an ethnic or racial group, that is genocide. Both genocide and ethnic cleansing are now underway in Darfur.

Cultural genocide can also be practised as occurred in Australia with the 'stolen generations'.

ethnocentric the attitude that one's own culture is superior to others, that one's own beliefs, values and behaviour are more correct than others; and that other people and cultures can be evaluated in terms of one's own culture. A tendency to understand the world only from the viewpoint of one's own culture.

eugenics meaning literally 'normal genes'. Sir Francis Galton (1822–1911) (Darwin's cousin) was the founder of the eugenics movement. Eugenics aims to improve the genetic constitution of the human species by selective breeding. There are several forms:

1   **positive**: selective breeding using 'superior' genetic material (for example, sperm donated by a Nobel scientist);
2   **negative eugenics**: forced sterilisation, ethnic cleansing, genocide;
3   **intra-societal eugenics**: social problems – crime, poverty, disease seen as product of less highly evolved genes;
4   **inter-societal eugenics**: imperial notions of 'progress' and 'civilisation' based on evolutionary principles. Focus on the need to compete and defeat other nations. War is seen as a necessary and 'natural' aspect of existence.

Although Darwin was anxious that evolutionary theory was not used in a negative way, certain readings of his work can be seen to have set such discourses in motion. 'When a species increases inordinately in numbers in a small tract, epidemics often ensue; and here we have a limiting check independent of the struggle for life' (Darwin 1979: 72). Darwin does seem to have believed that the mechanisms of natural selection are thwarted by human civilisation. One of the objectives of civilisation is somehow to help the underprivileged ones, therefore to be opposed to the natural selection responsible for extinction of the weakest.

ex-nomination a term used by Roland Barthes (1972) to identify one of the ways in which the dominance of the ruling class goes unexamined precisely because it is not named as such: the process of ex-nomination ensures that we see the values or attributes of dominant groups not as the product of particular class interests, but simply as apolitical, intrinsic human values that are, therefore, as unsuitable for critique as a grapefruit or any other 'real thing'. Ex-nomination also works to legitimate the dominance of specific racial and cultural groups by failing to acknowledge or 'mark' their distinctive qualities (for example, white, heterosexual), thereby assuming their universality.

genocide the Genocide Convention defines genocide as 'the intentional destruction, in whole or in part, of a national, ethnical, racial, or religious group' (Stanton 2004) The formal definition came in the 1948 Convention for the Prevention and the Punishment of the Crime of Genocide. Genocide is defined in the Convention as any of the following acts committed with intent to destroy, in whole or in part, a national, ethnic, racial or religious group, as such: a) killing members of the group; b) causing serious bodily or mental harm to members of the group; c) deliberately inflicting on the group conditions of life calculated to bring about its physical destruction in whole or in part; d) imposing measures intended to prevent births within the group; e) forcibly transferring children of the group to another group (Becker (2000) *Genocide and Ethnic Cleansing*, Model United Nations Far West , 50th Session Issues, http://www.munfw.org/archive/50th/4th1.htm).

habitus a concept originally suggested by Marcel Mauss (1979) to designate both the living space and how social groups internalise their environments forming sets of dispositions including material effects, bodily attitudes and behaviours. The culture is expressed through a range of bodily functions (similar to Foucault's techniques of the self): basic activities as sleeping, eating, sitting, walking, having sex, giving birth, and so forth. These are thought of as natural functions but they are performed quite differently in different historical periods and cultures. The term has come to prominence in the work of Pierre Bourdieu (1977). Bourdieu extended the concept demonstrating the relationship between habitus and social class. It has also been applied to various other social contexts such as ethnicity and gender relations.

hegemony developed by the Italian Marxist Antonio Gramsci in the 1930s, hegemony refers to the way in which dominant groups in society are able to maintain their dominance over the less powerful groups without recourse to force or coercion, but instead are able to actively gain their consent. This has the effect of making dominance of certain groups appear legitimate and natural, 'the way of the world'. Hegemony, in Gramsci's view, is never total but operates by constant negotiation with other emergent forms of resistance. For example the 'moral panics' which operate sporadically in western society.

hybridity 'in-between' stage, between the pre-colonial subject's identity and the identity internalised through colonialisation. Hybridity describes the inevitable process of cultural translation which is inevitable in a world where communities, peoples, cultures, tribes, ethnii, are no longer homogenous self-sufficient autochthonous entities tightly bound within by kinship and tradition and strongly boundaried in relation to the outside world (Hall 2000). Similar is the concept of 'border-crossing' in which the lack of fixed identities, uncertainty, mobility and the possibility of negotiating boundaries is emphasised.

ideal reader is a term which suggests that every text is presented with a particular class of reader in mind, marking preferences; values, attitudes and beliefs implicit in its reading. Kress (1988: 107) states:

> Every genre positions those who participate in a text of that kind: as interviewer or interviewee, as listener or storyteller, as a reader or a writer, as a person interested in political matters, as someone to be instructed or as someone who instructs; each of these positionings implies different possibilities for response and for action. Each written text provides a 'reading position' for readers, a position constructed by the writer for the 'ideal reader' of the text.

These reading positions can give the reader the clear impression that he or she is part of an 'Us' or 'Them'. Take, for example, the sample news headlines in Chapter 6. In this instance, and many like it, a group is presented as a threat to the moral order; the language used about them is in sharp contrast to that used about white citizens, tourists or the police. The values which emerge from a glance at these headlines are firmly white and middle class and imply that 'itinerants' are a problem because of their drinking and begging, bothering local business people and tourists. The same positioning is discernible (although not always as overtly) in all texts.

identity politics Postmodernism's culturally relative stance challenged and displaced the 'grand narratives' of history, meaning that old certainties associated with the project of modernity appeared untenable – such absolutes lead to the horrors of monocultural dominance. Instead the previously essentialised opposition to the state became fragmented; unified notions of black, feminist or working-class resistance to oppression, for example, are suggested to have been undermined by this 'cultural turn' in which relative values come to define groups through more and more finely drawn distinctions. This notion of identity politics has become something of a bête noire to left-leaning intellectuals and scholars as it embraces the notion of increasingly diffuse power relations making mass resistance impossible. The recent debate on multiculturalism (see Chapter 8) is a case in point. Kenan Malik, commenting on an article by David Goodhart entitled 'Too Diverse', which questioned whether diversity was compatible with social cohesion and a genuinely shared social system, made the following rejoinder:

> the real problem is not a surfeit of strangers in our midst but the abandonment over the past two decades of ideologically based politics for a politics of identity. The result has been the fragmentation of society as different groups assert their particular identities - and the creation of a well of resentment within white working class communities who feel left out.
>
> (Malik 2004)

ideological state apparatus Althusser (1977) argues that ideology is a 'system of representations' which mediate people's understanding of themselves and their relationship to society. Ideology actually forms social subjects, manipulating their unconscious desires as well as their rational interests in order to 'interpellate' them – that is, in order to gain their identification with certain social and cultural roles or identities. Ideology offers people particular identities with which they then identify. It constitutes the subject's '"lived" relation to the real'. James Kavanagh argues that this more sophisticated version of ideology might pave the way for highly sophisticated forms of criticism, taking into account multiple social and cultural differences:

> Ideology is less tenacious as a 'set of ideas' than as a system of representations, perceptions, and images that precisely encourages men and women to 'see' their specific place in a historically peculiar social formation as inevitable, natural, a necessary function of the 'real' itself. Notwithstanding its roots in a class-based understanding of history, contemporary ideology theory also recognises that perceived forms of social 'reality' and subjectivity are constructed within more than one system of differences. In various socially specific ways, differences of sex, race, religion, region, education and ethnicity, as well as class, form complex webs of determinations that affect how ideology works up in a 'lived' relation to the real.
>
> (Kavanagh 1995: 310–11)

ideology an underlying set of values or beliefs, but frequently ones which are not consciously questioned or even visible as such. The ideological process tends to normalise and naturalise covering its tracks. Stuart Hall defined ideology as: 'images, concepts and premises which provide frameworks through which we represent, interpret, understand and 'make sense' of some aspect of social existence' (2000: 271).

imagined communities Benedict Anderson's (1983) term for the way people's speculative realisation is all that really exists of an ethnic group or a nation state. Groups are often united by a powerful image of the nation which may be at odds with the current reality but provides an idealised or hoped-for state to which the group will return. Politicians are in the business of conveying this imagined holistic vision of the nation as it should be. The plurality of many modern states may seem as a threat to these visions and may make their core values harder to articulate. This can lead to break-away movements devising newer, more satisfying images of the community.

ineffability the notion that primordial attachments exert a powerful and unchangeable influence (are in fact ineffable). Hence such attachments are inescapable – outside of social influence.

institutional racism discriminatory racial practices built into such prominent structures as the political, economic, and education systems. Those accepted, established, evident, visible and respected forces, social arrangements, institutions, structures, policies, precedents and systems of social relations that operate and are manipulated in such a way as to allow, support or acquiesce to acts of individual racism and to deprive certain racially identified categories within a society a chance to share, have equal access to, or have equal opportunity to acquire those things, material and non-material, that are defined as desirable and necessary for rising in an hierarchical class society while that society is dependent, in part, upon that group they deprive for their labor and loyalty. Institutional racism is more subtle, less visible, and less identifiable but no less destructive to human life and human dignity than individual acts of racism. Institutional racism deprives a racially identified group, usually defined as generally inferior to the defining dominant group, equal access to an treatment in education, medical care, law, politics, housing, etc. (Knowles and Prewitt 1969).

internal colonialism a form of colonialism in which the dominant and subordinate populations are intermingled, so that there is no geographically distant 'metropolis' separate from the 'colony'. An explanation of society based on situations where there is a minority persistently exploited by capitalism. Some sort of de-facto segregation and exclusion is part of the equation. First developed with respect to England and its 'internal periphery'. This was mainly Wales and Ireland. The dominant culture uses the 'peripheral' areas to maintain supplies of cheap labour for industry. Other examples would include Turks within modern Germany, Blacks in South Africa (Bantustans) and Indians in Mexico (see Hechter 1995).

interpellation Louis Althusser, in his essay 'Ideology and Ideological State Apparatuses' (1977), describes interpellation as a process of identification, by which a subject (mis)recognises him or herself in an 'identity' or role which is offered them in society. Althusser uses the analogy of an address, or 'hailing'. An educator or a policeman, for example, might 'hail' me, by saying 'Hey you'. I might then turn around and recognise myself as the addressee. Thus Althusser hopes to show how ideologies either 'recruit' people to particular, acceptable subject positions in society, or else transform individuals into subjects who learn to identify with certain representations. Thus the agent addressing me might equally be a representation in a cultural text. Books, advertisements, TV programmes, films all contain representations of characters and situations with which we might identify. And bound up with such representations are certain societal norms, gender roles, attitudes towards certain groups, etc., which may be disseminated and normalised or satirised.

intersubjectivity the term implies the individual's subjectivity is dependent on networks of relationships. In a very real sense our identity is constantly negotiated and re-negotiated through communicative encounters with others. There are shared communicative codes within a culture. While we interpret images and other cultural codes uniquely through our own personal experiences and socio-cultural make-up we nevertheless recognise shared cultural meanings and interpretations. Examples of the 'myth' of whiteness and the contingent meanings of blackness in this text highlight the intersubjectivity of inter-pretations of race and ethnicity.

intertextuality the interrelationship between texts: usually one text's reference to another. This location of a cultural reference point (most often an historically prior one) usually takes the form of diffuse memories, echoes and reworkings of other texts. Intertextuality is particularly prevalent in 'postmodern' texts, which often play on the notion that everything is a reworking of something else to produce a 'pastiche aesthetic' (the hotchpotch of historical styles visible in postmodern architecture).

Kali Mai literally 'black mother'. Kali and Durga are two of the sisters or manifestations of a unitary power which are central to the beliefs of North Indians. The worship of Kali was brought to the Caribbean by North Indians during the indentureship period (1830s–1870s). A major feature of the religion is spirit possession and healing, there are ritual sacrifices in some churches and adherents have given proof of their spirit possession by permitting their arms and hands to be horse-whipped (with no apparent sign of pain or injury). Kali Mai worship in Guyana waned and reached its lowest period during the 1950s and 1960s (Bassier 1980, argues this coincides with Indian prominence in politics). There has since been revitalised movement of Kali Mai; African Guyanese have increasingly joined the church, and in some cases, as in the Rose Hall church I visited in 1991, an Africa 'Mother' was the presiding spirit medium. Many visited from different ethnic groups seeking solutions to a wide variety of personal problems both physical and psychological. The growth of the church in the 1990s reflects the need to transcend the political and economic realities in Guyana – now a very poor country. Similarly Rastafarian cults in Guyana have increased since 1978, again for the reason that the practices free the individual from the bonds of society and raise consciousness (by use of the sacred herb and practices that resist the materialism of society). 'The Rastas, like the Kali worshippers express disenchantment with the establishment and are incapable of having access to the scarce resources of society' (Bassier 1980: 37).

Manichean divide the Manicheans are adherents to a form of religious or philosophical dualism. Stemming from a religious dualism originating in Persia in the third century AD, Manicheans are said to have considered the universe as two irreconcilable forces of light and dark – hence the use of the term to mean a divide between irreconcilable opposites such as those listed below. These structural oppositions are considered by some structuralists to mirror the human psyche. Lévi-Strauss suggested that cultural patterns had developed from these largely unconscious human proclivity to categorise between stark oppositional categories, actually mirroring cognitive processes. Anomalous categories such as the serpent in the Garden of Eden are considered either magical or disturbing as they do not fit neatly into the existing categories. The tendency to divide the world in these terms, as expressed in the *Clash of Civilizations* (Huntington 1988), can be found in speeches by US presidents (Reagan/Bush references to an 'evil empire') particularly since 9/11 ('in the aftermath of 11 September George W. Bush moved to stifle dissent with the positively Procrustean pronouncement that "either you are with us or you are with the terrorists". There can be no middle way, for criticism is "unpatriotic"' (Macklin 2002)).

WHITE	BLACK
Culture	Nature
Good	Evil
Male	Female
Master	Slave
Adult	Child
Purity	Pollution
God	Satan
Reason	Emotion
law and order	Chaos
Civilization	Savagery
Us	Them

mirror stage Lacanian stage of development in the construction of the self. The child has no initial grasp of the boundaries between the self and others and the external world. During this phase, Lacan (see *Ecrits* 1977) argues (between the ages of 6 and 18 months – significantly before the acquisition of speech) the sight of oneself in the mirror creates a powerful embodied sense of self as an integrated whole, an 'illusion of a coherent and self-governing personal identity', yet the duality inherent in the experience is significant. Fanon (1967a) gives the example of the French child identifying (re-interpellating) him as a 'black man', thus shattering his illusory holistic self which had been formed within a colonial hierarchy.

misrecognition a term which stems from Lacanian speculation about the development of the ego. The child at a certain stage of infancy makes a primordial identification with his/her reflection in a mirror – this is the recognition of an ideal 'I'. The ego is seen emerging from the child's desire to completely identify with the reflected image (see **mirror stage**).

The term has also been applied to nationalism and the manner in which the migrant or the colonial subject identifies with the distorted mirror image the nation reflects back, internalising the misrecognised self (often manifest in a negative or contemptuous view of ones own kind). Misrecognition is defined in this instance as the opposite of recognition, and occurs when groups of people suffer because the people or society around them mirror back to them a confining or demeaning or contemptible picture of themselves (Taylor 1994: 25).

moral panic a recurrent feature of modern society, moral panics occur when society becomes convinced that it is under threat from some form of evil usually in human form. Stanley Cohen (1967) coined the term in reference to the clash between mods and rockers in the 1960s. Central to the concept is the instrumental actions of media in directing a spotlight on what are seen to be threats to the moral order or stability of society. Typical examples are street crimes and muggings (examined by Hall et al. in 1978) and more recently ecstasy and rave subcultures, video 'nasties' and paedophiles (Critcher 2003). Moral panics are frequently a reflection of society's anxiety, insularity and ignorance about others. Some examples are Islamophobia, news stories about terrorist activities in the UK, exaggerated images of black gang culture and gun crime.

multiculturalism term for an ethos, practices and policies through which the state manages diversity. There are several versions of multiculturalism; Lord Parekh's recent statement embodies the more progressive view:

> Multiculturalism is sometimes taken to mean that different cultural communities should live their own ways of life in a self-contained manner. This is not its only meaning and in fact it has long been obsolete. Multiculturalism basically means that no culture is perfect or represents the best life and that it can therefore benefit from a critical dialogue with other

cultures. In this sense multiculturalism requires that all cultures should be open, self-critical, and interactive in their relations with other each other.

More conservative interpretations reflect a concern that there should be a dominant strand of, for example, Britishness – as commented upon by Ruth Lea:

> every culture has the right to exist and there is no over-arching thread that holds them together. [. . .] That is the multiculturalism we think is so destructive because there's no thread to hold society together. It is that multiculturalism that Trevor Phillips has condemned and, of course, we are totally supportive. There is another way to define multiculturalism which I would call diversity where people have their own cultural beliefs and they happily coexist – but there is a common thread of Britishness or whatever you want to call it to hold society together.
>
> And that is clearly what I would support because you do accept that people have different cultures and you accept them. It a positive acceptance not a negative tolerance.
>
> (BBC News, 5 April 2004, see Parekh 2000)

the 'Other' a term which reflects the metaphysical self-referential perception of people who are seen as fundamentally different especially used to signify people from other cultures, non-hegemonic sexualities, gays or lesbians, transgressing gender norms – transsexuals, third sex, and so on. In short a concept which stems from existential thinkers such as Sartre and recognises the contingent nature of self identity as formed in relation to other alien subjectivities.

plural societies a plural society is one whose population is divided into two or more sub-populations where the members of each enclave are characterised by distinctive sets of values, beliefs occupational and social groups. In some cases political preferences may be drawn along ethnic lines. These societies are frequently the result of colonialism, where different nationals have been transported as a labour source. Guyana, Trinidad, Surinam, Mauritius, Fiji and Malaysia, are examples of societies where pluralism was created by migration for labour supply for sugar estates and other colonial production. The UK is a plural society due to the diaspora of subjects from former British colonies.

punctum the term Barthes uses to explain the instance by which a detail catches attention in a photograph and is able to radically alter the reading. In *Camera Lucida* he states: '. . . a "detail" attracts me. I feel that its mere presence changes my reading, that I am looking at a new photograph, marked in my eyes with a higher value' (1984b: 42). The 'punctum' to Barthes is that which 'rises from the scene, shoots out of it like an arrow, and pierces me' (p. 26). These details punctuate, disturb and rupture the *stadium*: that conscious investment in the image, a '. . . very wide field of unconcerned desire, of inconsequential taste: *I like/I don't like'* (p. 27); 'a kind of general, enthusiastic commitment, of course, but without special acuity' (p. 26). The example in Chapter 1 highlights this possibility that a detail in a photo can emerge and dominate the image.

scopophilia   a term used by Laura Mulvey (1975) to describe voyeurism and 'the look' in cinema. Derived originally from Freud's theoretical canon, Mulvey has convincingly shown that the look defines and possesses the other, furthermore by viewing films we are positioned as the voyeur. Some feminist theorists have employed the term as a way of discussing the 'male gaze' and the patriarchal and colonial view of the colonial female body.

'sous rature'   [under erasure] Derrida's (1976) concept which recognises the contested and problematic nature of certain concepts. Derrida developed a method of using such terms with a line through them to demonstrate that they were used out of necessity to convey a meaning which is in circulation but is a far from satisfactory use. 'Race' in particular (and due to its almost synonymous use 'ethnicity' too) would both be prime candidates for this treatment.

BIBLIOGRAPHY

African Reparation Movement (1997) from Lords' Hansard, available online at <http://www.arm.arc.co.uk/LordsHansard.html>.

Ahmad A. (1995) 'The Politics of Literary Postcoloniality', *Race and Class*, 36.

Aiken, R. and R. Poulsen (1997) *Militant*, 61, 44, 15 December.

Ali, T. (2002) *The Clash of Fundamentalisms: Crusades, Jihads, and Modernity*, London: Verso.

Althusser, L. 'Ideology and Ideological State Apparatuses (Notes Towards an Investigation)', in L. Althusser (1977) *'Lenin and Philosophy' and Other Essays*, London: New Left Books.

Anderson, B. (1983) *Imagined Communities: Reflections on the Origin and Spread of Nationalism*, London: Verso.

Anderson, S. E. (1995) *The Black Holocaust for Beginners*, London and New York: Writers and Readers.

Ankomah, B. (1999) 'The Butcher of Congo', *New African*, October, available online at <http://www.africasia.com/icpubs/na/oct99/nacs1002.htm>.

Anthias, F. and N. Yuval-Davis (1992) *Racialized Boundaries*, London and New York: Routledge.

Appadurai, A. (1990) 'Disjuncture and Difference in the Global Cultural Economy', in M. Featherstone (ed.) *Global Culture*, London: Sage, pp. 295–310.

Appignanesi, R. and C. Garrett (1995) *Postmodernism for Beginners*, Trumpington: Icon.

ARI (Ayn Rand Institute) (1998) 'Multiculturalism and Diversity: The New Racism', Available online at <http://multiculturalism.aynrand.org>.

Ashcroft, B., G. Griffiths and H. Tiffin (1998) *Key Concepts in Post-Colonial Studies*, London and New York: Routledge.

Ashcroft, B., G. Griffiths and H. Tiffin (eds) (1995) *The Post-Colonial Studies Reader*, London and New York: Routledge.

Aung San Suu Kyi (1994) 'Empowerment for a Culture of Peace and Development', 21 November, address to WCCD in Manila, available online at <http://www.ibiblio.org/freeburma/assk/assk3-2c.html>.

Aziz, R. (1992) 'Feminism and the Challenge of Racism: Deviance or Difference?' in H. Crowley and S. Himmelweit (eds) *Knowing Women: Feminism and Knowledge*, Cambridge: Polity Press.

Back, L. (2002) 'The Fact of Hybridity: Youth, Ethnicity and Racism' in D. T. Goldberg and J. Solomos (eds) *A Companion to Racial and Ethnic Studies*, Oxford: Blackwell, pp. 439–54.

Balandier, G. (1974) 'The Colonial Situation: A Theoretical Approach (1951)', in I. Wallerstein, *The Modern World System: Capitalist Agriculture and the Origins of the European World Economy in the Sixteenth Century*, London and New York: Academic Press.

Balibar, E. and E. Wallerstein, (1991) *Race, Nation, Class: Ambiguous Identities*, London and New York: Verso.

Banton, M. (1967) *Race Relations*, London: Tavistock.

Banton, M. (1987) *Racial Theories*, Cambridge: Cambridge University Press.

Barker, C. and D. Galasinski (2001) *Cultural Studies and Discourse Analysis: A Dialogue on Language and Identity*, London, Sage.

Barth, F. (1969) *Ethnic Groups and Social Boundaries: The Social Organization of Culture Difference*, London: George Allen & Unwin.

Barthes, R. (1972) *Mythologies*, selected and translated from the French by Annette Lavers, London: Cape.

Barthes, R. (1984a) *Image, Music, Text*, selected and translated by Stephen Heath, London: Flamingo.

Barthes, R. (1984b) *Camera Lucida*, translated by Richard Howard, London: Flamingo.

Bassier, D. (1980) *Kali Mai Worship in Guyana: A Quest for a New Identity*. WMZ, Bassier.

Baudrillard, J. (1983) *Simulations* New York: Semiotext.

Baudrillard, J. (1991) *La Guerre du golfe n'a pas eu lieu*, Paris: Galilee.

Bauman, Z. (2002) 'Holocaust', in D. T. Goldberg and J. Solomos (eds), *A Companion to Racial and Ethnic Studies*, Part 1, Oxford: Blackwell, pp 46–63.

BBC News (2004) 'Debate call on "multicultural" UK', 5 April, available online at <http://news.bbc.co.uk/1/hi/uk_politics/3599925.stm>.

BBC News (2004) 'So What Exactly is Multiculturalism?' 5 April, available online at <http://news.bbc.co.uk/1/hi/uk/3600791.stm>.

BBC World Service (2001) 'Mixed Race, Mixed Feelings', 1 September, available online at <http://www.bbc.co.uk/worldservice/people/highlights/010831_mixedrace.shtml>.

Beard, J. R. (1970) *The Life of Toussaint L'Ouverture, the Negro Patriot of Hayti: Comprising an Account of the Struggle for Liberty in the Island, and a Sketch of Its History to the Present Period*. First published 1853. Westport, Conn.: Negro Universities Press.

Beck, U. (1992) *The Risk Society*, London, Sage.

Beck, U. (2002) 'The Silence of Words and Political Dynamics in the World Risk Society', *Logos*, 1:4 (fall), Available online at <logosonline.home.igc.org/beck.htm>.

Becker, K. *Genocide and Ethnic Cleansing*, Model United Nations Far West, 50th Session Issues.

Benedict, R. (1961) *Patterns of Culture*, Boston, Mass.: Houghton Mifflin.

Benjamin, G. (1985) 'The Cultural Logic of Singapore's Multiracialism', in R. Hassan (ed.) *Singapore: Society in Transition*, Kuala Lumpur: Oxford University Press, pp. 115–33.

Bennett, D. and J. Stephens (1991) 'Postcolonial Critique' *Arena*, 96, (spring): 5.

Bentley, C. (1987) 'Ethnicity and Practice', *Comparative Studies in Society and History*, 29: 1, 24–55.

Bhabha, H. (1985) 'Signs Taken for Wonders: Questions of Ambivalence and Authority Under a Tree Outside Delhi', *Critical Inquiry* 12(1): 144–65.

Bhabha, H. (1994) *The Location of Culture*, London and New York: Routledge.

Bhabha, H. (1996) 'Culture's In-Between', in S. Hall and P. du Gay (eds), *Questions of Cultural Identity*, London and Thousand Oaks, Calif.: Sage, pp. 53–60.

Bilton, T., K. Bennett, P. Jones, M. Stanworth, K. Sheard and A. Webster (eds) (1987) *Introductory Sociology*, 2nd edn, London: Macmillan.

Black, E. (2001) *IBM and the Holocaust*, London: Little Brown.

Blainey, G. (1984) *All For Australia*, North Ryde: Methuen Haynes.

Blainey, G. (1988) 'Australian Australians Must Begin to Shout Loudly', *Weekend Australian*, 2–3 July, p. 22.

Blainey, G. (1993) 'Latham Memorial Lecture', *Australian*, 29 April, p. 3.

Blanchard, T. (2001) 'Model of a Modern Briton', Race in Britain Observer Special, 25 November, available online at <http://observer.guardian.co.uk/race/story/0,11255, 605343,00.html>.

Bleakley, J. W. (1929) *The Aboriginals and Half-Castes of Central Australia and North Australia*, Melbourne: Government Printer, available online at <http://www.usyd. edu.au/su/social/robert/arc/notes/bleakley.htm>.

Blonsky, M. (ed.) (1985) *On Signs: A Semiotic Reader*, Oxford: Basil Blackwell.

Blum, W. (2004) 'Killing Hope US Military and CIA Interventions Since World War II', available online at <http://members.aol.com/bblum6/webpagea.htm>.

Bolaffi, G et al. (eds) (2003) *Dictionary of Race, Ethnicity and Culture*, London and Thousand Oaks, Calif.: Sage.

Borges, J. L. (1975) *A Universal History of Infamy*, translated by Norman Thomas di Giovanni, Harmondsworth: Penguin.

Bourdieu, P. (1977) *Outline of Theory of Practice*, Cambridge: Cambridge University Press.

Bourdieu, P. (1989a) *Distinction: A Social Critique of the Judgement of Taste*, London and New York: Routledge.

Bourdieu, P. (1989b) *The Logic of Practice*, Cambridge: Polity Press.

Bourdieu, P. (1990) *In Other Words: Essays toward a Reflective Sociology*, Oxford: Polity.

Bourdieu, P. and L. Boltanski (1976) 'La production de l'idéologie dominante', *Actes de la Recherche en Sciences Sociales*, 2/3(June): 4.

Boylan, J. (1992) MA thesis, University of Washington.

Brah, A. (1996) *Cartographies of Diaspora, Contesting Identities*, London and New York: Routledge.

Bramann, J. K. (1999) *Multiculturalism and Personal Identity*, Preliminary draft of the Philosophical Forum presentation for 26 October, available online at <http://faculty. frostbury.edu/phil/forum/multicult.htm>.

Bronowski, J. (1974) *The Ascent of Man*, London: BBC Books.

Bufton, S. (2004) 'Social Class', in G. Taylor and S. Spencer (eds) (2004) *Social Identities: Multidisciplinary Approaches*, London and New York: Routledge

Bullivant, B. (1983) 'Australia's Pluralist Dilemma: An Age-Old Problem in a New Guise', *Australian Quarterly*, (winter): 136–48.

Carmen, L. (1996) 'Reading Gender and Culture in Media Discourses and Texts', in G. Bull and M. Anstey (eds) (1996) *The Literacy Lexicon*, New York and Sydney: Prentice-Hall.

Cashmore E. and J. Jennings (eds) (2001) *Racism: Essential Readings*, London and Thousand Oaks, Calif.: Sage.

Cashmore, E. (1988) *Dictionary of Race and Ethnic Relations*, 2nd edn, London and New York: Routledge.

Cashmore, E. (1996) 'Ethnicity', in E. Cashmore (ed.) *Dictionary of Race and Ethnic Relations*, New York: Routledge.

Castles, S. and A. Davidson (2000) *Citizenship and Migration: Globalisation and the Politics of Belonging*, London: Macmillan.

Castles, S. and G. Kossack (1985) *Immigrant Workers and Class Structure in Western Europe*, 2nd edn, Oxford: Oxford University Press.

Centre for Contemporary Cultural Studies (1982) *The Empire Strikes Back*, London: Macmillan.

Centre of International Studies (2001) 'Resolving Self-Determination Dispute Through Complex Power Sharing Arrangements Workshop', Cambridge University 9–10 February, available online at <http://www.ecmi.de/cps/download/background1.pdf>.

Chandler, D. (1999) *Semiotics for Beginners*, available online at <http://www.aber.ac.uk/media/Documents/S4B/semiotic.html>.

Chin, U. H. 'The Chinese of South-East Asia Raped for Being Chinese' available online at <http://www.minorityrights.org/Profiles/profile.asp?ID=16>.

Chinweizu (1987) *The West and the Rest of Us: White Predators, Black slavers and the African Elite*, 2nd edn, Lagos: Pero.

Cohen, R. (1997) *Global Diasporas*, London: UCL Press.

Cohen S. (1967) *Folk Devils and Moral Panics: The Creation of the Mods and Rockers.* London: MacGibbon and Kee.

Cohen, S. (2002) *Folk Devils and Moral Panics*, 3rd edn, London and New York: Routledge.

Cohen, S. and J. Young (eds) (1981) *The Manufacture of News: Social Problems, Deviance and the Mass Media*, London: Constable.

Comaroff, J. and J. Comaroff (1992) *Ethnography and the Historical Imagination*, Boulder, Col.: Westview Press.

Commonwealth of Australia (1978) *Migrant Services and Programs: Report of the Review of Post-arrival Programs and Services for Migrants*, Canberra: AGPS.

Connell, R. W. (1987) *Gender and Power.* Stanford, Calif: Stanford University Press.

Cooray, M. (1988) 'Multiculturalism in Australia', available online at <http://www.ourcivilisation.com/cooray/multcult>.

Cornell, S. and D. Hartmann (1998) *Ethnicity and Race: Making Identities in a Changing World*, London and Thousand Oaks, Calif.: Pine Forge Press.

Cottle, S. (ed.) (2000) *Ethnic Minorities and the Media*, London: Allen & Unwin.

Coward, R. (1984) *Female Desire: Women's Sexuality Today*, London: Granada.

Cowlishaw, G. (1994) 'Policing the Races', *Social Analysis* 36: 71–91.

Cox, O. C. (1976) *Race Relations: Elements and Social Dynamics*, Detroit, Mich.: Wayne State University Press.

Critcher, C. (2003) *Moral Panics and the Media*, Milton Keynes: Open University Press.

Crowley, H. and S. Himmelweit (eds) *Knowing Women: Feminism and Knowledge*, London: Polity Press.

Cuff, E. C., W. W. Sharrock and D. W. Francis (1992) *Perspectives in Sociology*, 3rd edn, London and New York: Routledge.

Culler, J. (1983) *Barthes*, London: Fontana.

Curtis, L. et al. (1984) *Nothing but the Same Old Story: The Roots of Anti-Irish Racism*, London: Information on Ireland.

Curtis, M. (2001) *Web of Deceit*, London: Verso.

Curtis, M. (2004) *Unpeople: Britain's Secret Human Rights Abuses*, London: Vintage.

Cuvier, Baron (1890) *The Animal Kingdom*, London: W.H. Allen.

Dabydeen, D. (1991) 'On Cultural Diversity', in M. Fisher and U. Owen, *Whose Cities?*, Harmondsworth: Penguin, pp. 97–106.

Dabydeen, D. and B. Samaroo (eds) (1987) *India in the Caribbean*, London: Hansib.

Daily Mirror (1980) 'Mirror Comment: They Eat Horses Don't They?' 10 September, p. 2.

Darwin, C. (1979) *The Illustrated Origin of Species* (abridged and introduced by Richard Leakey), London: Faber and Faber.

Dawkins, R. (1989) *The Selfish Gene*, 2nd edn, Oxford: Oxford University Press.

Day, W. B. (2001) 'Aboriginal Fringe Dwellers in Darwin: Cultural Persistence or Culture of Resistance?' Ph.D. thesis, University of Western Australia Department of Anthropology, available online at <http://www.country-liberal-party.com/pages/Bill_Day_Thesis.c.htm>.

Derrida, J. (1967) *Of Grammatology*, trans. Gayatri Chakravorty Spivak, France: Les Editions de Minuit.

Despres, L. (1967) *Cultural Pluralism and Nationalist Politics in British Guiana*, Chicago, Ill.: Rand McNally & Co.

Despres, L. (ed.) (1975) *Ethnicity and Resource Competition in Plural Societies*, The Hague: Mouton.

Dobbin, M. (1998) 'Unfriendly Giants', *ROB Magazine*, July, available online at <http://www.globalpolicy.org/socecon/tncs/unfriendlygiants.htm> (accessed 11 February 2005).

Dodd, V. (2004) 'Muslim Groups Infuriated by Anti-Terrorism Poster', *Guardian*, 14 May, available online at <http://www.guardian.co.uk/terrorism/story/0,12780,1216410,00.htm>.

Donald, J. and A. Rattansi (eds) (1992) *'Race', Culture and Difference*, London and Thousand Oaks, Calif.: Sage.

Drescher, S. and S. Engerman (1998) *A Historical Guide to World Slavery*, Oxford: Oxford University Press.

Drewe, R. (1976) *The Savage Crows*, Sydney: Collins.

Du Bois, W. E. B (1897) 'Strivings of the Negro People', *Atlantic Monthly* 80: 194–8, available online at <http://eserver.org/race/strivings.html> (accessed 11 February 2005).

Duggan E. J. M. (2000) *Digital Images: Lecture Notes*. February, available online at <http://www.ejmd.mcmail.com/digitalimages.htm>.

During, S. (1987) 'Postmodernism or Post-Colonialism Today,' *Textual Practice* 1.1: 32–47

Dyer, R. (1997) *White*, London: Routledge.

Eco, U. (1965) 'Towards a Semiotic Enquiry into the Television Message', in Corner and Hawthorn (eds) (1980) *Communication Studies: An Introductory Reader*, London: Edward Arnold, pp. 131–50.

The Electronic Telegraph (1998) 'The Trial of the Race Commission', 22 Sept. 1998, available online at: <http://amren.com/pdf/98November>.

Erdogan, N. (2000) 'Veiled and Revealed: Review of Meyda Yegenoglu, *Colonial Fantasies: Towards a Feminist Reading of Orientalism*', available online at <http://www. iath.virginia.edu/pmc/text-only/issue.100/10.2.r_erdogan.txt>.

Essed, P. and D. T. Goldberg (eds) (2002) *Race Critical Theories*, Oxford: Blackwell.

Eze, E. C. (ed.) *Race and the Enlightenment*, Oxford: Blackwell.

Fanon, F. (1961) *The Wretched of the Earth*, Harmondsworth: Penguin.

Fanon, F. (1967a) *Black Skin, White Masks*, New York: Grove Press.

Fanon, F. (1967b) *Toward the African Revolution*, Harmondsworth: Pelican.

Featherstone, M. (1991) *Consumer Culture and Postmodernism*, London and Thousand Oaks, Calif.: Sage.

Featherstone, M. (1995) *Undoing Culture*, London and Thousand Oaks, Calif.: Sage.

Featherstone, M. (ed.) *Global Modernities*, London and Thousand Oaks, Calif.: Sage.

Fenton, S. (1999) *Ethnicity: Racism, Class and Culture*, London: Macmillan.

Fenton, S. (2003) *Ethnicity*, London: Polity.

Fenton S. and H. Bradley (eds) (2002) *Ethnicity and Economy: 'Race and Class' Revisited*, Basingstoke, Palgrave.

Finnigan, G. (2001) *City of Port Phillip Aboriginal Resource Primer*, March.

Fiske, J. (1987) *Television Culture*. London: Routledge

Fiske, J. (1990) *Introduction to Communication Studies*, 2nd edn, London and New York: Routledge.

Fiske, J. and J. Hartley (1978) *Reading Television*, London: Methuen.

Fiske, J., B. Hodge et al. (1987) *Myths of Oz*, London: Allen & Unwin.

Fleras, A. (1994) in Mark Charlton and Paul Baker, *Contemporary Political Issues*, second edition, Scarborough, Nelson Canada, 1994, p. 26).

Foley, G. (1997) 'Muddy Waters: Archie, Mudrooroo and Aboriginality', available online at <http://www.kooriweb.org/foley/essays/essay_10.html>.

Foucault, M. (1972) *The Archaeology of Knowledge*, London: Tavistock.

Foucault, M. (1977a) *Discipline and Punish*, London: Allen Lane.

Foucault, M. (1977b) 'Intellectuals and Power: A Conversation Between Michel Foucault and Gilles Deleuze', translated by D. F. Bouchard and S. Simon, in D. F. Bouchard (ed.) *Language, Counter-Memory, Practice: Selected Essays and Interviews by Michel Foucault*, Ithaca, NY: Cornell University Press, pp. 205–17.

Foucault, M. (1980) *Power/Knowledge: Selected Interviews and Other Writings 1972–1977*, edited by C. Gordon, Brighton: Harvester Press.

Foucault, M. (1984) *The History of Sexuality: An Introduction*, Harmondsworth: Penguin.

Frankenberg, R. (1993) *White Women, Race Matters: The Social Construction of Whiteness*, London and New York: Routledge.

Frederickson, G. M. (2002) *Racism: A Short History*, Princeton, NJ: Princeton University Press.

Fukuyama, F. (1999) 'Economic Globalization and Culture', Merrill Lynch Forum, available online at <http://www.ml.com/woml/forum/global_s.htm> (accessed 27 November 1999).

Furnivall, J. S. (1948) *Colonial Policy and Practice: A Comparative Study of Burma, Netherlands and India*, New York: New York University Press.

Galton, F. (1996) *Essays in Eugenics* Washington DC: Scott-Townsend Publishers.

Gandhi, Mohandas Karamchand (1964) 'On Means and Ends', in *Gandhi on Non-Violence*, New York: New Directions.

Gardiner-Garden, J. (2000) 'The Definition of Aboriginality', *Social Policy Group Research* 18, 5 December, available online at <http://www.aph.gov.au/library/pubs/rn/2000-01/01RN18.htm>.

Gardiner-Garden, J. (2003) 'Defining Aboriginality in Australia', *Current Issues Brief* 10, Social Policy Group, 3 February.

Geertz, C. (1973) *The Interpretation of Cultures*, New York: Basic Books.

Giddens, A. (2000) *Runaway World: How Globalization is Reshaping Our Lives*, New York: Routledge.

Giddens, A. (ed.) (1994) *The Polity Reader in Social Theory*, Cambridge: Polity.

Gilbert, O. (1850), 'Narrative of Sojourner Truth' (based on information provided by Sojourner Truth), *A Celebration of Women Writers*, available online at <http://digital.library.upenn.edu/women/truth/1850/1850.html>.

Gilroy, P. (1993) *The Black Atlantic*, London: Verso.

Gilroy, P. (2000) *Between Camps, Nations, Cultures and the Allure of Race*, London and New York: Routledge.

Gilroy, P. (2004) *After Empire: Melancholia or Convivial Culture*, London and New York: Routledge.

Glasgow University Media Group (1976) *Bad News*, London: Routledge.

Glasgow University Media Group (1980) *More Bad News*. London: Routledge & Kegan Paul.

Goffman, E. (1972) *Interaction Ritual*, Harmondsworth: Penguin.

Goffman, E. (1984) *The Presentation of Self in Everyday Life*, London: Pelican.

Goldberg, D. T (1992) 'The Semantics of Race', in *Ethnic & Racial Studies*, 15, 4, October.

Goldberg D. T. (1993) *Racist Culture*, Oxford: Blackwell.

Goldberg D. T. (ed.) (1994) *Multiculturalism: A Critical Reader*, Oxford: Blackwell.

Goldberg D. T. and J. Solomos (eds) (2002), *A Companion to Racial and Ethnic Studies*, Oxford: Blackwell.

Goldsmith, O. (1876) *A History of the Earth and Animated Nature*, A Fullarton & Co: London & Edinburgh

Gonzalez, G. (2005)'Code of conduct for TNCs reappears', Third World Network (online) http://www.twnside.org.sg/title/code-cn.htm.

Gonzalez, M. (2001) 'Zapatistas After the Great March – A Postscript', *International Socialism Journal*, 91 (summer), available online at <http://pubs.socialistreviewindex.org.uk/isj91/gonzalez.htm>.

Goodhart, D. (2004) 'Too Diverse: Is Britain becoming too diverse to sustain the mutual obligations behind good society and the welfare state?' *Prospect magazine*, February 2004,available online at <http://www.geocities.com/jjrinst/DavidGoodhart-Immigration-Prospect.htm>.

Gray, J. and J. McGuigan (1993) *Studying Culture: An Introductory Reader*, London: Edward Arnold.

Grillo, R. (1998) *Pluralism and the Politics of Difference: State, Culture and Ethnicity in Comparative Perspective*, Oxford: Clarendon Press.

Grossberg, L. 'Identity and Cultural Studies: Is That All There Is?' in S. Hall and P. du

Gay (eds) (1996) *Questions of Cultural Identity*, London and Thousand Oaks, Calif.: Sage.

Guan, L. H. (2000) 'Ethnic Relations in Peninsular Malaysia: The Cultural and Economic Dimensions', *Social and Cultural Issues* 1.

The Guardian (2000) Anna Pha: 'The Evil Empire of TNCs', available online at <http://www.cpa.org.au/garchve2/1016glob.html>.

The Guardian (2004) Brian Whitaker and Luke Harding in Baghdad and Associated Press in Cairo: 'American beheaded in revenge for torture', available online at <http://www.guardian.co.uk/international/story/0,3604,1214758,00.html>.

The Guardian (2005) Jonathan Steele and Richard Norton-Taylor: '25,000 Iraqi civilians killed since invasion' US military 'responsible for one-third of deaths', Wednesday, 20 July 2005, available online at <http://www.guardian.co.uk/Iraq/Story/0,2763,1532157,00.html>.

Gunew, S. (2001) 'Postcolonialism and Multiculturalism: Between Race and Ethnicity', Available online at <http://www.english.ubc.ca/~sgunew/race.htm>

Guyana Chronicle (2004) '"You know wha' is bedding"? Folklore By Hazel Robinson', 23 May.

Habermas, J. 1970. 'On Systematically Distorted Communication.' *Inquiry* 13: 205–18.

Hall, S. (ed.) (1978) *Policing the Crisis: Mugging, the State and Law and Order*, London: Macmillan.

Hall, S. (1980) 'Race, Articulation and Societies Structured in Dominance' in S. Cohen and J. Young (eds) *The Manufacture of News: Social Problems, Deviance and the Mass Media*, London: Constable.

Hall, S. (1981) 'The Determinations of News Photographs', in S. Cohen and J. Young (eds) *The Manufacture of News: Social Problems, Deviance and the Mass Media*, London: Constable, pp. 226–43.

Hall, S. (1991) 'The Local and the Global: Globalization and Ethnicity', in A. King (ed.), *Culture Globalization and the World System*, London: Macmillan, pp. 19–40.

Hall, S. (1992) 'The Question of Cultural Identity', in S. Hall, D. Held and T. McGrew (eds) *Modernity and its Futures*, Cambridge: Polity, pp. 274–316.

Hall, S. (1993) 'What is this "Black" in Black Popular Culture? (Rethinking Race)' *Social Justice*, (spring–summer) 20, available online at <http://www.brynmawr.edu/Acads/GSSW/schram/stuarthall.htm>.

Hall, S. (1994) 'Cultural Identity and Diaspora' in P. Williams and L. Chrisman (eds), *Colonial Discourse and Postcolonial Theory*, New York: Columbia University Press.

Hall, S. (1996a)'New Ethnicities', in D. Morley and K. H. Chen (eds), *Stuart Hall, Critical Dialogues in Cultural Studies*, London and New York: Routledge, pp. 441–9.

Hall, S. (1996b) *Race, the Floating Signifier*, film, directed by Sut Jhally Hall, (videotape lecture), Northampton, MA, Media Education Foundation.

Hall, S. (ed.) (1997) *Representation: Cultural Representations and Signifying Practices*, London and Thousand Oaks, Calif.: Sage.

Hall, S. (2000) 'The Multicultural Question', Political Economy Research Centre, Lecture, Available online at <http://www.shef.ac.uk/uni/academic/N-Q/perc/lectures/Hall.html>.

Hall, S. and P. du Gay (eds) (1996) *Questions of Cultural Identity*, London and Thousand Oaks, Calif.: Sage.

Hall, S., du Gay, P., et al. (1997) *Doing Cultural Studies: The Story of the Sony Walkman*, London: Sage/The Open University Press.

Halsey, A. H. (1997) *Education Culture Economy Society*, Oxford: Oxford University Press.

Hamilton, W. D. (1964) 'The Genetical Evolution of Social Behavior. II,' in G. C. Williams (ed.) *Group Selection*, Chicago, Ill.: Aldine Atherton.

Hammerton, J. (1933) *Peoples of All Nations*, London: Amalgamated Press.

Hartley, J. (1998) *The Politics of Pictures*, London: Polity.

Harvey, D. (1989) *The Condition of Postmodernity*, Oxford: Basil Blackwell.

Hechter, M. (1975) *Internal Colonialism: The Celtic Fringe in British National Development*, London: Routledge & Kegan Paul.

Hechter, M. (1995) 'Explaining Nationalist Violence', *Nations and Nationalism* 1(1): 53–68.

Henderson M. (2000) 'Liverpool Faces the Past – and the Future for a Change', April–May.

Herman, E. S. and N. Chomsky (1995) *Manufacturing Consent: The Political Economy of the Mass Media*, London: Vintage.

Hernández Cuevas, M. P. (2005) *African Mexicans and the Discourse on Modern Nation*, University Press of America.

Hill Collins, P. (1990) 'Defining Black Feminist Thought', in P. H. Collins, *Black Feminist Thought: Knowledge, Consciousness, and the Politics of Empowerment.* New York: Routledge, pp. 19–40, available online at <http://www.hsph.harvard.edu/Organizations/healthnet/WoC/feminisms/collins2.html>.

History of Race in Science (1995) 'Bring back the Hottentot Venus', *In Media*, 15 June, available online at <http://www.racesci.org/in-media/baartman/ baartman_m&g_june95.htm>.

Hobsbawm, E. J. (1996) *Age of Extremes: The Short Twentieth Century 1914–1991*. London: Abacus.

Hochschild, A. (1998) *King Leopold's Ghost: A Story of Greed, Terror, and Heroism in Colonial Africa*, New York: Houghton Mifflin.

Hofstadter, R. (1955) *Social Darwinism in American Thought*, Boston, Mass.: Beacon Press.

Hohman, K. (2000) 'Race Relations: Whiteness Studies: A Look at White Privilege and Whiteness Studies and How They Pertain to Race Relations', available online at <http://racerelations.about.com/library/weekly/blwhiteprivilege.htm>.

hooks, b. (1989) *Talking Back*, Boston, Mass.: South End Press.

Horne, D. (1964) *The Lucky Country* Ringwood: Penguin.

Horowitz, D. (1985) *Ethnic Groups in Conflict*, Berkeley, Calif.: University of California Press.

Horowitz, D. L. (2003) 'The Cracked Foundations of the Right to Secede.' *Journal of Democracy* 24 (2): 5–17.

Howard, J. (1996) 'Robert Menzies Lecture', Parliamentary Library Research Paper 5, 1997–98.

Howe, D. (2005) 'To Refer to Muslims, Hindus and Sikhs, Rather than Asians, Undermines Secularism', *New Statesman*, 17 January.

Hughes, I. (1995) 'Dependent Autonomy: A New Phase of Internal Colonialism', in *Australian Journal of Social Issues* 30(4) (4 November 1995): 369–88.

Hughes, R. (1987) *The Fatal Shore: A History of the Transportation of Convicts to Australia*, London: Collins Harvill.

Human Rights Watch (1998) Press Advisor, Internal Security Act (ISA), 21 September, available online at <http://www.hrw.org/press98/bck-brif/my-isa.htm> (accessed 8 January 2005).

Hume, L. J. (1991) 'Another Look at the Cultural Cringe', available online at <http://www.therathouse.com/Another_look_at_the_Cultural_Cringe.htm>.

Huntington, S. (1998) *Clash of Civilizations and the Remaking of World Order*, London and New York: Touchstone.

Hutchinson J. and A. D. Smith (eds) (1996) *Ethnicity*, Oxford: Oxford University Press.

Inglis, F. (1990) *An Introduction to Media Theory*, Oxford: Blackwell.

James, C. L. R. (1963) *The Black Jacobins: Toussaint L'Ouverture and the San Domingo Revolution*. Rev. edn. New York, Vintage.

Jenkins, R. (1992) *Pierre Bourdieu*, London: Routledge.

Jenkins, R. (1996) *Social Identity*, London and New York: Routledge.

Jenkins, R. (1997) *Rethinking Ethnicity: Arguments and Explorations*, London and Thousand Oaks, Calif.: Sage.

Jenkins, R. (2003) 'The Limits of Identity: Ethnicity, Conflict and Politics', Sheffield University, available online at <http://www.shef.ac.uk/socst/Shop/2jenkins.pdf>.

Jenks, C. (ed.) (1998) *Core Sociological Dichotomies*, London and Thousand Oaks, Calif.: Sage.

Jensen, K. B. (1995) *The Social Semiotics of Mass Communication*. Thousand Oaks, Calif.: Sage.

John, C. (2002) 'Changing Face of Britain: Britain's Blurring Ethnic Mix', available online at <http://news.bbc.co.uk/hi/english/static/in_depth/uk/2002/race/changing_face_of_britain.stm>.

Jordan, T. (2000) *Cyberpower: The Culture and Politics of Cyberspace and the Internet*, London and New York: Routledge.

Jupp, J. (2002) *From White Australia to Woomera*, Cambridge: Cambridge University Press.

Kafka, F. (2000) *Metamorphosis, In the Penal Colony and Other Stories*, New York: Scriber Paperback Fictions.

Karvelas, P. (2004) 'Aborigines Rewarded for Face-Washing', *Sunday Times*, 9 December.

Kavanagh, J. (1995) *Critical Terms for Literary Study*, 2nd edn, ed. F. Lentricchia and T. McLaughlin, Chicago, Ill.: University of Chicago Press.

Kellas, J. G. (1998) *The Politics of Nationalism and Ethnicity*, 2nd edn, New York: St Martin's Press.

Kennedy, B. M. *The Cybercultures Reader*, London and New York: Routledge.

Khair, T. (1999) 'Why Post-colonialism Hates Revolutions', *Biblio: A Review of Books*, 4, 5–6, May–June, available online at <http://www.biblio-india.com/articles/mj99_ar9.asp?mp=MJ99>.

King, B. (2004) 'Mass Media' in G. Taylor and S. Spencer (eds) *Social Identities: Multidisciplinary Approaches*, London and New York: Routledge.

Knightley, P. (1975) *The First Casualty: The War Correspondent as Hero, Propagandist and Myth Maker*, New York: Harcourt.

Knowles, C. (2004) *Race and Social Analysis*, London and Thousand Oaks, Calif.: Sage.

Knowles, C. and S. Mercer (1992) 'Feminism and Antiracism: An Exploration of the

Political Possibilities', in J. Donald and A. Rattansi (eds) *'Race', Culture and Difference*, London and Thousand Oaks, Calif.: Sage.

Knowles, L. L. and Prewitt, K. (eds) (1969) *Institutional Racism in America*, Englewood Cliffs, NJ: Prentice-Hall.

Kohn, M. (1996) *The Race Gallery*, London: Verso.

Kolakowski, L. (1985) *Main Currents in Marxism*, Oxford: Oxford University Press.

Kolko, B., L. Nakamura, R. Gilbert (eds) *Race in Cyberspace*, London and New York: Routledge.

Korner, B. and D. Garrard (2005) 'Is It Wrong to Be Racist? Dealing with Emotion and Discomfort in Classroom Discussions of "Race" and Ethnicity', in S. Spencer and M. Todd (eds) *Reflecting on Practice: Teaching and Learning Issues in Race and Ethnicity*, Birmingham: University of Birmingham Press.

Kress, G. (1988) *Communication and Culture*, Kensington: New South Wales University Press.

Kress, G. R. and Hodge, R. (1979) *Language as Ideology*, London: Routledge and Kegan Paul.

Kuper, L. (1981) *Genocide: Its Political Use in the Twentieth Century*, New Haven, Conn.: Yale University Press.

Kuper, L. (1996) 'Genocide and the Plural Society', in J. Hutchinson and A. D. Smith (eds), *Ethnicity*, Oxford: Oxford University Press.

Kymlicka, W. (1995) *Multicultural Citizenship: A Liberal Theory of Minority Rights*, Oxford: Clarendon.

Lacan, J. (1977) *Ecrits. A Selection*, New York: Norton.

Laclau, E. and C. Mouffe. 1985. *Hegemony and Socialist Strategy: Towards a Radical Democratic Politics*. London: Verso

Lamarck, J.-B. (1801) *Philosophie zoologique*, Vol. I, Part 1, Ch. 7, available online at <http://www.mala.bc.ca/~johnstoi/LAMARCK/lamarck7.htm>.

Lambe, M. (2003) 'NT Labor Continue Traditional Dry Season Racism' Part 1, 15 April 2003, available online at <http://www.country-liberal-party.com/pages/Kenbi-Claim-shell-game.htm#family>.

Langton, M. (1993a) 'Rum, Seduction and Death: "Aboriginality" and alcohol', *Oceania* 63(3): 195–206.

Langton, M. (1993b) *Well, I Heard it on the Radio and I Saw it on the Television*, Sydney: Australian Film Commission.

Langton, M. (1997) *The Long Grass People of Darwin*, PARITY magazine.

Langton, M. (2002) 'Langton Warns of Poverty Trap', *Uni News*, University of Sydney, 25 October, available online at <http://www.usyd.edu.au/publications/news/022510 News/2510_poverty.html>.

Langton, M., L. Ah Matt, B. Moss, E. Schaber, C. Mackinolty, M. Thomas, E. Tilton and L. Spencer (1991) 'Too Much Sorry Business: The Report of the Aboriginal Issues Unit of the Northern Territory. Royal Commission into Aboriginal Deaths in Custody', National Report Volume 5. Canberra: Australian Government Publishing Service.

Leakey, R. (1979) *The Illustrated Origin of Species*, London: Faber & Faber.

Lewis, R. (1996) *Gendering Orientalism: Race, Feminity and Representation*, London and New York: Routledge.

Lim, S. P. 'The Question of Diaspora in International Relations: A Case Study of Chinese Diaspora in Malaysia and South-East Asia', Dissertation, MA in International Relations, University of Sussex.

Linnaeus (Carl von Linne) (1806) *A General System of Nature Through the Three Grand Kingdoms of Animals, Vegetable, and Minerals*, London: Lackington, Allen and Company.

Loomba, A. (1993) 'Overworldling the "Third World"', in P. Williams and L. Chrisman (eds) *Colonial Discourse and Postcolonial Theory*, New York: Columbia University Press, pp. 305–23.

Loomba, A. (1998) *Colonialism/Postcolonialism*, London and New York: Routledge.

Lott, T. L. (1999) *The Invention of Race*, Oxford: Blackwell.

Luke, C. (1996) 'Reading Gender and Culture in Media Discourses and Texts', in G. Bull and M. Anstey (eds) *The Literary Lexicon*, New York/Sydney: Prentice-Hall.

Lyell, C. (1830) *Principles of Geology*, London: John Murray.

Mac an Ghaill, M. (1999) *Contemporary Racisms and Ethnicities*, Oxford: Oxford University Press.

McCaskell, T. (1994) 'A History of Race/ism', Equity Department, Toronto District School Board, available online at <http://www.ameno.ca/docs/A520History%20 of%20Race.doc>.

McGuigan, J. (1999) *Modernity and Postmodern Culture*, Milton Keynes: Open University Press.

McKenna, M. (1997) 'Different Perspectives on Black Armband History', Research Paper 5 1997–8, Politics and Public Administration Group, 10 November.

Macklin, G. (2002) in a review of Gore Vidal, 'Perpetual War for Perpetual Peace', Clairview, online document, available at <http://www.spokesmanbooks.com/ Spokesman/PDF/reviews77.pdf>.

McLeod, J. (2000) *Beginning Postcolonialism*, Manchester: Manchester University Press.

McQuail, D. (ed.) (1972) *Sociology of Mass Communications*, Harmondsworth: Penguin.

McQuail, D. (1994) *Mass Communication Theory* (3rd edn), London and Thousand Oaks, Calif.: Sage.

McQuail, D. (1987) *Mass Communication Theory*, 2nd edn, London and Thousand Oaks, Calif.: Sage.

Malesevic, S. (2004) *The Sociology of Ethnicity*, London and Thousand Oaks, Calif.: Sage.

Malik, K. (1996) *The Meaning of Race*, London: Macmillan.

Malik, K. (1998) 'Race, Pluralism and the Meaning of Difference', *New Formations*, 33 (spring), available online at <http://www.kenanmalik.com/papers/new_formations. html>.

Malik, K. (2002) 'Against Multiculturalism', *New Humanist* (summer), available online at <http://www.kenanmalik.com/essays/against_mc.html>.

Malik, K. (2004) 'Too Diverse' (A Response to David Goodhart), Kenan Malik website Debates at http://www.kenanmalik.com/debates/prospect_diversity.html (accessed 10/11/2005).

Manne, R. (ed.) (2003) *Whitewash: on Keith Windschuttle's Fabrication of Aboriginal History*, Melbourne: Black Inc. Agenda.

Marcus, S. (1974) *Engels, Manchester and the Working Class*, London: Weidenfield & Nicolson.

Marx, K. (1961) *Capital*, Vol 1, Moscow: Foreign Languages Publishing House.

Marx, K. and F. Engels (1982) *Selected Correspondence*, London: Progress.

Mason, D. (2000) *Race and Ethnicity in Modern Britain*, Oxford: Oxford University Press.

Mauss, M. (1979) 'Body Techniques', in *Psychology and Sociology: Essays*, London: Routledge & Kegan Paul.

May, S. (ed.) (1999) *Critical Multiculturalism: Rethinking Multicultural and Antiracist Education*, London: Falmer.

May, S. (2000) 'Multiculturalism', in D. T. Goldberg and J. Solomos (eds) *A Companion to Racial and Ethnic Studies*, Oxford: Blackwell, pp. 124–43.

May, S., T. Modood and J. Squires (eds) (2004) *Ethnicity, Nationalism and Minority Rights*, Cambridge: Cambridge University Press.

Mayne, A. (1997) *Black Armband History: The Future for History in Australia*, Melbourne: University of Melbourne Press.

Melville, P. (1991) *Shape Shifter*, Harmondsworth: Penguin.

Mercer, K. (1994) *Welcome To The Jungle: New Positions in Black Cultural Studies*, New York: Routledge.

Mercer, K. (2000) 'Identity and diversity', in L. Back and J. Solomos (eds) *Theories of Race and Racism: A Reader*, New York: Routledge.

Metropolitan Borough of Oldham Council (2005) Meeting of the Cabinet, 30 March, Report of the Acting Executive Director of Education and Cultural Services, available online at <http://decision.oldham.gov.uk/DET05030140.Doc>

Miles, R. (1989) *Racism*, London and New York: Routledge.

Mills, S. (1997) *Discourse*, London and New York: Routledge.

Modood, T. (ed.) (1997) *Ethnic Minorities in Britain: Diversity and Disadvantage*, London: Policy Studies Institute.

Modood, T. (2000) 'Anti-Essentialism, Multiculturalism, and the 'Recognition' of Religious Groups' in: W. Kymlicka and W. Norman (eds) *Citizenship in Diverse Societies*, Oxford: Oxford University Press, pp. 175–95.

Modood, T. and P. Werbner (eds) (1997) *Debating Cultural Hybridity: Multi-Cultural Identities and the Politics of Anti-Racism*, London and New York: Atlantic Highlands and Zed Books.

Montesquieu, Baron de (1748) *Spirit of Laws*, Book 15, 'In W <http://www.lonang.com/exlibris/montesquieu/sol-15.htm>.

Moore J. H. (1933) *Savage Survivals*, London: Watts.

Morley, D. and C. Kuan-Hsing (eds) (1996) *Stuart Hall*, London and New York: Routledge.

Mosse, G. L. (1978) *Towards the Final Solution, A History of European Racism*, New York, Harper Colophon Books, Harper & Row.

Muecke, S. (1982) 'Available Discourses on Aborigines', in P. D. Botsman *Theoretical Strategies*, Sydney: Local Consumption Press.

Muecke, S. (1992) *Textual Spaces: Aboriginality and Cultural Studies*, Sydney: New South Wales University Press.

Mulvey, L. (1975) 'Visual Pleasure and Narrative Cinema', *Screen* 16: 6–18.

Nakamura, L. (2000) 'Race In/For Cyberspace: Identity Tourism and Racial Passing on the Internet', in D. Bell and B. Kennedy (eds) *The Cybercultures Reader*, London and New York: Routledge.

Nakayama, T. K. and J. N. Martin (1998) *Whiteness: The Communication of Social Identity*, London and Thousand Oaks, Calif.: Sage.

Nasser, Haya El (1997) 'Measuring Race: Varied Heritage Claimed and Extolled by Millions', *USA Today*, 8 May, p. 1A.

Neumann, I. (1999) *Uses of the Other: 'The East' in European Identity Formation*, Minneapolis, Minn.: Minnesota University Press.

Nkrumah, K. (1965) 'Neo-Colonialism: The Last Stage of Capitalism', available online at <http://www.marxists.org/subject/africa/nkrumah/neo-colonialism/introduction.htm>.

O'Sullivan, T., J. Hartley et al. (1983) *Key Concepts in Communication*, London: Methuen.

Ortner, S. (1984) 'Theory in Anthropology since the Sixties', *Comparative Study in Society and History*, 26, 1: 126–66.

Orwell, G. (1945[1971]) *Animal Farm: A Fairy Story*, London: Secker and Warburg.

Parekh, B. (ed.) (2000) *The Future of Multi-Ethnic Britain*, London: Methuen.

Parker, D. (2004) 'Mixed Race: The Social Identities of the Future?' in G. Taylor and S. Spencer *Social Identities: Multidisciplinary Approaches*, London and New York: Routledge.

Pearson, N. (2000) 'Misguided Policies a Toxic Cocktail: Aborigines Must Renew Family Life and Eradicate Drug Abuse', *Australian*, 24 October, p.13.

Petkovic, J. (1983) *Frame on Dreaming* (film).

Pfaff-Czarnecka J. et al. (1999) *Ethnic Futures: The State and Identity Politics in Asia*, London and Thousand Oaks, Calif.: Sage.

Phelan, S. (1989) *Identity Politics*, Philadelphia, Pa.: Temple University Press.

Pickering, M. (2004) 'Racial Stereotypes' in G. Taylor and S. Spencer (eds) *Social Identities: Multidisciplinary Approaches*, London and New York: Routledge.

Pieterese, J. N. (2001) *Development Theory: Deconstructions/Reconstructions*, London and Thousand Oaks, Calif.: Sage.

Pieterse, J. N. (2002) 'Europe and Its Others Over Time', in D. T. Goldberg and J. Solomos (eds) *A Companion to Racial and Ethnic Studies*, Oxford: Blackwell.

Pieterese, J. N. and B. Parekh (1995) *The Decolonization of the Imagination: Culture, Knowledge and Power*, London: Zed Books.

Pilger, J. (1986) *Heroes*, London: Pan.

Pilger, J. (1989) *A Secret Country*, London: Vintage.

Pilger, J. (2002) 'The Treatment of Asylum Seekers Beggars Belief' *New Statesman*, 25 January, available online at <http://www.country-liberal-party.com/pages/Refugees.b.htm> (accessed 14 July 2005).

Pinkus, J. (1996) 'Foucault', available online at <http://www.massey.ac.nz/~ALock/theory/foucault.htm>.

Popeau, J. (1998) 'Race/Ethnicity', in C. Jenks (ed.) *Core Sociological Dichotomies*, London and Thousand Oaks, Calif.: Sage, pp. 166–78.

Poulantzas, N. (1973) *Political Power and Social Classes*, London: New Left Books.

Powell, J. (1997) *Derrida for Beginners*, London: Icon.

Prakash, G. (ed.) (1995) *After Colonialism: Imperial Histories and Postcolonial Displacements*, Princeton, NJ: Princeton University Press.

Premdas, R. (1992) 'Ethnic and Racial Conflict in the Caribbean', in B. Samaroo and C. Debidin (eds) *Ethnicity and Indians in the Caribbean*, London: Macmillan.

Premdas, R. (1972) *Voluntary Associations and Political Parties in a Racially Fragmented State*, Georgetown: University of Guyana.

Project for the New American Century (1997), available online at <http://www.new americancentury.org> (accessed 7 December 2005).

Radio Nederland (2001) Pieternel Gruppen (RN African Affairs editor): 'Civil War in Congo: 2.5 Million Deaths', 4 May 2001.

Rand, A. (1998) (ARI) 'Multiculturalism: An Assault on the Individual', *Impact News Letter of the Ayn Rand Institute*, available online at <http://www.aynrand.org/site/ DocServer/newsletter_multiculturalism.pdf?docID=162>.

Randall, M. (2003) 'Guest Media Lens Alert: Asylum and Immigration, Comparing the *Daily Telegraph*, *Guardian* and the *Independent*', 8 December, available online at <http://www.medialens.org/alerts/03/031208 _Asylum_Immigration.htm>.

Ratcliffe, P. (2004) *'Race', Ethnicity and Difference*, Milton Keynes: Open University Press.

Read, P. (1996) Unpublished paper, Aboriginal Citizenship conference at the ANU in February.

Research Development and Statistics Directorate (2004) 'Ethnicity, Victimisation and Worry about Crime: Findings 237', from the 2001/2 and 2002/3 *British Crime Surveys*, June, available online at <http://www.crimereduction.gov.uk/racial12.htm>.

Rex, J. (1970) *Race Relations in Sociological Theory*, London: Weidenfeld and Nicolson.

Rex, J. (1973) *Race, Colonialism and the City*, London and New York: Routledge.

Rex, J. (1980) 'Theory of Race Relations: A Weberian Approach', in *Sociological Theories, Race and Colonialism*, Paris: Unesco, pp. 169–186

Rex, J. (1986) 'The Role of Class Analysis in the Study of Race Relations: A Weberian Perspective', in J. Rex and D. Mason (eds) *Theories of Race and Ethnic Relations*, Cambridge University Press, pp. 64–83.

Rex, J. (1986) *Race and Ethnicity*, Milton Keynes: Open University Press.

Rex, J. and M. Guibernau (eds) (1997) *The Ethnicity Reader: Nationalism, Multiculturalism, and Migration*, Cambridge: Polity.

Rex, J. and D. Mason (eds) (1986) *Theories of Race and Ethnic Relations*, Cambridge: Cambridge University Press.

Rex, J. and R. Moore (1967) *Race, Community and Conflict: A Study of Sparkbrook*, Oxford: Oxford University Press.

Rex, J. and S. Tomlinson (1979) *Colonial Immigrants in a British City*, Routledge and Kegan Paul.

Reynolds, V., V. Falger and I. Vine (1987) *The Sociobiology of Ethnocentrism*. London: Croom Helm.

Robertson, R. (1995) 'Glocalisation: Time-Space and Homogeneity-Heterogeneity', in M. Featherstone et al. (eds), *Global Modernities*, London and Thousand Oaks, Calif.: Sage.

Robins, D. (1991) 'Tradition and Translation: National Culture in its Global Context', in J. Corner and S. Harvey (eds), *Enterprise and Heritage: Crosscurrents in National Culture*, London and New York: Routledge.

Robinson, H. (2004) 'You know wha' is "bedding"?' *Guyana Chronicle*, 23 May, available online at <http://www.landofsixpeoples.com/news402/nc4052318.htm>.

Roche, B. (2002) 'Devolution and Britishness Conference', Queen Elizabeth II Centre,

21 February, available online at <http://archive.cabinetoffice.gov.uk/ ministers/2002/ Barbara%20Roche/Devolution%2021.02.htm>.

Rodney, W. (1972) *How Europe Underdeveloped Africa*, Harrare: Zimbabwe Publishing House.

Rodney, W. (1981) *A History of the Guyanese Working People, 1881–1905*, Kingston and London: Heinemann.

Roy, A. (2005) 'British Asians in Identity Crisis, Post 9/11', *Calcutta Telegraph*, 14 January, available online at <http://www.telegraphindia.com/1050114/asp/nation/story_424 5977.asp> (accessed 20 January 2005).

Rushdie, S. (1988) *The Satanic Verses*, New York and London: Viking.

Russell, B. (1991) *History of Western Philosophy*, London and New York: Routledge.

Said, E. (1985) *Orientalism*, Harmondsworth: Penguin.

Said, E. (1993) *Culture and Imperialism*, New York: Vintage.

Salleh, M. (2003) 'The Lie of Benevolence: Book Review of *Web of Deceit* by Mark Curtis', July, available online at <http://www.socialistreview.org.uk/article.php? articlenumber= 8536>.

Sansom, B. (1980) *The Camp at Wallaby Cross: Aboriginal Fringe Dwellers in Darwin*, Darwin: Australian Institute of Aboriginal Studies.

Sardar, Z. (1998) *Postmodernism and the Other: The New Imperialism of Western Culture*. London: Pluto.

Sardar, Z. (1999) in J. McGuigan (ed.) *Modernity and Postmodern Culture*, Milton Keynes: Open University Press.

Sardar, Z. (2004) 'Islam and the West in a Transmodern World', 18 August, available online at <http://www.islamonline.net/english/Contemporary/2002/05/Article20. shtml>.

Seabrook, J. (1996) 'Internationalism Versus Globalisation', *Third World Network Features*, 8 August.

Shamsul, A. B. (2002) 'Malaysia's International Role Post-September 11', Universiti Kebangsaan Malaysia, Bangi, Malaysia, November article published in IDSS Commentaries, available online at <http://www.ntu.edu.sg/idss/Perspective/Research_ 050229.htm> (accessed 4 January 2005).

Sharrad, P. (1993) 'Blackbirding: Diaspora Narratives and the Invasion of the Bodysnatchers', *Span, Journal of the South Pacific Association for Commonwealth Literature and Language Studies*, 34–5.

Short, A. (1970) 'Communism, Race and Politics in Malaysia', *Asian Survey* 10(12) (December 1970): 1089.

Sibley, D. (1995) *Geographies of Exclusion: Society and Difference in the West*, London and New York: Routledge.

Sivanandan, A. (1986) *From Resistance to Rebellion: Asian and Afro-Caribbean Struggles in Britain*, Institute of Race Relations.

Smart, B. (1993) *Postmodernity*, London and New York: Routledge.

Smith M. G. (1974) *The Plural Society in the British West Indies*, London: University of California Press.

Smith R. T. (1962) *British Guiana*, London: Oxford University Press.

Smith, C. and G. K. Ward (eds) (2000) *Indigenous Cultures in an Interconnected World*, St Leonards: Allen & Lane.

Smith, M. G. (1974) *The Plural Society in the British West Indies*, London: University of California Press.

Smith, R. (1997) *Fontana History of the Human Sciences*, London: Fontana.

Smith, R. T. (1962) *British Guiana*, Oxford: Oxford University Press.

Smith, R. T. (1965) *The Negro Family in British Guiana: Family Structure and Social Status in the Villages*, London: Routledge & Kegan Paul.

Sollors, W. (2002) 'Ethnicity and Race', in D. T. Goldberg and J. Solomos (eds) *A Companion to Racial and Ethnic Studies*, Oxford: Blackwell, pp. 97–103.

Solomos, J. and L. Back (1996) *Racism and Society*, London: Macmillan.

Sotiropoulou, A. (2002) 'The Role of Ethnicity in Ethnic Conflicts: The Case of Yugoslavia', MA in Contemporary European Studies, University of Bath, available online at <http://unpan1.un.org/intradoc/groups/public/documents/UNTC/UNPAN 019076.pdf>.

Soysal, Y. N. (2000) 'Citizenship and Identity: Living in diasporas in Post-War Europe?' *Ethnic and Racial Studies*, 23: 1, January.

Spencer, H. (1860) *System of Synthetic Philosophy: First Principles*, London: George Manwaring.

Spencer, S. (2005) *'Framing the Fringe Dwellers': Visual Methods for Research and Teaching Race and Ethnicity: A Sample Case Study*, Birmingham: University of Birmingham Press.

Spencer, S. (forthcoming) 'Contested Homelands: Darwin's "itinerant problem"', *Pacific Journalism Review*.

Spencer, S. (forthcoming) *A Dream Deferred: Ethnic Conflict in Guyana*, Chichester: Dido Press.

Spencer, S. and M. Todd (2005) *Reflecting on Practice: Teaching and Learning Issues in Race and Ethnicity*, Birmingham: University of Birmingham Press.

Spivak, G. C. (1985) 'Can the Subaltern Speak', in P. Williams and L. Chrisman (eds) (1994) *Colonial Discourse and Postcolonial Theory*, New York: Columbia University Press.

Stanton, G. H. (2004) 'Genocide Emergency: Darfur, Sudan', available online at <http://www.genocidewatch.org/Never%20Again.htm>.

Stone, A. R. (1995) *The War of Desire and Technology at the Close of the Mechanical Age*, Cambridge, Mass.: MIT Press

Sverker, F. 'Postcoloniality and the Postcolony: Theories of the Global and the Local', MA Department of Cultural Anthropology and Ethnology, Uppsala University, available online at <http://www.scholars.nus.edu.Lsg/landow/post/poldiscourse/finnstrom/finnstrom1.htm>

Tatz, C. (1999) 'Genocide in Australia', *AIATSIS, Research Discussion Papers* 8, available online at <http://www.aiatsis.gov.au/rsrch/rsrch_dp/genocide.htm>.

Taylor, C. et al. (1994) *Multiculturalism: Examining the Politics of Recognition*, Princeton, NJ: Princeton University Press.

Taylor, G. and S. Spencer (eds) (2004) *Social Identities: Multidisciplinary Approaches*, London and New York: Routledge.

Thompson, K. (1998) *Moral Panics*, London and New York: Routledge.

Tizzard, B. and A. Phoenix (1993) *Black, White or Mixed Race? Race and Racism in the Lives of Young People of Mixed Parentage*, London and New York: Routledge.

Tobach, E. and B. Rosoff (1994) *Challenging Racism and Sexism, Alternatives to Genetic Explanations*, New York, The Feminist Press.

Turpin, T. (1990) *The Social Construction of Immigrant & Aboriginal Ethnic Group Boundaries in Australia*, Ph.D. thesis, La Trobe University.

Tweedie, N. (1998) 'Shock Posters Send Police on the Trail of Race Commission', *Electronic Telegraph*, 22 September, available online at <http://www.amren.com/pdf/98November.pdf>.

UN Economic and Social Council (1999) Substantive Session, Geneva, 5–30 July, available online at <http://www.unhchr.ch/Huridocda/Huridoca.nsf/0/658a0ff32e3ef7de80 256862005316b9?Opendocument>.

UNESCO (1995) 'Multiculturalism: A Policy Response to Diversity', Global Cultural Diversity Conference, 26–8 April, and 'MOST Pacific Sub-Regional Consultation', 28–9 April, Sydney, Australia, available online at <http://www.unesco.org/most/sydpaper.htm>.

Urry, J. (1990) *The Tourist Gaze*, London and Thousand Oaks, Calif.: Sage.

US Census Bureau (1999) 'National Population Projections, Cheeseman Day', available online at <http://216.239.59.104/search?q=cache:A9Sgd6xAv3EJ: www.census.gov/population/www/pop-profile/natproj.html+rate+of+growth+Hispanic+population and hl=en#>.

Valdaverde, M. (1995) 'Online Book review of Robert Young's *Colonial Desire: Hybridity in Theory, Culture and Race*', available online at <http://www.utpjournals.com/product/chr/781/desire41.html> (accessed 23 February 2004).

Van den Berghe, P. (1967) *Race and Racism: A Comparative Perspective*, New York: John Wiley.

Vasil, R. K. (1984) *Politics in Bi-Racial Societies: The Third World Experience*, New Delhi: Vikas.

Vaughan, A. T. (1982) 'From White Man to Redskin: Changing Anglo American Perceptions of the American Indian', *American Historical Review* 87: 917–51.

Waddington, D. (2004) 'Music', in G. Taylor and S. Spencer *Social Identities: Multidisciplinary Approaches*, London and New York: Routledge.

Walker, A. (1983) *In Search of our Mothers' Gardens: Womanist Prose*, San Diego, Calif.: Harcourt Brace Jovanovich.

Wallerstein, I. (1974) *The Modern World System: Capitalist Agriculture and the Origins of the European World Economy in the Sixteenth Century*, London and New York: Academic Press.

Wallerstein, I. (1988) 'The Ideological Tensions of Capitalism: Universalism Versus Racism and Sexism', in E. Balibar and I. Wallerstein, *Race, Nation, Class, Ambiguous Identities*, London and New York: Verso.

Waters, M. (1996) *Globalization*, London and New York: Routledge.

Weber, M. (1978) *Economy and Society: An Outline of Interpretive Sociology*, Berkeley, Calif.: University of California Press.

Weedon, C. (1987) *Feminist Practice and Poststructuralist theory*, 2nd edn, Oxford: Blackwell.

West, C. (1995) 'Race Matters', *College Literature* 22 (June): 13442.

Wheeler, H. (ed.) (1935) *Peoples of the World in Pictures*, London: Odhams.

Williams, B. F. (1991) *Stains on My Name; War in My Veins*, Durham, NC: Duke University Press.

Williams, B. F. (1995) 'From Class to "Trash" to Hybrid Nation: A Conversation with Brackette Williams', *Crosscurrents*, 3:1 (fall), available online at <http://www.jhu.edu/~igscph/fall95bw.htm>.

Williams, P. and L. Chrisman (1993) *Colonial Discourse and Post-Colonial Theory: A Reader*, London and New York: Harvester Wheatsheaf.

Williams, R. (1977) *Marxism and Literature*, Oxford: Oxford University Press.

Williams, R. (1983) *Keywords*, London: Fontana.

Windschuttle, K. (2004a) *The Fabrication of Aboriginal History, Volume One: Van Diemen's Land 1803–1847*, Sydney: Macleay Press.

Windschuttle, K. (2004b) *The White Australia Policy: Race and Shame in the Australian History Wars*, Sydney: Macleay Press.

Woodlock, R. (2002) 'Muslim Feminists and the Veil: To Veil or Not to Veil – Is That the Question?' available online at <http://www.islamfortoday.com/feminists_veil.htm>.

Woodward, K. (1997) *Identity and Difference*, London and Thousand Oaks, Calif.: Sage.

Yegenoglu, M. (1998) *Colonial Fantasies: Towards a Feminist Reading of Orientalism*, Cambridge: Cambridge University Press.

Young, C. (1976) *The Politics of Cultural Pluralism*, Madison, Wisc.: University of Wisconsin Press.

Young, J. (1971) *The Drugtakers: The Social Meaning of Drug Abuse*, London: MacGibbon & Kee.

Young, L. (1996) *Fear of the Dark: 'Race', Gender and Sexuality in the Cinema*, London: Routledge.

Young, R. J. C. (1995) *Colonial Desire: Hybridity in Theory, Culture and Race*, London and New York: Routledge.

Younge, G. and J. Henley (2003) 'Dissenters in Europe Become the First Victims – of a War of Words', *Guardian*, 11 February.

Zickmund, S. (2000) 'Approaching the Radical Other; The Discursive Culture of Cyberhate', in D. Bell and B. M. Kennedy, *The Cybercultures Reader*, London and New York: Routledge.

Žižek, S. (1990) 'Eastern Europe's Republics of Gilead', *New Left Review* 183: 50–62.

INDEX

RACE AND ETHNICITY

Broad-ranging and comprehensive, this incisive new textbook examines the shifting meanings of 'race' and ethnicity and collates the essential concepts in one indispensable companion volume. From Marxist views to post-colonialism, this book investigates the attendant debates, issues and analyses within the context of global change.

Using international case studies from Australia, Malaysia, the Caribbean, Mexico and the UK and examples of popular imagery that help to explain the more difficult elements of theory, this key text focuses on everyday life issues such as:

- ethnic conflicts and polarised states
- racism(s) and policies of multiculturalism
- diasporas, asylum seekers and refugees
- mixed race and hybrid identity

Incorporating summaries, questions, illustrations, exercises and a glossary of terms, this student-friendly text also puts forward suggestions for further project work. Broad in scope, interactive and accessible, this book is a key resource for undergraduate and postgraduate level students of 'race' and ethnicity across the social sciences.

Stephen Spencer is Senior Lecturer in Sociology at Sheffield Hallam University. His recent publications include: *A Dream Deferred: Ethnic Identity in Guyana* (Dido Press, forthcoming) and *Social Identities: Multidisciplinary Approaches* with Gary Taylor (Routledge 2004).

Printed in the United States
134949LV00001B/2/P